ENTERTAINING CHICAGO

Remembering the Places,
Performers and Stories
Throughout the 20th Century

by **Neal Samors** and **Bob Dauber**

Entertaining Chicago:
Remembering the Places, Performers
and Stories Throughout the
20th Century

Copyright 2019
by Neal Samors and Bob Dauber

All Rights Reserved
Published in the United States of America
in 2019 by Chicago's Books Press, an imprint
of Chicago's Neighborhoods, Inc.

First Edition, October, 2019

Edited by Neal Samors, Bob Dauber,
and Jennifer Ebeling.
Produced by Neal Samors and Bob Dauber.
Designed by Sam Silvio, Silvio Design, Inc.
Printed in Canada by Friesens Corporation.

ISBN: 978-0-9961417-2-7

Library of Congress Control Number: 2019913253

Front and back covers:
A collage of photographs from
various sources.

**For more information on this book
as well as the authors' other works, visit
www.chicagosbookspress.com or email
the authors at NSamors@comcast.net
or BB3fingers@sbcglobal.net**

Acknowledgements and Dedications

To my wife, Freddi, daughter and son-in-law,
Jennifer and Michael Ebeling, and granddaughter,
Audrey Elizabeth Ebeling
Neal Samors

To my life-partner, Renee, and my children,
David and Jami. Validation of so many of the
stories I've bored you with over the years.
Bob Dauber

The authors wish to express their deep
appreciation to **Lee Stern** for his total financial
support for this book. It wouldn't have
happened without his encouragement.

Thank you to Gary Johnson for another
brilliant introduction.

Special thanks also to the book's designer,
Sam Silvio, for his usual outstanding work in
creating another unique publication.

TABLE OF CONTENTS

INTRODUCTION

by Gary T. Johnson
President
Chicago History Museum

When you are a museum president as I am, consultants appear with the message that today's young people don't accumulate consumer products, they collect experiences. Well, I've got news for you. In 20th Century Chicago, they were collecting experiences, too, as Neal Samors and Bob Dauber so richly demonstrate.

Consider Barney Balaban and the Chicago Theatre. His movie theater was built like a palace complete with murals by Louis Grell, an artist whose works later adorned the Century of Progress World's Fair. My grandfather was born in 1901, so he came of age when the theater opened in 1920. Sixty years later when the structure had fallen on hard times, he used to tell me stories of seeing the stars who played there. He was skeptical that any restoration could do it justice. Why? "Because Barney Balaban only offered the best." How's that for brand across generations!

The authors' selection of venues might seem surprising: what does a bowling alley have to do with the Civic Opera House or the Plugged Nickel to do with the Chez Paree? Here's the answer. Each venue offered its own atmosphere, but in its own unique way. Each developed loyalty with regulars, while also welcoming curious newcomers. Each offered an indelible experience.

This book itself is an experience because it offers an immersion in history, images, and memories. The venues are thoughtfully chosen and the contexts carefully explained. I am proud that so many of the images came from the Chicago History Museum. Among them were our newly-acquired works of Raeburn Flerlage, a photographer who documented Chicago's blues and jazz scenes.

What makes the "experience" offered by Samors and Dauber most worth seeking is not the history or even the images, but the stories. The interviews were collected over decades and draw on memories from all corners of the twentieth century. The storytellers include old-timers still with us today such as comedian Shecky Greene, radio DJ Clark Weber, and civic leader Josephine Baskin Minow. There are voices from the departed that take stories back even farther in time, such as business leader Dempsey Travis, Second City co-founder Joyce Sloane, and jazz musician Johnny Frigo. Stories are here too from those who departed too soon, such as actor and writer Harold Ramis. Listen to all their stories and understand the magic of these venues from their special points of view.

My personal favorite, though, is hearing from bowling legend Carmen Salvino, still with us today, after a lifetime of service to his sport, first as a champion bowler and later in a long career with Brunswick, the maker of bowling alleys and equipment. Why does

Chicago Theater
(Courtesy of Chicago
Historical Society,
ICHi 024875)

Carmen Salvino resonate with me? Because he takes this baby boomer back to childhood memories when bowling was one of the most popular sports on television. Meet the world of "Whispering" Joe Wilson, the ranking broadcast announcer in the era of the bowling venues explored in this book. My sister and I watched those shows when we were kids. I rooted for Johnny King, while my sister rooted for Chicagoan Salvino, a great bowler who she also thought was a heartthrob.

Chicago's venues offered more than local experiences; they often set national standards. Chicago's jazz and blues scenes were among the tops in the country. Everyone knew that. There were national musical broadcasts from the Edgewater Beach Hotel, Aragon Ballroom, and Blackhawk Restaurant. The Chicago Theatre was the flagship for the national fleet of Balaban and Katz theaters. Second City was the home for improvisational comedy that supplied talent to the nation, including *Saturday Night Live*. Who in the world didn't know about the original Playboy Club?

Regrets, I have a few. I was old enough to have visited the nightclubs that my parents had loved so much, but I never set foot in the Gaslight Club or the Chez Paree. Not even once. I kick myself for never having visited the Gold Star Sardine Bar. I always thought I would make it to that tiny little venue with the fabulously curated talent, but then it was closed. I used to live a couple of blocks from the original Old Town School of Folk Music. When I walked by, I could hear the music through the open window. Once it was the deep voice of its founder, Win Stracke. I should have walked in just to thank him.

The best part about this book for me is that I can immerse myself in so many of the places that I never entered and get a sense of why each and every one of them was an experience worth collecting. **Thank you Neal Samors and Bob Dauber!**

Gary T. Johnson

MEMORIES OF CHICAGO ENTERTAINMENT

Neal Samors

I grew up in Chicago and lived in the city from 1943 until 1976 except for years away at college. In 1976 my wife, daughter, and I moved to the suburbs but still came into the city regularly to enjoy the variety of entertainment venues from movie theaters, concerts, and plays to sporting events, comedy clubs, and an occasional jazz and folk club. My earliest recollection was going with my parents to hear classical music by sitting on the lawn near the original Grant Park band shell on the south end of the park near the Field Museum. Several times I went with my family to the Riverview Amusement Park on Western Avenue. When I was in grammar school I was part of a group of classmates who went downtown regularly to a classical concert series at the Symphony Hall on South Michigan Avenue across from the Art Institute. It was there that I developed an enjoyment and appreciation of classical music.

I also spent a lot of time roaming around the Loop when I was young and would see live shows on stage at the Chicago Theater including a memorable one by Roy Rogers, Dale Evans, and Trigger. My family and I would also come downtown regularly for dinner at the city's many restaurants and go to the Balaban and Katz theaters for the major, first-run movies. One time we saw *Around The World in Eighty Days*, and another time it was *The Bridge On The River Kwai* at the spectacular State and Lake Theater. As I grew up and attended high school, I went on dates in the city including after senior prom taking my date to the Gate of Horn, and, on one New Year's Eve, I double dated and went to the Chicago Theater to see *Butterfield Eight.* I had a class in high school called Literature of the Drama and, one day, our class went to the Blackstone Theater to see the great play, *Raisin in the Sun*. I also regularly went with family, friends, or on dates up to Highland Park to hear many concerts at Ravinia, including ones by Peter, Paul and Mary, Aretha Franklin, Tony Bennett, and, of course, the Chicago Symphony Orchestra.

While in college, I went with friends to the Plugged Nickel on Wells Street to hear the Horace Silver Quintet and to the No Exit Cafe to hear Art Thieme, the great folk singer and brother of a college friend. When I got married, my wife and I went to see *Jacques Brel is Alive and Well and Living in Paris* at the Happy Medium and to the London House to have dinner and hear Ramsey Lewis, and throughout the 1970s we often went to Second City and to plays at many of the theaters in the downtown area including Steppenwolf on Halsted Avenue. I began following the Chicago Cubs in 1952 thanks to my father who was a diehard baseball fan. Throughout all my years in Chicago, I attended numerous Cubs and White Sox games, a few Bears and Blackhawk games, did a lot of bowling at the Howard Bowl in Rogers Park, and played a lot of 16" softball. Obviously, Chicago offered its residents a wide variety of entertainment opportunities.

MY KIND OF TOWN

Bob Dauber

Quite often, I make the statement, "I am so fortunate to have grown up *where* and *when* I did—Chicago, in the 20th century."

Of course, as it was unfolding, I don't think I realized the impact it would have on me in so many ways, until I started looking back. It never dawned on me that the panoply of entertainment choices presented to me was not available to so many people who weren't here to experience what so many others and I had.

An obvious first recollection would be the Chicago Theater where I was exposed to a first-run feature film followed by a complete stage show consisting of comedians, musicians, circus-type acts all of the caliber that appeared on the weekly *Ed Sullivan Show* on TV. As I recall, we were charged the grand sum of 75 cents for all of this. Quite often, the actors and actresses who appeared in the movies on display were on hand to sign autographs at the end of the day.

Another facet of entertainment in Chicago was the number of broadcast events that originated here, that we were able to attend while they were being sent LIVE over the airwaves. *The Breakfast Club* on radio and *Garroway at Large* on TV, to name just a couple. For the kids, *Kukla, Fran and Ollie* came from Chicago and were created by Chicagoan Burr Tillstrom, who grew up in Rogers Park. There were talent shows akin to *America's Got Talent*, originating from television studios in the Chicago Tribune Tower.

Live music. The London House. Mister Kelly's. Wise Fools Pub. The Plugged Nickel. The Blue Note. Sutherland Lounge. Concerts performed by the Chicago Symphony Orchestra at Orchestra Hall and outdoor performances at the Grant Park Band Shell, later renamed the James C. Petrillo Shell in honor of the late leader of the American Federation of Musicians. The Marine Dining Room at Edgewater Beach Hotel. The Boulevard Room at the Conrad Hilton. The Empire Room at the Palmer House. The Camelia Room at the Drake Hotel.

Theater and comedy? The Goodman. The Schubert. The Blackstone. Second City. The Civic Opera House.

Sports? You name it. Wrigley Field. Comiskey Park. Soldier Field. Chicago Stadium. The arenas that were home to the Chicago Cubs, Chicago White Sox, Chicago Blackhawks, Chicago Bears, and the Chicago Bulls. So many memorable events that took place at these shrines.

Entertaining Chicago? What follows in this book are deliciously retold memories by so many who experienced them or actually performed at some of the aforementioned venues. These are the things that make Chicago—and for those of us who grew up and/or lived here in the 20th century—*my kind of town!*

Blue Note on Clark Street, (Courtesy of Chicago Historical Society, ICHi-027861)

JAZZ CLUBS

DOWNTOWN

THE BLUE NOTE

Located first at 56 W. Madison Street, near Dearborn Street, in downtown Chicago, the club was owned by Frank Holzfeind who opened the venue on November 25, 1947. The offerings included an eclectic mix of music from Dixieland, and big band swing to modern jazz. In 1953, Holzfeind moved the Blue Note to North Clark Street, but ended up closing in 1960 mainly because the fees charged by the big bands and star jazz performers just became too expensive. Among the jazz greats who could be heard at the Blue Note were Duke Ellington, Louis Armstrong, Dizzy Gillespie, George Shearing, Lionel Hampton, and Jack Teagarden. The Blue Note also created recordings by Woody Herman, Stan Kenton, Benny Goodman, Dave Brubeck, the Oscar Peterson Trio, and Harry James.

TOM HOLZFEIND | SON OF OWNER OF THE BLUE NOTE

Before my father opened the Blue Note he was working at the Northwestern Railroad. Dad started a bowling league since bowling was really popular then. The owner of the bowling alley was a guy named Harold Wessel. Wessel also owned a club in downtown Chicago called Lipp's Lower Level. The strength of his organization was with the bowling league and the various leagues managed by my father. Mr. Wessel also made my father the manager of Lipp's Lower Level, a post-WWII club for folks to come and just listen to music, not necessarily jazz. I'm not sure of the amount of time that this took, but, eventually, my father managed to buy the option to own the place from Harold Wessel in 1946. Dad decided to operate it as a jazz club because he loved that type of music. It also happened that at that time there was a disc jockey who had a radio show and who occasionally played jazz. His name was Dave Garroway, the eventual host of the original *Today Show*. It turned out that my father consulted with Garroway about jazz and who were

the best musicians he should hire to perform at the club. Dave and my father became quite close, and it was Garroway who made a really important point to my father about operating the Blue Note. Garroway told Dad that if he was going to have a jazz club that it had to be an integrated club, and that was a huge milestone in the 1940s. Garroway said that the club should be integrated in terms of the audience as well as having black and white jazz players performing there.

One of my father's great accomplishments was to have that type of club. Over the years, Dad won awards from the Urban League and organizations like that. According to an Urban League statement from the award: "...for your courageous pioneering policy and practice in Chicago's entertaining world of admitting guests solely with respect to their good manners, and of employing musicians at the Blue Note solely with respect to their artistry—thus setting a pattern of decency and democracy." So, Garroway was the one who put that thought in my dad's mind and boy, "it was off to the races" after that for the Blue Note. In addition, the jazz performers at the Blue Note, even from the very beginning, were remarkable people from the club's heyday in the late 1940s until the club closed around 1960.

The great Duke Ellington played at the Blue Note more than any other person. In fact, he and my father became quite close and, over the years, they corresponded regularly and Duke would perform with his band at the club a couple times a year. What was unusual was that when he came he would stay for two weeks. So, for example, over the Christmas break, always, he came for two to four weeks which gave the musicians and their families the chance to stay in place for more than one or two nights. Other big names who performed at the club included Count Basie, Stan Kenton, Dave Brubeck, Oscar Peterson, Ella Fitzgerald, Sarah Vaughan, and Billie Holiday. So the really major players of the time performed at the Blue Note. In fact, one of the great lines from Duke Ellington was when he called the Blue Note the "Metropolitan House of Jazz." Those were the kinds of players who performed there.

Ahmad Jamal, formerly Fritz Jones, also performed at the club in the early 1950s when he was only 19-20 years old, and there is a great story my father told about him when he first played at the club. At the end of his performances, my father gave him a $1,000 bonus and, he was so touched that he left for Paris, France, where his career took off. Ahmad was always so grateful to my father for his generosity. I think that he came back and played at the club several times again. Those were the kinds of people who were at the Blue Note.

In 1947, Dad moved the Blue Note to another venue at 3 North Clark Street, right in the heart of downtown. In those days, that was the place to be and there were a couple of interesting things about that place. One was that it was a very large venue and it had a very big stage, which was one of the few places that could accommodate the big bands. You know, Ellington and Basie had 20+ piece bands, so you had to have room for them to perform. The other thing that was sort of interesting about it was that my father created this thing called the Teen Terrace. The idea was that he had a section of the club that was located at a higher level, stage right (if you were in the audience, it was on the left) which had a sort of picket fence and was four or five steps up, but still very close to the stage. But, that is where people who were under 21 years old could come, buy a Coke, and listen to the greatest jazz musicians of all time. Dad was very proud of the fact that he was able to introduce young people to jazz. When I was still living in Chicago, I would run into people and after I told them who I was, they would tell me that they experienced jazz at the club. The Blue Note closed in 1960, but when it was open it was a pretty big deal.

There are a few theories concerning why the club ended up closing. First, the costs of performers increased. One example was Nat King Cole who played at the Blue Note a couple of times. After he had the hit song, *Nature Boy*, his price charged just skyrocketed and my father said, "I just can't afford you." He was paying the Count Basie Band something like $5,000 a week (today that is nothing,

but this is back in 1950), and, at one point, the cost just doubled and he could not afford to pay those prices. A side note to that was that when Duke Ellington played at the Blue Note, his rate never increased from the very beginning in the late 1940s up until the club closed in 1960. He was just a good buddy of my dad's and they had great rapport. I think that the price of talent just skyrocketed overnight and the business was moving a lot away from the Loop down to the Rush Street area northward. That was probably the other reason for the change and the club's closing. These guys started playing in convention halls and big amphitheaters, and small clubs couldn't afford the musicians' price increases. Then, there was the movement away from the inner Loop when Chicagoans started staying away from the Loop in the evenings. But, despite all of those factors, I don't think that Dad ever considered moving the club further north.

I was born in 1946, so I was a teenager when it closed, but all of my memories are from when I was still in grammar school. My mother took us down to the club for Sunday matinees, regularly, so we were exposed to that music during all my early life. We lived on the Northwest Side near Foster and Cicero in a neighborhood called Forest Glen which was just off Elston Avenue.

There is another important story about the club that relates to Evanston. One night my father wanted to take Duke Ellington out to dinner during the mid 1950s but he could not find a restaurant that would serve him and an African American for dinner, even someone with the stature of one of the greatest entertainers and intellectuals in the history of music. Finally, he decided to call the owner of Fanny's Restaurant in Evanston. Dad said to her, "Here's the deal. I've got this incredible man I want to take to dinner and his name is Duke Ellington." According to the story that I heard, Fanny said to him, "Well, I don't like it, but because it is you, I'll do it." So, this is one of those incredible stories about integration that, in that day and age, a man of Ellington's international stature couldn't be served in a white-owned restaurant.

Duke Ellington,
(Courtesy of Chicago
Historical Society,
ICHi-024875)

SONDRA FARGO | EDUCATOR

As for jazz places in the Loop, the Blue Note was the primary place, and probably the only place that we frequented. Sometimes they would have jazz concerts at the Civic Opera House, or, sometimes, at Orchestra Hall, but the Blue Note was the place that you would go to hear Count Basie or Duke Ellington or Woody Herman bands.

BOB DAUBER | AUTHOR

I remember the time we went to the Blue Note after my senior prom to hear Duke Ellington. On our way there, I said to my girlfriend, "It's going to be great to see the Duke again." She said, "Do you know him?" I said, "Sure!" So, we went to Blue Note, and who was standing at the maitre d' stand but Duke Ellington. He took a look at me and said, "Man, how are you doing, great to see you." My girlfriend looked like her jaw was going to hit the floor. I said, "It's good to see you." I couldn't have scripted it any better, especially when you consider the fact that he didn't even know me. It was just one of those very happy accidents.

JOE LEVINSON | MUSICIAN

For jazz, the Blue Note on Randolph was extremely popular. The biggest names worked there, including Duke Ellington, Dizzie Gillespie, Harry James, Charley Barnet, The Sauter-Finnigan Band, Dave Brubeck, and Les Brown. There was just an amazing array of artists who appeared there, and it became known as one of the world's greatest jazz rooms.

THE BLACK ORCHID

Founded by Al Greenfield in 1949, the upscale nightclub was located at Rush and Ontario Streets on the city's Near North Side. Frequented by celebrities that included Hugh Hefner and Tony Bennett, it was also the place that Johnny Mathis was claimed to have gotten his first big break. Greenfield sold the club in 1956 to Paul Raffles, Pat Fontecchio, and Bill Doherty. The group also were the owners of the Cloister Inn at 900 N. Rush Street. The Black Orchid had such famous performers as Harry Belafonte, Diahann Carroll, Ray Charles, Billy Eckstine, Buddy Hackett, Mort Sahl, Mel Torme, Dinah Washington, and Jonathan Winters. The owners of the club declared bankruptcy in 1959 and never reopened.

BOB DAUBER | AUTHOR

I would go to the Black Orchid, and I remember when we went there and saw Johnny Mathis in 1957 or 1958 when he was already a big star. His warm-up act was a guy I never heard of by the name of Professor Irwin Korey who was billed as "The World's Foremost Authority." He came out wearing a beat-up tuxedo, was rather disheveled looking, and he would walk back and forth across the stage without saying a word for about three or four minutes. Then, he would pick up somebody's drink, take a sip, put it back down, and his opening line was always the same. He'd stop and look like he was about to say something, and then he would start walking back and forth again. Then, he'd stop and, finally, he'd say, "However…" That was always the opening line to his act.

THE BIRDHOUSE

A small jazz club that was created by jazz saxophonist Fred Anderson in the 1960s in a second-story loft at Dearborn and Division, it lasted until 1978. The club catered to an under-21 year-old clientele by not serving alcohol. However, major jazz performers like Oscar Peterson and Ramsey Lewis offered their music to the young listeners at The Birdhouse.

BILL BENJAMIN | ASHEVILLE, NC

I became a big fan of jazz in my teens. And, of course, Chicago offered up a great menu of jazz clubs and big-name performers. The problem was that being underage, there weren't too many places I could go to and listen to that wonderful music. There was a place, though, that opened up that had specifically tried to appeal to the younger crowd to try to expose them to real live jazz. It was called

The Birdhouse and it was located on Dearborn between Division and Goethe. The club was unique because it had a section for underage folks called The Peanut Gallery and there was also a separate section for imbibers. So, the place was literally split in half for those who could legally drink alcohol and those who could not. While the club was short-lived, we youngsters were able to come listen to the likes of Gene Ammons, Sonny Stitt, Bill Henderson, Quincy Jones, Slide Hampton, and Thelonius Monk, to name just a few.

One of the great things about growing up in Chicago was having access to some terrific radio jazz shows·and I remember, specifically, three jazz DJ's – Sid McCoy, Daddy-O Daylie and of course, Dick Buckley. They did so much to promote the exposure to great jazz music. There were a couple of other jazz DJ's during the 50s, 60s and early 70s and it was a great time for jazz music on the radio. Of course, all of that has changed with the advent of the Internet and access to resources like Sirius, etc.

TED YOUNG | EDUCATOR
THE NETHERLANDS

The Birdhouse was my favorite jazz place, not because of its alcohol policy that made my admission possible, but because of its intimacy and the excellence of its artists. Remembering things past: Oscar Brown, Jr. (*Mr. Kicks*), Lambert, Hendricks & Ross (*Cloudburst*), The Horace Silver Quintet (*Song for My Father*), and Art Blakey & His Jazz Messengers (*Caravan*)—a feast!

Eisenhower was in the White House, soon to be followed by that young guy from Massachusetts, and Hanoi and Selma were far, far away. We were teenagers in Chicago and the music was sweet. We were first generation rock-and-rollers but it is the jazz and folk that I remember most. Live and on radio, they were there for the asking.

"Hey babe and you, too, old bean, it's the real McCoy" was the sign-on of Sid McCoy on his late-night jazz program on AM radio. Here I was introduced to Frank, Ella, and Miles. On the FM side there was "Midnight Special" with Norm Pelligrini,

the most eclectic (and long-lasting!) folk program one could imagine. Eclectic meaning that in one broadcast you could hear Tom Lehrer, Josh White, and Mohammed el-Bakkar and his Oriental Ensemble.

As teenagers, live music was limited to the weekends. In symbiosis with the radio, it provided the sounds, the mannerisms, and the smells to truly flesh-out the broadcast experience. I saw Gibson and Camp at the old Gate of Horn and Theodore Bikel, Judy Collins, and Lenny Bruce at the new Gate of Horn. The performers were all extraordinary but the old venue trumped the new.

And then, in 1959 there was the first Playboy Jazz Festival. We were not quite 16 and the Chicago Stadium was anything but intimate, but my classmate Dave Beck and I were there. The jazz and the crowd were wonderful; the Bunnies were absent.

These memories are secure but those times were a bubble. For me, the bubble burst on August 29, 1968. And, like all things Chicago, it had a soundtrack, *Prologue* and *Someday* from Chicago Transit Authority. The whole world, you see, really was watching.

RAMSEY LEWIS | MUSICIAN

In 1950, I was 15 years old and still in high school at Wells High School. I had just joined the musicians' union and when I told them I was 16 they didn't ask for any proof. I started playing with a band called the Cleffs, led by Wallace Burton, who invited me to come over to his house and told me what jazz records to buy and listen to and showed me chord symbols rather than writing the chord out. Wallace was the one who whetted my appetite for jazz.

There were girls there, and I was in high school and my first year of college. In addition, you picked up $5 or $6 a weekend and, in those days, it wasn't loose change. I also pretended to play piano, but, I think that in my heart it was still going to be classical music for my career. I went to the University of Illinois for my academics, but I also studied music at the Chicago Musical College which, today, is part of Roosevelt University. I took music and piano classes with Dorothy Mendelsohn, who was the piano teacher at both Chicago Musical College and DePaul University. I had met Red Holt and Eldee Young, the drum and bass players, respectively, with the Cleffs. They were part of that seven-piece group.

The Korean War broke up our seven-piece group, and Red went into Service for a year and a half. Eldee Young and I were the only two guys who didn't go. In those days, if you were in college, you were deferred from military service until needed. While Red was in the Army we used a drummer named Butch McCann, but when Red got out of the Army, the three of us got together between 1954 and 1956. Chess Records produced our first records and we were playing in a nightclub called the Lake Meadows Lounge on 35th and South Parkway, later King Drive. We were pretty much part of the wallpaper there because we played music but people weren't as attentive as we wanted them to be. A few people came in just to hear us, and one of them was Daddy-O Daylie, a big-time disc jockey/jazz jockey in Chicago and he was on WAIT-AM in those days. He would come in there to hear us, and we must have played there for a year or more.

One of the times he came in and said, "You know, you guys are pretty good. You guys should have a record deal." We had heard that before, but he came back in a couple of weeks and he said, "I've arranged for an audition for you with a record company. On Saturday, show up at 48th and Cottage Grove at a stationary store that is owned by the Chess brothers who are just starting a label. In fact, they have already started the label that focuses on the blues, but they are looking to expand into jazz." So, we showed up that Saturday afternoon and they had a piano back in the shipping department. We set up and played three or four songs, and Phil Chess was smoking his pipe and said, "Yeah, yeah, you guys are pretty good." So Phil called Sonny out of the shipping department, and he asked him, "What do you think of these guys?" We played a couple more times and Sonny said, "These guys are really good." Phil said, "You think they're all right?" Sonny said, "Yeah, they're very good."

So, Phil told us that he wanted to talk to his brother, Leonard, and he would get back to us. About a week later, Daddy-O called us and told us that they wanted to sign our trio. So, we got our first record deal and they recorded it under the Argo label. In those days, they recorded their blues under Chess and Checker and their jazz under Argo. They eventually had to give up that name because some other company was using the Argo name, so they changed their jazz label to Cadet. We continued to record with them until 1969 or 1970. Then we went with Columbia Records.

In the early days, with the Chess family they had already recorded the blues and they knew the best blues makers because they ended up with some of the best blues artists ever. They kind of left it up to us as to what to play because they didn't know quite what to do, although Phil Chess used to say. "Play more high notes, play more high notes!" But, I didn't know what that meant. He was honest and sincere about it, and he just liked the sound of the high end of the piano. But, we were pretty much left up to our own devices and we recorded the first album called *The Gentlemen of Swing* and there was a song on there called *Carmen* that got a fair amount of air play. The next album was called *Gentlemen of Jazz* and there was a song on there called *Delilah*, which even got more air play. The first album after they recorded us sat on the shelf for a while, and they were not certain if they wanted to put it out. Daddy-O Daylie said to them, "If you put it out, at least in Chicago, I guarantee that I will play it." So, they did put it out in Chicago, he played it, and then Marty Faye and others played it, so we became fairly well known because of their support. And, because of their help they released the album in Philadelphia and Washington, DC and both of the first two albums caught on there. We recorded 17 albums by the time we had our first big hit. In those days, you recorded two albums a year. Every six months you went into the studio and did another album, and every new album became more popular and we were pretty happy.

JAZZ SHOWCASE Since 1947
WHERE JAZZ LIVES IN CHICAGO
(312)670-BIRD
(& CLARK)

EXIT

CHICAGO JAZZ

1st Annual Chicago Jazz Festival

THE FINEST IN JAZZ SINCE 1939
BLUE NOTE

As we approached 1965, we were recording our seventeenth album and we put it out. A couple of months after it was out, we got a call from the record company saying that we had a big hit on our hands. We didn't quite understand quite what that meant because we didn't record albums in those days to be "big hits." We recorded them because that's the way we felt about music at that time. So, we were like, "What song are they playing? Why is it a hit?" And they told us, it was the song called *The In Crowd*. We found that to be very humorous because *The In Crowd* was the final song we put on the album and it was sort of the "dessert," and we thought that we had the "meat and potatoes" and we wanted something light and gay, so we put that on and that song caught on. That was also the name of the album, and that became our first big, national hit. After that, there were several other hits and Joe Glazer got involved and booked us all over the United States in the major concert halls and nightclubs.

It was still the three of us as a trio, but in January 1966 after we had become a huge hit (we had been together since 1954 or 1955), we decided to break up the group. The money was coming left and right, and there was great notoriety, and although we had great album sales and concerts, we just decided to break up the group.

THE JAZZ SHOWCASE

Founded in 1947 by Joe Segal, The Jazz Showcase has been at over 60 locations in Chicago over the years, including its current one on South Plymouth Court next to the Dearborn Station. The club has been a venue for many of the greats of jazz, including Ahmad Jamal, McCoy Tyner, Kenny Burrell, Eddie Harris, Bill Evans, Sonny Stitt, Gene Ammons, Joe Williams, Art Blakey and the Jazz Messengers, Ornette Coleman, and Marian McPartland.

JAZZ, LTD.

Jazz, Ltd. was a Dixieland jazz band managed by Bill Reinhardt from June 1947 to April 1978 that included the great Sidney Bechet. It was also a nightclub in existence from June, 1947 to February 1972 that was managed by Bill's wife, Ruth. First located at 11 E. Grand Avenue it was also situated at 164 E. Grand Avenue. Bill and Ruth co-owned the club. It was estimated that over 700 musicians played at the jazz club over the years including Bechet, Barrett Deems, Eddie Higgins, Art Hodes, Jimmy McPartland, Chet Roble, Jack Teagarden, and Franz Jackson. And, finally, Jazz, Ltd. was also a record label that produced over a dozen albums.

GOLD STAR SARDINE BAR

Located at 680 N. Lake Shore Drive at Erie and founded by Bill Allen, it probably got its name from the fact that it could only seat a maximum of 50–60 people. It was in operation from 1982 until 1997. The club never charged a minimum or a cover charge, took no reservations, offered free cigarettes, and was open for lunch as well as late evenings. Some of the big names in jazz who performed at the Gold Star were Tony Bennett, Bobby Short, Buddy Rich, Stan Getz, Julie Wilson, and Woody Herman.

BILL ZWECKER | ENTERTAINMENT REPORTER AND TELEVISION PERSONALITY
The Gold Star Sardine Bar is a great story. I remember going there one night and seeing Liza Minnelli who was in town. She was great friends with Bill Allen, who was a wonderful cabaret kind of guy and who co-owned the club. He loved that kind of music and was the one who launched the Sardine Bar. Liza had been performing at the Lyric Opera House and came over to the Gold Star Sardine Bar afterwards when we were all there. Of course, I saw Bobby Short there a couple of times when he came to town and he loved that place because it was so intimate

and obviously much, much smaller than the Carlyle where he performed regularly in New York. But, he just loved the intimacy of the Gold Star.

ANDY'S JAZZ CLUB

The club was first opened in 1951 as Andy's 11 E. Lounge just east of State Street near Mother Hubbard's, the preeminent River North sports bar. The club served as a hangout for newspaper workers from the nearby *Chicago Tribune* and *Chicago Sun-Times*. It grew into a renowned jazz club and restaurant and, in 1975, a group of investors bought the club and changed its name to Andy's. Among those jazz stars who have performed at Andy's were Chuck Hedges, Larry Coryell, Franz Jackson, Barrett Deems, Art Hoyle, and Von Freeman.

CAROL MARKER | GURNEE, IL

One of our favorite places was Andy's. We went there a lot, and it was where we would see a different band each week. Still, we loved taking the out-of-towners there to show off our Chicago clubs jazz scene. So Monday night was a key night to escape your reality and go out in Chicago and have a ball.

I would add that my husband was a dentist and he totally understood embouchure and the importance of it to musicians who played instrument using their mouths. So, not only were these people musicians, but they also were patients of his and ultimately became social friends of ours, as well. There was no bigger fan of these musicians and their music than my husband.

OLD TOWN

PLUGGED NICKEL

The club was located in Old Town on North Wells Street. Miles Davis recorded several famous albums at the club, and bands like the Horace Silver Quintet performed there.

PENNY LANE | BROADCAST PERSONALITY AND ENTERTAINMENT CONSULTANT

It was a blistering, cold Chicago winter night. My husband, Wayne, and I had gone to the Plugged Nickel on Wells to see Buddy Rich and his big band. After the show, we were beginning the drive home. We were on Clark St. around North Avenue and we stopped for the light. Standing on the corner, trying to keep his coat closed as the wind was blowing gale force along with the snow was Buddy Rich. I said, "Look, honey, that's Buddy Rich standing there. We should give him a ride." So we pulled over and I lowered the window and said, "Mr. Rich, do you need a lift?" He gratefully accepted. Now, we were driving a ratty old car, but at this point I don't think he cared. I hopped into the back seat, and Buddy sat up front with Wayne. He was staying at the Playboy Mansion and that's where we took him. He was so appreciative and just thanked us profusely. A nice ending to a terrific evening.

UPTOWN, EDGEWATER AND ROGERS PARK

GREEN MILL COCKTAIL LOUNGE

The jazz club is located at 4802 N. Broadway in Chicago in the Uptown neighborhood on the North Side. It originally opened in 1907 as Pop Morse's Roadhouse and was renamed Green Mill Gardens just a few years later. It was a favorite of Al Capone during the Prohibition Era. It appeared in several movies including *Prelude to a Kiss* and *High Fidelity*. Other North Side jazz clubs included Club Laurel, Key of C, 1111 Club, Club Silhouette, Club Detour, Marios, and Bar-O, some of which were either located in the Uptown and Edgewater neighborhoods or on Howard Street in the Rogers Park neighborhood.

LARRY BEERS | MUSICIAN | CHICAGO

I'm from downstate Illinois, and I studied at the U. of I. and had some wonderful teachers over the years who helped prepare me for the move to Chicago. Champaign could be considered as the springboard

Bobby Short,
Gold Star Sardine Bar,
1988

Andrea Marcovicci,
Gold Star Sardine Bar,
1988

to jump to Chicago. I believe the first club I played at professionally was the now-defunct, Orphans. It was on Lincoln. I think this was around 1982. When I moved up to Chicago in the mid-80s, around '86 or so, a good friend of mine, a bass player named Angus Thomas was playing with Ghallib Ghallab and some other players at a place called Kiku's and I sat in one night. After doing it, they asked if I wanted the gig. I was waiting tables at the time, so I jumped at the opportunity and started playing with them.

We played all kinds of joints for about a year— places like The Backroom and The Cotton Club, which didn't do very well. It was on South Michigan. This was when the Bulls were still kind of not at the top of the NBA rankings, but I remember one night when Michael Jordan walked in with Horace Grant and Scottie Pippen and this was before they became big stars. One night, McCoy Tyner and Stanley Turrentine came in and they sat in with us. They played a couple of tunes with us and that was a major big deal; kind of a happening—a brush with greatness, if you will. McCoy Tyner and Stanley Turrentine are two iconic legends and I never dreamed that I would be playing with them.

Over the years, getting to know a lot of people, I would play at other places like The Bop Shop and the Green Mill, which is a legendary fixture in Chicago. I was also playing in rock clubs like The Avalon, formerly called Tuts on Belmont. There were other places, half of which I can't remember because they were there for only a short while. But, the Beat Kitchen, which is still there was one of the clubs. Alan Baer opened it before he sold it to the present owner.

I played with a real fun group—The Action Figures that included Kevon Smith, Angus Thomas, myself, and another player who Angus really taught how to play bass. His name is Darryl Jones and he's gone on to a little gig to play with a small rock band called The Rolling Stones. Darryl Jones also went on to play with a trumpet player you might have heard of—Miles Davis. The Action Figures was a funk/rock band that we'd put together. This was around 1988 and we had formed a pretty solid rock quartet that held court and played different rock venues for over three years. We had a steady Monday night gig at a place called Esoteria and another called the Big Nasty. So many of the musicians were off on Monday nights, so they would come and sit in with us. Buddy Miles was a regular in Chicago in those days, so he would often come and sit in with us. Sometimes, he would take over my drums for a couple of tunes or he would just sing. One time, he surprised all of us and played guitar. Turned out he had learned guitar while he was working with Jimi Hendrix. After about a year at Esoteria and then a year at the Big Nasty, we moved over to a place called The Union, which was just south of the Vic. The Monday night culture resulted in all kinds of musicians showing up to play with us, like Dave Mick from the Big Twist and Larry Nolan, also from the Big Twist. Derek Frigo, Johnny's son and a guitarist from Enuff Z'Nuff.

In the late 80s and into the early 90s, I worked with a wonderful musician, Nick Tremulis and we did a series of benefits called The Waltz. Nick took the name from the film, *The Last Waltz*, which was a Martin Scorcese-directed documentary of The Band's final performance. There were five of them in total and these were done to benefit homeless teenagers. They were held at The Metro. Nick was able to really pull some strings in terms of attracting musicians to perform at these events. In fact, the first one of them that we did, Rick Danko from The Band came to perform. The list of people who came to do these shows were folks like Mavis Staples, Ronnie Spector, Ian Hunter from Mott The Hoople, and so many other big-name performers.

A lot of memorable moments for me, as a musician in Chicago.

BOB CUNNIFF

On Argyle, there was the Tail Spin, and further west on Argyle there was the place where Charlie Parker and Lester Young played at the Green Mill, and on Bryn Mawr there was the 1111 Club that was right by the "L." We also went up to Howard Street after the War, and Art Tatum was performing at the Club Silhouette in an empty room. So, I got my own personal "audience" with Art Tatum.

DEMPSEY TRAVIS | AUTHOR

Club Laurel on north Broadway was a place that we went to a lot of times. Count Basie used to play there all the time. They had society singers there and it was a high-class place. The Green Mill on north Broadway was one of the original jazz places and opened in the early '30s. We used to go there after the Aragon Ballroom to have a beer and listen to some good jazz after listening to waltzes by Wayne King.

There was also the 1111 Club on the North Side that was famous because of a guy named George Brunies who was a great trombone player, and who played with all the top jazz people including the band leader Paul Whiteman. But, Brunies didn't like playing with a big band and preferred a small group where he could feature his jazz trombone. He actually would lay on his back and play the trombone with his feet.

JOE LEVINSON | MUSICIAN

Many of the jazz clubs located along the "L" on the North Side were just storefronts. One of them was the Key of C, which was located on Broadway around Wellington. They had jam sessions in there all the time, and that was where I met Fred Karlin, who later won the Oscar for *For All We Know* from the movie *Lovers and Other Strangers*. He was a trumpet player from Winnetka who had graduated from Amherst College at the age of 18 and he was brilliant. Fred had formed an octet that was rehearsing in his home, and the group played his own arrangements. He not only played the trumpet, but also the piano and he was a great arranger. A lot of the local musicians went up to Winnetka to play in his octet, and I was one of them. That was where I learned the art of "chamber music jazz," playing tightly arranged, highly difficult, and exciting

arrangements. A lot of them were original compositions, and some of them were tunes that were standards.

Clubs like the Key of C existed all over the city of Chicago, including the Club Laurel and the Green Mill, probably the longest running jazz club in the world at a single location. In fact, I played there in the '40s and early '50s with a bunch of local musicians like Sandy Moss and Eddie Avis. There was also a place on Milwaukee Avenue and Webster called Mario's. Mario was an Italian bar owner, and he had a band there on weekends and a little stage in this bar, and it was the dumpiest place. My friend, Eddie Avis, the trombone player, was part of that band. They didn't have a bass, but they had a vibraphone, trombone, tenor sax, and guitar. In those years, I was starting to do a lot of society work and playing dance bands, and, on the weekends; playing weddings in hotels downtown. I'd be done at midnight on a job on a Saturday night, and I would drive my Chevy with my bass over to Mario's. The sun was just coming up on Sunday morning, and I had played all night at Mario's with these jazz players and it was just wild. I played in a lot of the joints. In those days, sitting in was a lot easier and almost expected in a lot of the places, even in the more sophisticated rooms. If you were a good enough player, and they knew you, they'd say, "I'll take a rest, you play bass for a set." I got to play with an awful lot of people, including Ahmad Jamal on the South Side in a joint on 64th and Cottage Grove in the Pershing Hotel. When I knew Ahmad he was called Fritz Jones, and he played piano and his bass player, Israel Crosby, worked at the post office. One night Ahmad asked me to sit in with his group even though I was 16 at the time.

The 1111 Club was in Uptown right by the "L" on Granville, and they had a Dixieland band that played there with George Brunies and a drummer named "Hey Hey" Humphrey, who was a wonderful character. I also heard about all this music that was being played in Rogers Park in clubs on Howard Street. Traveling from Drexel Square on the South Side to Howard Street on the Far North Side was a

Andy's Jazz Club

The Green Mill, (Courtesy of Chicago Historical Society, ICHi-051416)

pretty big hike, especially in those days, since the expressways didn't exist. But, my dad was real good about it. He let me have the car, and I'd go to Howard Street and park it there. It was easy. But, one thing you got to know about Howard Street, both during and after the War, was that it was jammed with servicemen. They came from Great Lakes Naval Training Station, Glenview Naval Air Base, and Fort Sheridan located to the north of the city and Howard Street could be reached with the Chicago and Northwestern or North Shore trains.

The beautiful thing about Howard Street was that it was also located at the end of the line for the Chicago Howard Street "L" line. Howard Street was to the North Side what Rush Street was to downtown. It was a jumping street, at least on the south side of the street where liquor could be served while the Evanston side of the street was "dry." The two places that I knew about were the Club Silhouette and The Club Detour. I actually sat in the Club Detour when I was 17 years old. I wasn't old enough to be in there, but I probably conned my way in…certainly, the bartender didn't bother me. I only had a ginger ale since I wasn't a drinker in those days.

Both of those clubs were within a few blocks of one another just east of the Howard Street "L" station. When I'd go into the Silhouette… remember, again, that I wasn't old enough to be in there, I'd sneak in, and maybe they'd throw me out, and maybe they wouldn't. I remember listening to Herbie Fields and Charlie Ventura at the Silhouette. I remember seeing the Herbie Fields Octet or Septet there at the Silhouette, and that was a real powerhouse group that was sort of trying to be a Bop group. They were trying to get into that kind of thing. Swing music, the Benny Goodman and Tommy Dorsey kind of stuff was beginning to be passe among the hip musicians of the time. By the way, I was hep when it was hip to be hep. Anyhow, in those days I was hep, but I was not a hep cat because I didn't have the zoot suits and

the big shoulder stuff and the chain, and all that. And, a lot of the hep cats would wear a beret and let their goatee grow, and try to be like Dizzy Gillespie. And, there were a lot of guys who were smoking joints and doing all kinds of stuff with needles, but I never got into that, thank G-d.

I can't remember when the clubs closed, but I saw Art Tatum in the Club Detour one night when I went down there. I sat at the bar at the Detour and it was the kind of one of those bars with the piano and the little bandstand was behind the bartender. It was like a round bar surrounding the platform where the band was. And, here was Tatum all by himself up there, on a grand piano, in the middle of this bar playing and hardly anybody was in the club. Either nobody knew he was there, or they hadn't advertised very much, or I don't know what, but I sat there completely blown away. He was the greatest jazz piano player that I'd ever heard up 'til then, you know, and he was so advanced it was scary. There was his technique and his ideas and his harmonics and everything. It was like a graduate school course in how to be totally great on your instrument.

SONDRA FARGO | EDUCATOR

In the early to middle 1940s I remember going to the jazz clubs on Howard Street. In those days everybody danced. I was not drinking at that point, unlike some of the other kids I knew, but I loved to dance. And, so, except for the Aragon, the nearest place to where I went to school, at Evanston Township High School, was Howard Street. We went to such places as the Bar-O and the Club Silhouette, which was where I first saw Sarah Vaughn. They might have been postage-stamp sized places but they had some sort of dance floor. The fact is, I remember the Silhouette was really a nice nightclub located east of Paulina, close to Marshfield. We just hung out on Howard Street in those years after high school. I remember seeing Billy Eckstine there even though nobody had really heard of him yet.

SOUTH SIDE

CLUB DELISA

The Club DeLisa was located at 5521 S. State Street near Garfield Avenue on the city's South Side and was one of Chicago's most famous and important African American jazz clubs. It opened in 1934 and was owned by the four DeLisa brothers. The original building burned down in 1941 but was soon replaced by the New Club DeLisa. The club provided entertainment in the format of a variety show that featured singers, comedians, and dancers along with the DeLisa chorines. At the height of its popularity in the 1930s and 1940s, Club DeLisa was open 24 hours a day offering continuous entertainment. The Red Saunders Band was in residence at the club from 1937 to 1945 and 1947 to 1958, and other well known entertainers of the time included Fletcher Henderson, Count Basie, Joe Williams, Albert Ammons, and LaVern Baker. The club was closed in February 1958 following the death of two of the four DeLisa brothers.

JIM DELISA | SON
AND NEPHEW OF OWNERS

The Club DeLisa opened right after Prohibition. When my dad, Jim, came from Italy he first stopped in New York to visit relatives and friends. My dad became a carpenter, my uncle Mike became a tailor, and my uncle Louis became a shoemaker. After they arrived in America on the boat in New York City, my dad decided to come to Chicago.

He called my uncle Mike and my uncle Louis and said, "you gotta come to Chicago because there are bushels of money being made here." This was in the 1920s, and it was moonshine that was providing the money. So, they came and opened up five moonshines and a beer tavern on the South Side. After Prohibition ended, they established Club DeLisa in 1933 and when they first started, it was pay for your beer. But they would also give free pretzels and popcorn to draw the crowds. The original club seated 350 people but, on weekends, over 500 were

squeezed into the Club DeLisa. The crowds kept getting bigger and bigger, but then the first club at 55th and State Street burned down because of an electrical fire on February 11, 1941. So, they decided to open up the New Club DeLisa at 5521 S. State Street. People were laughing because they said that they wouldn't be able to build another club that quick, but my dad said that he was going to make it happen. And he and his brothers did just that in about two and one-half months. The new club was bigger and better than the original club, had central air conditioning, employed 150 staff, and accommodated 1,000–1,500 people and it had a stage with settings under the floor and you could hear Red Saunders with the band beating on his drums. The stage would rise and there would be Red Saunders, Louis Armstrong, and whoever was performing there. The stage would be raised so that there wasn't a bad seat in the house. And they did nightly floorshows.

At the old club, the actor John Barrymore would come there from the Blackstone Hotel in his robe and he would be eating salami, drinking, and flirting with the women. Bob Hope would also come to the club, as well as John Wayne. The Kirbys, the Eckstines, Joe Williams, La Verne Baker, Moms Mabley: they all started there, and even Sammy Davis Jr, along with his dad, when they came through Chicago. My dad and his brothers fed them when they didn't have enough money to eat.

All of the top jazz people came to Club DeLisa, and on Monday they had a breakfast show at six in the morning. Everybody who was appearing in Chicago would come to the club, do their thing on the stage, and then watch the other performers. Radio personality Daddy-O Daylie used to broadcast a radio show from the Club DeLisa.

On Saturday, my dad would have kiddie shows at the club. But when you went downstairs, the chorus girls were dressing, and there was gambling. One day, when U.S. Congressman William Dawson came to the club with his wife, my mom was sitting at a table, and the Congressman asked if he could join my mother. And, Mom said, "Of course you can," but Mrs. Dawson said that there was no way. She wanted

Club DeLisa, 1954

Red Saunders

Dancers, Rhumboogie Nightclub, Chicago, April 1941. Photo by Russell Lee, (Library of Congress)

the table for just her and the Congressman. She had no idea who my mom was. So, when Mrs. Dawson said to my mother, "You can leave now." My mom's answer was, "My name is Georgia DeLisa, and I would love for you to join me." So, they did and Dawson, who was the most powerful politician on Chicago's South Side, was a gentleman and sat with Mom.

TED SAUNDERS | SON OF DRUMMER RED SAUNDERS

My dad, Red Saunders, performed regularly at Club DeLisa. He started there in 1936, was the lead drummer, and Albert Ahmons was the first bandleader at the club. My father came up to Chicago from Memphis, Tennessee with my auntie on the Illinois Central Railroad. They arrived in Chicago around 1917 or 1918, and Lill Armstrong, Louis Armstrong's wife, had just come up from Memphis too. Many other musicians and entertainers came to Chicago from the south since Chicago was the key place for entertainment and for musicians from the 1920s on. The hottest recorders were the Red Hot Five and the Red Hot Seven who played in Chicago at the Grand Terrace. Lill Armstrong was the piano player with the group and also the one who wrote the records. It turned out that a nun taught Dad how to play drums. Lill was the one who used to sit down and teach each of the musicians their parts. They played at the Grand Terrace on 35th Street, and then it moved to 38th and Grand Boulevard (later King Drive).

We lived in back of a place called the Rhumboogie that was one of the city's top jazz clubs, but the Club DeLisa was the place in Chicago. The Club DeLisa was the first one that blacks and whites could go in and mix and sit down and watch the shows together. There were white acts and black acts in the show. They called them "black and tan" and it was the only place in town like that. In New York, the Cotton Club in Harlem was segregated. Blacks performed there but could not go in the club. If you were a musician and you were serious about playing music, you came to Chicago. So, all of the key musicians, including W.C. Handy, who was considered the "father of the blues," came and lived in Chicago. Nat King Cole came to Chicago in the 1940s, but he was a struggling musician who used to play at the Grand Terrace. He learned to play from Earl "Fatha" Hines who was at the Grand Terrace at that time. Nat used to go in and stand at the back door and watch Earl Hines play the piano.

My dad's full name was Theodore Dudley "Red" Saunders. "Red" was the name they gave him because many of the people in Memphis, at that time, were called Red. He was a light-skinned black man and, therefore, they called him "Red." One of his first major gigs was with John Phillip Sousa, playing drums with the band because the military band was made up of civilians who traveled with Sousa. That was how he got started. From there, he played in a group called the Walkathons, who traveled around the country, had dance contests and offered prizes. On the Walkathon that Dad was on, Red Skelton was the comedian and emcee of the show, and they got to be very close friends.

My mother and father were on the road with a show called *Harlem's Scandals* and my dad was the drummer who was making $75 a week which was considered a fortune in the early 1930s. My mother was a dancer in the show, and, actually, she came from a prominent family, because my grandfather was a lawyer and he was the man who was in charge of streets and driveways for the city of Chicago for 58 years. His name was Madison James Washington. My dad was playing at Club DeLisa during the War, and he was making records for Vee-Jay Records. Everybody came into the Club DeLisa including John Barrymore. Bob Hope lived in Chicago and worked here, and his manager used to book some of the acts at the club. His name was Charlie Hogan, and he was the main booker for the Regal Theater. One of the major things at the Club DeLisa was the security. Nobody bothered you when you went into the Club DeLisa, and one of the major reasons was the bouncers including Punjai. Those bouncers all seemed to be 6' 8" tall and weigh 300 pounds, and nobody messed with them. They looked out after everybody. When you came in the club, and you had the money or you were a prominent person, you had a front seat. They would grab a table and put you up front, right in the center, no matter what your color was.

JESSE WHITE | ILLINOIS SECRETARY OF STATE

I remember Club De Lisa that was located near 55th and State, and it was the place to go for live entertainment for African Americans. The fellow who owned the place was the father of someone who works for me, Jim DeLisa. The club really mattered to the African American community in Chicago because it was the place to go and be seen. Whenever there was good entertainment for African Americans in town you had to get a ticket to get in there. Since I was old enough to go there I do recall seeing the great pianist Red Saunders who played there. I also remember going to the Chicago Theater to hear my good friend Nat King Cole. What was strange about that was we were sitting in the back of the theater and there was someone who was so enthusiastic about the music that she yelled out, "Sing it Mr. Cole, sing it!" Then, of course, there is the fantastic Ramsey Lewis, who we honored recently for his commitment to providing entertainment to people across the State of Illinois.

RHUMBOOGIE CAFE/ RHUMBOOGIE CLUB

The club was located at 343 East 55th Street, but it was only in business for a short time from April 1942 until May 1947. The Rhumboogie was owned by world champion boxer, Joe Louis, and Charlie Glenn. Although the club closed after a fire on December 31, 1945, it did reopen in June 1946, but because business never came back to earlier heights, it closed a year later. When it originally opened, the first orchestra was Tiny Bradshaw and His Orchestra, which was followed by Horace Henderson, T-Bone Walker, and Milt Larkin. Other acts over the five years of the club's

existence included Sarah Vaughan and Charlie Parker. In October 1944, a Rhumboogie Recording Company was created with a house band that included Red Saunders, famous for playing at Club DeLisa. The label went out of existence in 1946.

GRAND TERRACE/SUNSET CAFE

Originally called the Sunset Cafe at 35th and Calumet, it later became the Grand Terrace. When it was the Sunset Cafe it was considered to be one of the hottest jazz venues in Chicago in the 1920s where such stars as Bix Beiderbecke, Benny Goodman, Gene Krupa, and Tommy and Jimmy Dorsey performed. In April 1926, Louis Armstrong joined the Sunset Cafe's band, becoming the band leader in 1927. Armstrong's master of ceremonies was Cab Calloway, and the band included Earl "Fatha" Hines. The club was raided on November 5, 1927 for openly selling bootleg whiskey. The Grand Terrace, originally located at 39th and King Drive opened in place of the Sunset Cafe and Earl Hines became the bandleader. The band broadcast on WMAQ. The Grand Terrace would close in 1940.

GRAND BALLROOM

The Grand Ballroom was located near 63rd and Cottage Grove which was previously known as the Frank Loeffler Building. In November 1923, Loeffler had purchased the previous building on the lot from Mayor "Big Bill" Thompson and had that structure demolished. The new Frank Loeffler building was constructed on that site. Next to the Loeffler Building was the 3,200-seat Tivoli Theater movie palace and the seven-story Pershing Hotel. The Loeffler Building became known as the Grand Ballroom where they would have lavish pageants and dances. The Pershing Hotel would become black-owned in 1943 and host such important black artists as Earl "Fatha" Hines, Ahmad Jamal, and Charlie Parker.

Regal Theater,(Courtesy of Chicago Historical Society, ICHi-139740)

Sutherland Hotel / Lounge (Courtesy of Chicago Historical Society, ICHi-021461)

DEMPSEY TRAVIS | AUTHOR
I started playing piano at five years of age, and I became interested in jazz when I was even younger because my father was a piano player.

In terms of the jazz clubs on State Street, the first ones that I can remember as a kid were on 35th Street and included the Grand Terrace at 35th and Calumet, on the southwest corner. I also went to the State Theater and to the Dreamland. Most interesting to me was seeing people going home at 9 or 10 in the morning dressed as if they were going out for the evening although they were just coming home after being out all night. You would see them leaving the various clubs, like Club DeLisa, Swinger, Rhumboogie, and Grand Terrace. I started going to the clubs when I was 15 and 16 because I was playing in them which I did until 1942 when I went into the Army.

In the '40s, Club DeLisa was probably the biggest club on the South Side, and in the city. The club burned down and they rebuilt it.

ROBERTS SHOW LOUNGE

The Show Lounge was open from 1954 to 1961 and operated by Herman Roberts at 6622 South Park Way although the sign in front said Roberts Show Club. During those years, Roberts booked such major stars as Count Basie, Nat King Cole, Lionel Hampton, Sam Cooke, Brook Benton, Jackie Wilson, and Sam Cooke. Roberts also opened the Roberts Motel Chain on the South Side and booked such stars as Ramsey Lewis, Bobby Bland, Billie Eckstine, and Esther Phillips.

SUTHERLAND LOUNGE

A very popular venue for music during the heyday of Chicago's jazz scene, it was located in the Sutherland Hotel that was completed in January 1919 at 4659 S. Drexel Boulevard on the city's South Side. It was originally designated a military hospital and then assigned to the US Public Health Service. In 1925, the six-story hotel was purchased by a real estate consortium including its partner, William J. Sutherland, and the hotel was named for him. When jazz music began a revival in the 1950s, the Sutherland Lounge was advertised as "Where the Stars and Celebrities Meet." Such jazz stars as Thelonius Monk, John Coltrane, Louis Armstrong, Dizzy Gillespie, Billie Holiday, Bill Evans, Sarah Vaughan, Nancy Wilson, Nina Simone, and Miles Davis performed at the lounge. It closed for repairs in 1963 and briefly reopened in 1964 before finally closing that year.

BILL GOLDMAN | LINCOLNSHIRE, IL
Here's one story I really remember about the Sutherland Lounge. I was dating a young lady and wanted to take her to hear some jazz. This was in the early 60s and the Sutherland was kind a legendary place. I used to go there often, and it was situated in a primarily black neighborhood. It was definitely off the beaten path of the usual Rush Street clubs like the Cloister Bar at the Maryland Hotel, the Black Orchid, and others. As I recall, it cost about 3 bucks to get in. When we got there, we were treated to the music of Sonny Stitt, a magnificent tenor sax player. But, the offshoot of this story is that I married Joyce and remarkably, we're still together after 57 years. I guess she was really impressed that I would lay out that kind of money to take her to a great entertainment venue like the Sutherland.

PHIL HOLDMAN
I think that I was at the Club DeLisa about twice because it was a long distance from where we lived on the West Side. I went there with one of my friends who liked big bands. His father had a brand new DeSoto and he would get the car and say, "Phil, where do you want to go because I'm getting the car this Saturday night?" I said to him, "Let's go to the Club DeLisa." I told him that it was at 55th and State and, boy, that was a thrill because they had good food like fried chicken. It was a "black and tan" club, which meant it had African Americans and whites attending the club. Jimmy Noone

had a great dance band there, and he was a talented clarinet man. In fact, when Benny Goodman got done playing at the Sutherland Lounge he used to take the band and go to Club DeLisa to hear Jimmy Noone, who was one of his idols. We saw beautiful dancers and beautiful floorshows, heard great music, and the night wasn't expensive because you could get it all for about a dollar. A fried chicken dinner was $.35 and it was a real plush club, although it was rather compact, so no matter where you sat you were close to the band and close to the show and there were chorus girls with scanty clothing. It was a lot of fun. I also saw Red Saunders there who was the house drummer, and he performed at Club DeLisa for many years.

There was a club on the South Side at 63rd and Western where the guys drove their fathers' cars to take a load of us West Side guys who were friends and liked good music. It was called Jump Town, and it featured the singer Anita O'Day. The club featured all the great jazz singers and jazz trios of the day, and it was a very hot spot.

I never went to the Sutherland Lounge but I knew about it. Benny Goodman played there, and it was in the Southmoor Hotel at 47th and Drexel. The Cloister Inn at the Maryland Hotel was another place that I went to a couple of times because I liked Lenny Bruce, the comedian. I was friendly with him and he was brilliant. But, he didn't perform there until the '50s.

RICH SAMUELS | TELEVISION PERSONALITY
During my high school years I lived in the suburbs, but I did get into Chicago a lot because I was with a group of kids who were jazz musicians, or so we fancied ourselves. So, quite often, we would go down to the Blue Note, which used to be at Clark and Madison, and, later on, when we had driver's licenses, we would go south to the Sutherland Lounge at 47th and Drexel in the Sutherland Hotel, where the jazz musicians would play, the Regal Theater at 47th and South Parkway (King Drive), and McKies Disc Jockey Lounge at 63rd and Cottage Grove. As for the Club DeLisa, it was more of a place

for floor shows. We went to places, particularly, where they had jazz acts, although there were some more exotic things that they could only play in Bronzeville, like Redd Foxx at the Sutherland back when he was doing "party records" before his television career. At the Regal, we saw Moms Mabley, who was not in the mainstream at that point.

KENT BEAUCHAMP | RECORD PROMOTER
I spent a lot of time on the South Side of the city because I loved jazz and blues music. I would also sit up and listen to Sid McCoy on his all-night radio show. I was fairly street smart, and I knew my way around and knew where to go and where not to go. I hung out at the different blues and jazz clubs, and I remember seeing Ramsey Lewis at the Croydon Inn off Rush Street and Ahmad Jamal at the Pershing Room. The Club DeLisa had just closed by the late '50s and early '60s, and the Crown Propeller may have still been in existence by then. The Blue Note had also closed by then.

I got to know the Chess family quite well. The real recording of blues music was going on at their studio on South Michigan Avenue where they did Chess, Checker and Argo recordings. I got to know a lot of record artists and radio people, and they included Eydie Gorme and Steve Lawrence, Ferrante and Teicher, and Martin and Lewis. I remember the time that Van Morrison came to Chicago, and he was a very talented kid and I had to take him around to the television and radio stations for interviews. Ironically, his interviews were good and he was talkative with the interviewers even though he was quiet when we were traveling around the city. Another guy who was like that was Neil Diamond, and he was one of the great show business personalities who you could ever imagine. But, although he was not real talkative, he was friendly to me.

During the early '60s, I was dealing with some of the best known black recording artists, like Aretha Franklin.

I also worked with Dick Gregory, Ramsey Lewis, and Ahmad Jamal. I was promoting rock and roll

records and we would visit the big radio stations, like WIND to meet with Howard Miller. WLS came later in the early '60s with Dick Biondi, Gene Taylor, and Clark Weber. In those days, WCFL and WJJD were the rival stations for WLS.

THE BEEHIVE LOUNGE

Located at 1503 E. 55th Street in the Hyde Park neighborhood on Chicago's South Side, The Beehive Lounge was one of the city's premier jazz clubs in the 1950s. The Beehive opened in 1948 and from the mid-1940s to the mid-1950s, it was a place to hear bebop and hard bop in Chicago by such great musicians as Coleman Hawkins, Al Hibbler, Milt Jackson, Art Blakey and the Jazz Messengers, Max Roach, Thelonius Monk, Gene Ammons, Cannonball Adderley, Dexter Gordon, and Sonny Rollins. It was known as a "black and tan" club because of its multiracial audience, and the house pianist from 1948 to 1951 was Jimmy Yancey, while Junior Mance performed at the Lounge from 1953 to 1954.

PALM TAVERN

In 1933, James Knight, the first "Mayor" of Bronzeville opened the Palm Tavern at 446 E. 47th Street on the city's South Side. When he retired in 1956, ownership of the tavern was transferred to Geraldine "Mama Gerri" Oliver who would operate the establishment as Gerri's Palm Tavern until July 3, 2001. The Palm Tavern had a major impact on the nurturing of black musical culture in Chicago. Over the decades, the Palm Tavern provided a venue for such diverse African American musicians as Duke Ellington, James Brown, Count Basie, Quincy Jones, Dizzy Gillespie, and Muddy Waters.

REGAL THEATER

Built in 1928, the very popular theater that seated over 3,000 people was part of the Balaban and Katz chain and was located at 47th and Grand Boulevard (later renamed South Parkway, and, then, in 1968, Martin Luther King Drive). It was a key night club and music venue on the city's South Side, was lavishly decorated with plush carpeting and velvet drapes, and offered customers motion pictures and live stage shows. Those shows included such stars as Nat "King" Cole, Cab Calloway, Ella Fitzgerald, Louis Armstrong, Lena Horne, Sarah Vaughan, Miles Davis, Lionel Hampton, Duke Ellington, Dizzy Gillespie, Sammy Davis Jr., and, in the 1960s, Aretha Franklin. Other acts included Sam Cooke, Jackie Wilson, The Supremes, The Four Tops, Della Reese, Herbie Hancock, Dionne Warwick, James Brown, John Coltrane, and Martha and the Vandellas. In June 1962, "Little" Stevie Wonder recorded his hit single *Fingertips* at the Regal in a Motortown Revue that included Smokey Robinson and the Miracles, Marvin Gaye, Mary Wells and the Marvelettes, and BB King. In 1968, The Jackson 5 opened for Motown acts that included Gladys Knight and the Pips. The Regal closed in 1968 and was demolished in 1973.

WARNER SAUNDERS | TELEVISION PERSONALITY

My father was a Pullman porter and my mother was a maid, and we lived up over the grocery store and other stores near 47th and South Parkway. It was an exciting life because the Regal Theater was right around the corner and the Savoy Ballroom was there, and the alley with the back door to the Regal literally faced the front of our house. You talk about "people watching." There were 10 children who lived in the apartment building where we lived, and we were all about the same age. So, we used to stand outside and literally watch the stars go by, and they included every entertainer, athlete, and businessperson. It almost became common place to see all the famous people..."Oh, there's Joe Louis, there's Count Basie, there's Ella Fitzgerald, there's Billy Eckstine…" It was like State and Madison for the black community, and it was the center of everything. There was a large department store across the street called the South Center Department Store, and it was very much like a mini-Marshall Field's. The Regal and the Savoy Ballroom drew a lot of people, and there were lines around the corner waiting for the stage shows. So, we used to go outside and hang out on 47th Street and just watch because we didn't have to go anywhere.

I had a strong interest in jazz when I was growing up, but I wasn't old enough to go to the Club DeLisa. It was a jazz place for my parent's generation. Into the 1950s, the downtown clubs were opening up, like the Blue Note, the Black Orchid, the London House. I was a young man at that time, and it was the hip thing to do to go there.

BOB KRYZAK | GRAPEVINE, TX
Some friends and I had gone to the Regal Theater to see James Brown. He was a fabulous entertainer, and he had this shtick he would do that involved a cape. He would be onstage, singing and dancing and sweating and really getting after it, when all of a sudden he would drop to a knee and come to a dead stop. He would act as if he just couldn't continue. Then, one of his fellow musicians would come out carrying a cape and proceed to drape it over Brown and try to coax him back into performing. Suddenly, he would stand up and start to move and groove, like he had amazingly been revived. It truly was a sight to see. He would do this several times during his act and of course, the audience would roar with approval each time he did it. I'll never forget it. He was a truly incredible performer.

BURNING SPEAR/HIGH CHAPARRAL
One of the South Side clubs owned and operated during the 1950s and 1960s by radio personality Pervis Spann. The club was located at 55th and State, and Spann booked major acts to perform at the club including the Jackson 5, Aretha Franklin, and B.B. King. After Spann's overnight slot at WOPA-AM radio ended, the station was bought by Phil and

Leonard Chess in 1963 and the call letters were changed to the popular WVON-AM, a 24-hour blues station.

MCKIE'S DISC JOCKEY SHOW LOUNGE
Created by popular disc jockey McKie Fitzhugh, McKie's Disc Jockey Show Lounge was opened in 1956 at 63rd and Cottage Grove on the city's South Side. Among the many performers at the lounge were Sonny Rollins, Bill King, Gene Ammons, John Coltrane, Fontella Bass, Brook Benton, and Sonny Stitt. After the club closed in the late 1960s, Fitzhugh died in 1970 and the hotel where the club was located went vacant soon after.

MARC DAVIS | AUTHOR
FREELANCE WRITER
In 1969, Gene Ammons, the great tenor sax man, was released from Joliet prison after serving a seven-year stint for narcotics possession; his second imprisonment for a dope rap. To celebrate his liberation, he got together with another great tenor player, Sonny Stitt, with whom he used to perform regularly and they scheduled a night of music at McKie's, a South Side club.

I was there with my wife and some friends, along with a packed house three-deep and more at the bar, in a relatively small room. The air was dense with the aroma of weed and the mood was jubilant. The crowd was mixed—both black and white. Ammons and Stitt were at the peak of their virtuosity, blowing their warm, rich, resonant tones, with astoundingly complex improvisations and mind-boggling fingering.

They stood under a single spotlight, side by side on a small stage over the bar, taking turns at "cutting" each other with memorable solos, each successive "call and response" more beautiful and enchanting than the one before. They played long sets, late into the night and into the half light of the following early dawn.

Beyond the great jazz of that never-to-be forgotten night, was the joyous spirit of their playing, two great friends and musical colleagues, reunited after many years apart, each inspiring the other to play at the very best of their capability.

JOHNNY FRIGO | MUSICIAN

On the South Side, I would sit in at the black jazz clubs after my gigs. I would park my car in an alley on a Saturday night at 2:00 a.m., take my violin, and walk right into some jazz club, like Club DeLisa. On Sunday mornings they had what was called a "Milkman's Matinee." that included eight dancing girls, and Albert Ammons, who was the son of the great tenor player, Gene Ammons, and his band. I would go in there. and they would let me sit in. One night, I was tired. But when you sat in you played one or two sets and then let somebody else play. I was so ignorant that I walked up there and although I decided I wasn't going to stay there too long, I just kept playing. When I finished, the announcer said, "OK, Johnny, let Teddy Wilson play on piano."

I played my music at a lot of clubs on 63rd Street. Mostly, I played bass at the Trianon Ballroom with Wayne King, and at the Aragon Ballroom with Dick Jergens. In 1942, I played with Chico Marx at the Blackhawk Restaurant. They would broadcast every night. I sang with Mel Torme, and we had the quartet. Mel had just gotten out of high school and he was from the Hyde Park area. I traveled with Chico Marx. It was during the time that I was with him that I signed up for World War II in 1942. I picked the Coast Guard. They heard that I played violin, so they sent me to Ellis Island. I had a physical, and little did I know that there was something wrong with my back, so I was on "light duty." So, I played bass with the band, and I played tuba and trumpet with the military band. I was in the military from 1942 to 1945, but I mainly played with the band and did concerts at Walter Reed Hospital and radio programs. Then, from Ellis Island, life was good. As long as you passed muster, you were able to get out every night to go to Manhattan. People would give us tickets to everything, so I went to all the clubs, saw the Glenn Miller show, Broadway plays, and, at one point, next to Carnegie Hall, a new USO opened.

After I got out of the Service in 1945, I came right back to Chicago and began traveling with Chico Marx. I joined him at Tower Theater in Kansas City, and we did theaters all over the country. And, when he saw that I played violin, he asked me to bring my violin on stage one day, and we sort of fell into a comedy routine. He had an Italian accent, and we would do stupid stuff and improvise routines like "You noodle on the fiddle, and I'll spaghetti on the piano." The audiences liked it, and when Mel Torme couldn't make it at times, I sang with Chico and I sang some Irish songs.

About 1951, I introduced myself to everyone in Chicago again since I had been away for so long. I happened to stop at the Streamliner Club near Union Station on Madison Street, west of the Loop. George Shearing was playing there. and he had me sit in and he played Detour Ahead. Later, I went to the Pump Room, where I had played with David LeWinter, the pianist for Paul Draper, the tap dancer, and LeWinter had a nice dance band. I remember picking my fiddle and playing Sleepy Lagoon on a Sunday afternoon to a dance tempo, and Jascha Heifitz was sitting in front of me.

JOE LEVINSON | MUSICIAN

Chicago was rife with clubs in the 1940s and 1950s. Some were very sophisticated and some were real dives, and I played in both types of clubs. Since I was born in 1929, during the '40s I was too young to play in those places, but I went to hear music there. I hung out and I haunted all those clubs. I remember many of them, and even if I couldn't get in I would stand in the doorway or I would go around to the back alley and listen through the window. I would catch neighborhood guys and local bands. Some of the places were expensive and classy, and I went there too. I grew up playing classical violin. As an 11-year-old, I had never really paid attention to jazz. But, my parents went to the clubs, not particularly because of the music, but because they liked the food and they took me with them. I would just sit there and I remember hearing Fats Waller and his Rhythm

Band. Then, I found out that my father loved Benny Goodman and he was the one who introduced me to big band music. There was a radio broadcast of jazz coming out of New York City that he loved to tune in on, and Dinah Shore used to sing on that program. In 9th grade we moved to the South Side from the North Side, and when I completed grammar school, my father thought that I should attend a good high school. Even though I was all set to go to Lake View High School, my father said, "No, I think that we are going to send you out to University High." He was able to do that because he was a visiting professor at the University of Chicago in legal medicine.

We moved to Hyde Park and lived at 915 Hyde Park Boulevard, right at Drexel Square. We had some brilliant people in that school, including those who were jazz musicians and had great jazz record collections. That was when I started collecting jazz records.

When I finished 10th grade in 1945, I had two choices: I could either go to Hyde Park High or stay on in the four-year college at the University of Chicago. The U of C students were a number of years older than me and much more worldly, experienced, and serious students. So, I really wasn't doing very well. But, what I was doing well was playing violin in a high school orchestra in the U-Hi dance band and listening to jazz records by Ellington, Jimmy Blanton playing bass in his band. I listened to that sound and said, "That's it, that's it, that's the perfect sound and rhythm!" I went to a band rehearsal at U-Hi one day and they had a bass fiddle standing in a corner and nobody played it. It was a cheap bass, a plywood bass. I picked it up, and it looked like a violin with a thyroid condition. So, I realized that I could play, and I understood what was happening with it because it was like the violin I was already playing. I said to the bandmaster that I could play the bass, and he said that he would rather have me on bass than on violin because they didn't have a bass player. It was a terrible band.

Then, I heard that a bunch of guys living in the Burton-Judson dormitory on the U of C Midway had formed a dance band, and a lot of them were military veterans who had come in and even had some professional experience with bands. They were 7 to 10 years older than me, and I went over there to hear the band one day. They were rehearsing in the dining room, and I noticed that they didn't have a bass player, so I boldly said, "Can I play in your band?" So, one day I borrowed the bass out of the high school band room, walked into this rehearsal with the school's bass, and said to them, "I've come to play in the band!" They decided to let me try, and I blew them away because I knew what I was doing. So, I was immediately a member of a band in which I was the youngest person, and they were playing college proms, fraternity parties, and all kinds of things around the campus. I was actually even making money.

These guys introduced me to the jazz clubs around Chicago's South Side. They snuck me in with them, including the Bee Hive on East 55th Street, and I saw Charlie Parker and Max Roach and others of that caliber. I was only 15 or 16 years old but it didn't matter if you were white or black, and we would go to jazz clubs up and down 63rd Street. I even went downtown with them to places like the Cloister Inn at the Maryland Hotel. Bronzeville was the euphemism for the Black Belt, especially along South Parkway and 63rd down to 47th Streets. I even remember going to the Regal Theater at 47th and South Parkway and seeing Pearl Bailey. Down the street from the Regal Theater was a record shop called the Groove Record Shop. I used to ride my bike up there after school, and they had jazz records galore.

There were a lot of jazz piano, stride piano and blues piano players in Chicago. One of them, who recorded a lot was Jimmy Yancey. And, Mama Yancey, his wife, was a blues shout, and some of the guys in the band took me over to Jimmy's apartment with my bass. They were having a rent party and, of course, he had a beat-up old, upright piano in his apartment on the second floor near Sox Park. And, I went in there with my friends from the college band, and Mama, who had one eye, was the nicest person, knew I was just a kid. So, I played blues with Jimmy Yancey, and Mama sang some songs, and, in between, whenever we weren't playing she would come over and hand me a ginger ale.

Guys took me all kinds of places around the South Side and downtown to hear jazz, including the Sutherland Lounge. I never went into the Club DeLisa on 55th and State because that was big-time and you had to have a lot of money. But, I knew guys who told me about it, and they had the "Milkman's Special" where the last show started at one in the morning and they came out about 7 o'clock in the morning and the band was still playing. Visiting dignitaries in the music business would stop by there after they did their thing. Club DeLisa was renowned.

JUDY ROBERTS | MUSICIAN AND LEGENDARY JAZZ ICON

My beginnings actually started with my father, who was a great guitar player and who did big band arrangements for the likes of Fletcher Henderson. My dad was born white and Jewish (like me!) and Henderson's bass player, the famed Israel Crosby, said to my father, "Man, you write some good bass parts for a white boy!" I guess it was okay to say things like that at the time, and my dad was thrilled. My dad is really the one who turned me onto the greats like Andre Previn, Oscar Peterson, Ella, Jackie and Roy, the incredibly talented jazz duo. I was around 5 years old when I started picking up on the greatness of that music. I don't read music, but I was picking things out on the piano and that's how it all began. So, you could say I was truly blessed by having a really cool father. His name was Bob Loewy. By the way, later when I started doing featured gigs, I decided to change my name from Judy Loewy to Judy Roberts—using my dad's first name for my last name was a sweet decision. In the 80s, we did a jazz quartet CD together called *My Heart Belongs To Daddy*, that featured both of us playing and singing. It was pretty cool. But, it all started because my dad was an arranger and he was generally home all day.

So, we listened to lots and lots of music together—all the greats—all the time. A wonderful foundation.

Now, how I started singing is really a funny story. When I was in high school, I became part of a very cool jazz quartet, but all I wanted to do was play piano. You know, I've never really considered myself a singer, but despite that, here's how it all began. We got booked into a club out in Addison (IL) that was owned by the Mob and one night, while we were playing, one of the mobsters came up to me and said, "Hey, I want to hear you sing *Fascination*." I told him, "I'm sorry, sir. I don't sing." He takes out a gun and puts it down on the bar and said, again, "Sing *Fascination*." So, I looked at the guys in the band and I began to sing, "It was fascination, I know..." And the next song I sang was, *Never Will I Marry* followed by *Save Your Love For Me*, you know, the Nancy Wilson songbook because I'd been listening to great singers for most of my life. So, that's how I began singing... at gunpoint!

My first real chance at success happened when I was still in my teens, and I got the house trio gig at The London House. That was something that really opened up some doors for me. I got to play opposite "the real people" five nights a week. That's how you get to not only listen, but also get to know them, get familiar with their style and find out what the real people were doing. During their sets we were able to sit in the audience, in the back, and can you just imagine? Getting to hear stars like Oscar Peterson five nights a week, three sets a night? Unbelievable! That's how I got to meet bassist Ray Brown. He came through with Oscar Peterson, and he liked me. I was young—like 19—and we went into a recording studio and did some fun things. I'm pretty sure it was Universal Recording on Walton and here was Ray Brown, the real deal and the nicest guy. He wasn't hitting on me or anything like that. He was solely interested in making music with me and that's what we did. Ray had an "in" at Mercury records, and he tried to get them to do something for us, but Mercury shut down right about the time we made the recording, so nothing ever happened with it. (I still have the acetate recording in my possession!) But that recording session paved the way.

Judy Roberts
(Courtesy of Judy Roberts)

The fans would line up outside when I had the London House gig. You know, we would start early there—around 6 o'clock and our trio would perform for the dinner crowd. Most of the time, the audiences were respectful of the musicians, but occasionally, there would be some yahoos who just didn't get it. There was this one time when some conventioneers had a table right up close to the band and my bass player, Fred Atwood, was taking his solo and these guys were just yakking it up. Well, the audience tried to shush them up but they weren't having any of it. This one guy was really being obnoxious. Now, when I played, I always took my shoes off because it was more comfortable for me. But, now here was this guy, talking loudly and being excessively rude so I got up, ran across the stage in my stocking feet and jumped down into the audience and grabbed this guy by the collar telling him to shut up. The audience applauded, however, the manager didn't think as much of my actions, so I got suspended for a week, but it was worth it to me. There's also a well-known story of mine about George Shearing playing at the London House and experiencing some loudmouths. The cool audience members were audibly making shushing noises to these idiots. Finally, Shearing himself, upon hearing the "shushing" wittily said into the mic, "I'm playing as softly as I can." It's a time-honored great story.

INTERNATIONAL AMPHITHEATRE

The International Amphitheatre was an indoor arena that was open from 1934 to 1999 located on the west side of Halsted Street at 42nd Street on the city's South Side, adjacent to the Union Stock Yards. The Amphitheatre replaced a horse-racing track that was destroyed by fire in 1934. It was among the first arenas in the country to be air conditioned. Not only did the Beatles perform there on September 5, 1964 and August 12, 1966, but it was home to the NBA Chicago Packers and, later, the Chicago Bulls in their inaugural season of 1966-67. It was also home for Chicago wrestling and the Chicago Auto Show as well as several national political conventions including the infamous Democratic National Convention in 1968.

NORTH SIDE

THE BACK ROOM
Located at 1007 N. Rush Street in Chicago, it lasted from the 1960s until 2014. It was one of the oldest jazz clubs in the city and offered excellent jazz by some of Chicago's best vocalists, trios, and quartets. It consisted of a small, carpeted room with exposed brick walls and a black drop ceiling and a tiny, wooden bar.

JUDY ROBERTS | MUSICIAN AND LEGENDARY JAZZ ICON
After my London House gig, I began playing at a very hip place on Rush Street called The Back Room. It was originally called Wil Sheldon's. This was also a big break for me because it was centrally located, right in the midst of all the Rush Street happenings. We were there five nights a week, too. A lot of the big-time musicians who happened to be in Chicago would come and sit in and it was a major thing that was going on there. So between Mr. Kelly's, the London House, and the Marienthals doing their thing, it turned out to be a big deal for me. That's also where I met my first electric bass player—Neal Seroka—and who shortly thereafter played guitar on my hit albums for Inner City and PAUSA. We still play together.

CAROL MARKER | GURNEE, IL
The Gaslight Club was a place you could go to in order to escape the everyday responsibility of taking care of toddlers and maintaining a home front. Every room in the club had a different motif, so depending on your mood, you were free to pick and choose your surroundings. Did you want a nice, quiet library with low-level blue lighting, very comfortable sofas and a piano player in the corner that you could barely hear? Then that was your room. Of course, being with someone special made for a very romantic setting with exceptional potential for that evening. Or did you want to go to a French bistro? You made a right

The Beatles, International Amphitheater, 1964

turn for one and a left turn for the other. But there you were with access to two different worlds just for the taking within that building. All of it wonderful. The bistro had, in the corner, a table with corned beef and marbled rye bread, so if you wanted a sandwich to go with your cocktails, you were in business. They had this every night. There was a big winding staircase that was housed in this mansion so if you felt like negotiating it, you'd find yourself upstairs, headed for the Speakeasy. When you got up to the entrance of this room, there was a phone booth and you'd go into it, pick up the phone and say, "Joe sent me." Once you got into the Speakeasy, there was always a jazz band playing and waitpersons rather scantily attired, taking care of the customers. My all-time favorite song the band would play was called, *I Wish I Could Shimmy Like My Sister Kate*. The tables in the room were all made of rugged wood and on the tables were wooden mallets that the customers could use to rap on the tables— keeping time with the music, which everyone did. It was total festivity, silliness, and joy! While I was not there for this particular period, I'd been told that the Gaslight Speakeasy was where you took your girlfriend—NOT your wife. Again, while I never saw it, I was told that the bar, instead of regular barstools, had saddles.

I also heard that in the corner, they had a fire pole so that if you needed to get down to the first floor without the wrong person seeing you, you slide down the fire pole. Now, this was before my time and I never saw these features, but I have no doubt they existed. It was this great Victorian mansion with all of these different rooms, and you could and spend the whole night being entertained by the magnificence of it all. The place was founded by Burton Browne, who must have been a highly creative and inventive person to come up with a concept like the Gaslight Club.

FACES

Faces, located at 940 N. Rush Street on the city's Near North Side, was the premier jet-setters' disco in the early 1970s. Individuals could become one of the approximately 16,000 lifetime members for $50 to get a nod from the doorman. It closed in 1989 and was the brainchild of Jimmy Rittenberg and three friends. When it opened, people said that Rush Street was like being in Las Vegas.

JIMMY RITTENBERG | GENERAL MANAGER OF FACES

During the mid '60s, Rush Street and Old Town became the center of my activities. We would have a couple of beers at Mister Kelly's, stop at the old River Shannon, go either to Old Town or Butch McGuires, and then walk around the corner to Rush Street. The place where I used to work was originally The Gate of Horn, and that was where Lenny Bruce got removed from the stage by the police and the club was shut down. When it got closed, three young guys bought it and transformed it into The Store, a post-college bar. By that time, State and Division had become the location of several college bars, whereas Rush Street still remained the place for the "Boys," including entertainment, the Whiskey A-Go-Go, the Candy Store, the strip joints, and the "dress-up" joints. So, the city's Near North Side was like three different cultures: Old Town, Rush Street, and State and Division. I worked in Old Town and tended bar at Chances R, and I was very fortunate because I had the opportunity to hear Steve Goodman, Bonnie Koloc, Johnny Prine, and many others.

I went to the college bars on a regular basis in the '60s and later became a mainstay at Mr. Kelly's, so I became known to performers like Jackie Mason, Shelley Berman, Joel Grey, Chad Mitchell, Bill Cosby, and Tom Jones. London House didn't have the big acts in the late '60s, but Happy Medium, Mister Kelly's, and the Empire Room all had major entertainers in those years. The clubs began to lose their clientele because of television and the fact that you could see the comedy acts on television every night. Then, the bands started hitting big, and they couldn't fit into the little clubs.

CAROL MARKER | GURNEE, IL

Briefly, one great place to talk about down on Rush Street was Faces—a disco club. 70s and 80s. Think younger people and disco and Motown. One thing that really stands out in my mind was the entrance to the place. When you walked in, it was done up all in silver, including the ceiling and you just had to stop to absorb it. When John Travolta did his movie—*Saturday Night Fever*—one of the gals in the neighborhood had learned all the steps. We're housewives, and we would practice in the driveways so we'd have long enough routines and learn the steps, so that when we went into clubs like Faces, we really knew what we were doing. It was an amazing amount of fun! That's what I remember about Faces and there wasn't a song they would play that we didn't know, and we would sing right along with them and it was incredible! So, you go from the Gaslight Club, to a jazz club or a Motown disco. That's Chicago!

WISE FOOLS PUB

In the 1970s, this became one of the city's most popular blues club. It was located at 2270 N. Lincoln Avenue on the city's North Side. Performers at the club included Muddy Waters, Howlin' Wolf, and Mighty Joe Young. After being sold twice, the club now is more likely to host local alt-rock and cover bands than blues performers.

JUDY ROBERTS | MUSICIAN AND LEGENDARY JAZZ ICON

There was a kind of heyday period for places on Lincoln Avenue in New Town. One of those spots was the Wise Fools Pub. People used to literally line up around the block to get into that venue. One of the things that some of the clubs would pride themselves in was getting people to remain quiet when there were performances taking place. I played Wise Fools five nights a week, and I was pretty popular there. I had this thing for when people would start yapping. I had a flashlight and if there were people making too much noise, I would shine the flashlight on them—you know—to draw attention to them. The whole room would applaud and of course, the offenders would either slink down in their seats to try and avoid the embarrassment or they would get up and walk out. And that was okay, because there were 50 more people waiting to get in! The flashlight shaming was actually very effective for controlling noisy patrons who were spoiling things for the true fans.

CAROL MARKER | GURNEE, IL

My second favorite place to go was the Wise Fools Pub on Lincoln Avenue—particularly on Monday nights. That's because Monday nights have always been slow nights for musicians, so they'd show up at Wise Fools. All the money they would get for playing was whatever was collected at the door. The musicians were encouraged to bring in their own arrangements of jazz standards and perform them there. It was a long room, always jam-packed and each waitress had to cover about 30 tables and the amazing thing was—they never missed a lick. The band that was always there, although it would vary by which players came in on a Monday night, was run by Dave Remington and given license to do whatever. My high point about that experience, as well as everybody else's was the improvisation that was encouraged by Remington. And the musicians who came in were all A-List musicians. The tune that Remington had selected was the theme from *2001–A Space Odyssey*. Some of the musicians I remember coming in to play included Sun Seals, Cy Touff, Bobby Lewis, and Bob Cousins on percussion. Dave Remington was blatantly honest, so he would not permit anyone to be on that bandstand that didn't have the chops to pull it off. Again, this would be the kind of night that you could step away from kids in diapers or the lawn needing tending and so forth and just escape for two or three hours. Also, when we would have out-of-town company, including people from Europe, we would take them to clubs like Wise Fools and others and they were hearing only the best!

NORTH SIDE ENTERTAINMENT VENUES

MERCURY THEATER

The building that houses the Mercury Theater at 3745 N. Southport Avenue was built in 1912 as a silent nickelodeon theater. In 1994, it was purchased and the Mercury Theater was born. A small theater, it only seats 290 patrons. It has become an anchor theater in the Southport community on the city's North Side.

MICHAEL RABIN | DEERFIELD, IL

A friend came in from out of town and as would often happen with him, we would go listen to music. On this particular occasion, we went to see Miles Davis at the Mercury Theater, kind of on the Near North Side of the city. It was a nice little theater—not built for large audiences, but good for music. This was in the 80s as I recall. Miles had kind of changed up the kind of music he was playing, and while the audience was hungry to hear the tunes he'd made famous on his recordings, that was not what was in store. So, the musicians in his group were out on stage and playing, but Miles just kind of stood there—trumpet in hand, but not playing. He had a scowl on his face, looking almost angry. And the music, again, was quite different from the tunes that had made him such a big name. After a bit, he started playing. He played a few bars, the crowd went nuts, and then he stopped. Now, we had heard that his life wasn't going so well at the time and that the music he played was reflective of it. And people were disappointed in what they were hearing, and he kind of had an attitude directed at the audience that said, "Screw you. This is what I'm playing so take it or leave it." Obviously, that didn't sit well. After a while, he did play some of the tunes that people wanted to hear, but he'd changed everything up and they didn't enjoy it. Another thing that happened was that at intermission, we went outside and you could see that there was a room where Miles Davis was and that I guess people were going to be able to meet him. There were a couple of guys standing outside of the room – guards, presumably and I was determined to go in there and meet Miles Davis. I got past the two guys but then a woman came up to me and said, "Whatever you do, don't go near Miles. He's not in a good mood." So, here was Miles, in a corner all by himself and nobody was going near him. In fact, there was about a 6-to-8 foot area that was devoid of people; just him in the corner. I just looked at him and walked out. It was kind of surreal.

PARK WEST

Formerly the Lane Court Theater from 1916 to 1935, then the Town Theater from 1935 to 1967 and the Town Underground Theater from 1967 to 1977 before becoming Park West in 1977. Located at 322 Armitage Avenue, the theater had an original capacity of 1,000 people, the building was purchased by Dale Niedermaier and John May and refurbished as Park West. It has hosted a wide range of musical performers and special events. Stars who have performed there have included Aretha Franklin, Genesis, the Eurythmics, Hall & Oates, Neil Sedaka, Patti Smith, Tina Turner, Whitney Houston, and U2. Metro Chicago, first opened in 1982, was formerly called Cabaret Metro and is a concert hall located at 3730 N. Clark Street on the city's North Side. The venue has played host to a wide variety of local, regional, and national bands and musicians including Nirvana, Liz Phair, Pearl Jam, Smashing Pumpkins, Chance the Rapper, and Bob Dylan.

SHELLEY HOWARD | CHICAGO, IL | "THE UNOFFICIAL MAYOR OF RUSH STREET"

It was 1958, and much of the music was on State Street, from Chicago Ave. to Division. I discovered some great dive bars, like the Store, and the Store Annex. But the center of the scene was State and Chestnut. Right where there is now an ugly high-rise today, was a courtyard and there were five bars in or about there. My favorite was Barnaby's, a dark dingy place with a small stage on a second level above the bar. I went there every weekend on my summer break to hear my good buddies from the Missing Links play. They were now calling themselves C.T.A. I usually hung out with Nick Fortuno from the Buckinghams

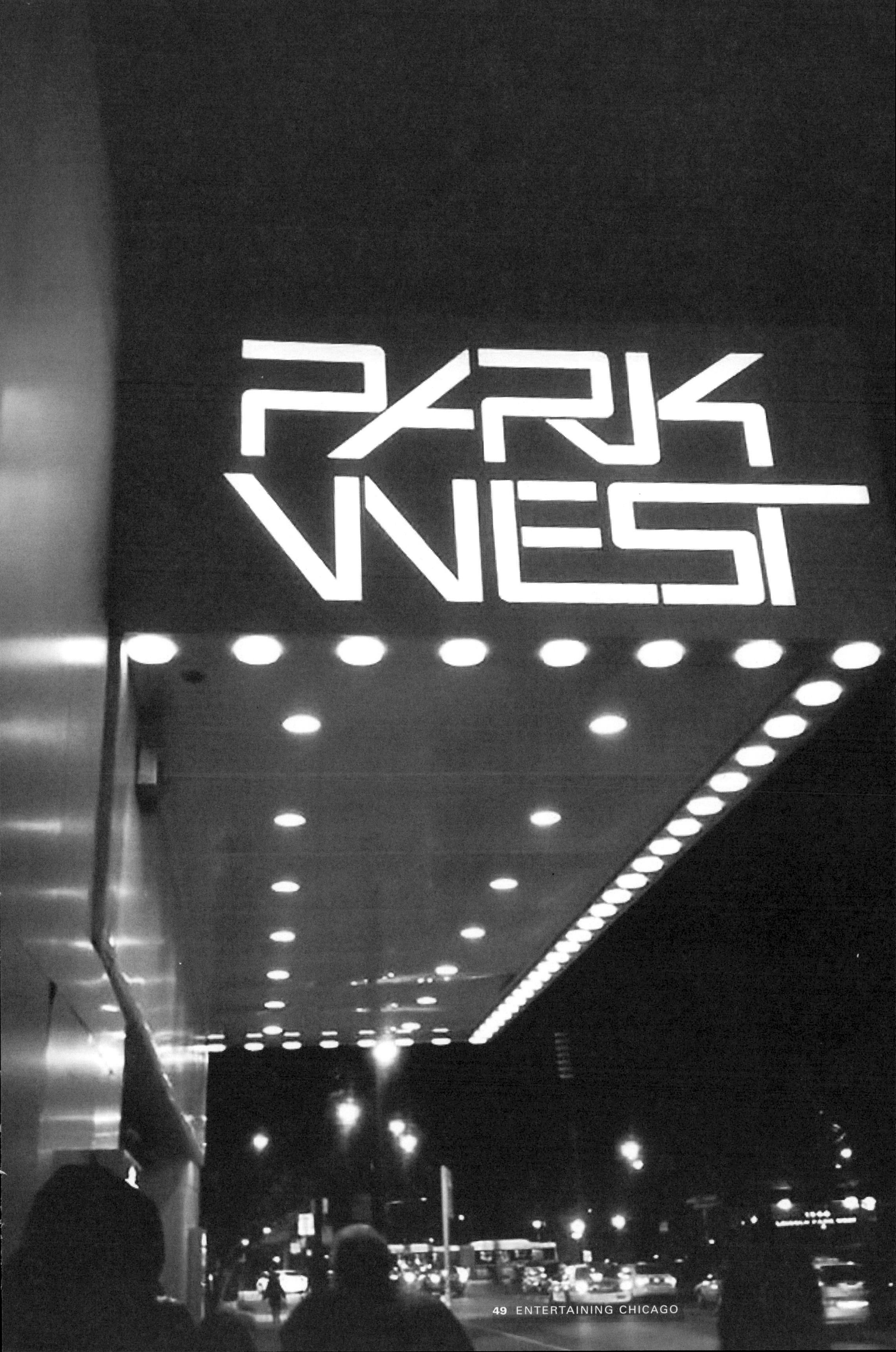
PARK
WEST

and we would always blow a J in the courtyard during the band breaks, while hitting on the various stewardesses that hung out there. This was years before they were called "flight attendants."

C.T.A. was like an all-star squad of top Chicago musicians. From the Missing Links was Danny Seraphine on drums, Walt Parazaider on sax, and Terry Kath was now jamming on lead guitar. They had found two guys from DePaul, Lee Loughnane and James Pankow to round out the horn section with Walt. A very talented guy, Robert Lamm was on keyboards. And, I was very happy to see the former bass player from the Exceptions, Peter Cetera, with this new group. Like most bands of the day, they played mostly cover songs. Because of their horn section and their wide range of vocals they were able to do tunes that sounded record perfect. I loved when they did *Darling* by the Beach Boys, with those great horn parts and Peter on vocals. And it turned out that Terry Kath was kick-ass on guitar. I remember that they covered a bunch of Hendrix songs, including *Fire* and *Purple Haze*. I thought Terry was better than Jimi. I later found out that Hendrix himself had said the same thing.

They would do cover songs for their first three sets. Then, about 1:00 a.m., when all the tourists and people from the burbs went home, the band got on stage and announced they would like to play some originals for their friends who had stuck around. I remember like yesterday, as they broke into Introduction, with Terry on vocals. That became the first song on their debut album, which they hadn't recorded yet. They followed that with *Does Anybody Really Know What Time It Is?* and then went right to *Beginnings*. History was in the making. After that it was *Question 67 and 68* and *Listen*. They always would finish the set with an extended version of Stevie Winwood's *I'm A Man* and left the stage with everyone in the band playing some sort of percussion instrument.

Well, we all know what happened to C.T.A. They eventually finished that first self-titled double album and after its release in 1969, it became a huge hit.

After the actual C.T.A. threatened to sue them, they changed their name to Chicago and released their second album in 1970. It also went gold and they band scored a number of top 10 singles. Of course by that time, they were no longer playing dives like Barnaby's, but they never forgot their original fans. Starting in 1969, and continuing on for a decade, they always played the Auditorium Theatre over Thanksgiving weekend. I never missed a show. And to this day, I still remember that summer of '68 when it was *Only the Beginning*.

I also remember when Roy Orbison played Park West in August of 1980. It was the first time in decades that the classic hit maker had toured and excitement was high. Could he still hit all those high notes? I couldn't wait to find out. He was always one of my favorites since high school, and I was not alone. Per usual, I sat in Booth One by the soundboard with some of my fellow Jam Productions mates. In Booth Two was David Bowie, who was staying in Chicago to perform in *The Elephant Man*. In Booth Three were Jerry Garcia and Bob Weir of the *Grateful Dead*, in town for a concert. Not too shabby an audience, right?

Roy began his set with his signature song *Only The Lonely*. Dum dum dum, dumby do wah. Oh yeah, the guy still had his chops. He played through most of his greatest hits. But the one I was waiting for was *Running Scared*, a song that never failed to move me. To a dramatic drumbeat, Roy would sing: "Just running scared, what would I do, if he came back and wanted you". During the final part of the song, Roy sang "My heart was breaking, which one would it be...you turned around and walked away with me," as his voice soared about four octaves.

Well, the place went completely nuts! Everyone just jumped out of their seats for a standing ovation. Yes, Bowie, the Dead, and me—standing, cheering! Roy looked amazed at the response, and with a wave of his hand, the band repeated the last verse, as he nailed the high part again. Same result—a wild standing ovation, perhaps louder than the first.

Well, why rest on your laurels? He did it again! Last verse repeated in all of its glory. I have never seen that type of loud applause and appreciation for any song. And this was from a group of musicians who were used to basking in the same thing. Roy clearly was moved by the reaction, and he said thank you and walked off the stage. We clapped until he returned for one more song. That encore was of course, *Oh, Pretty Woman*. On my list of best shows ever, (and I've seen a few), this performance ranks as number one. And I think there are a few who were there that agree with me.

I used to take my son, Shaun, with me whenever I would go to a concert. Metro was my favorite place because my show, Video Metro, was still active, and I had complete access to the upstairs booth where my tapes and equipment were stashed. There was also a small room, where the sound guys would take a break and chill on the small bed in there. Shaun, who was four at the time, fancied himself as a pirate. He would wear a fake eye patch, carry a plastic sword and loved to "capture" whoever was in the booth, force them to go into that small room and demand a "ransom" to let them out. Most folks got a giggle out of that and gave him a buck or two to gain their release. Big fun, right?

Well, one night back in the late 80s, we were there to see the Irish band, *The Cranberries*. Loved them. Who shows up in the booth but Sinead O'Connor, fresh from her SNL Pope picture tearing moment. She was there to cheer on fellow Irish singer, the late Dolores O'Riordan. Shaun was in full pirate mode and went up to Sinead, pointed his sword at her, and demanded that she go to the little room. Everyone around us just sort of went "Oh, no," expecting the worst. Instead, she played right along! She put her hands up and said, "Please don't hurt me, I'll pay your ransom," and then walked at sword point into that room, pretending to be frightened! We all breathed a sigh of relief, and her companion gave him a ten-spot to gain her release. I went up to her afterwards to apologize, and she said she loved kids and missed interacting when she was on the road.

He soon grew out of that silly game. And Sinead? Well, nothing compares to you, my lady.

DOWNTOWN AND NEAR NORTH SIDE CLUBS

MISTER KELLY'S

One of the most famous clubs in the history of Rush Street, it was owned by Oscar and George Marienthal and was in existence from 1953 to 1975. The Marienthals also owned and operated the London House and Happy Medium. The club, at 1028 N. Rush Street (now the location of Gibson's Restaurant) provided a venue for many entertainers, including comedians, jazz, folk, and popular singers. When the club opened on November 24, 1953, it had a restaurant that served steaks, seafood, the famous Green Goddess salad, a delicious dessert tray and Mister Kelly's added entertainment in 1954. A fire destroyed the club on December 8, 1955 but Mister Kelly's was rebuilt and reopened on August 29, 1956, becoming a springboard for many entertainers, including Barbra Streisand and Bob Newhart, some of whom recorded albums at the club like Ella Fitzgerald, Della Reese, Buddy Greco, Sarah Vaughan, Woody Allen, Lainie Kazan, Mort Sahl, Flip Wilson, and Freddie Prinze. Another fire destroyed the club in 1966, but it also reopened on May 15, 1967 before finally closing for business on August 25, 1975. Today it is the site of Gibson's Restaurant.

DAVID MARIENTHAL | SON AND NEPHEW OF THE OWNERS OF MISTER KELLY'S, LONDON HOUSE, AND HAPPY MEDIUM

My father and uncle, George and Oscar Marienthal founded, owned ,and operated three of the most famous clubs on the city's near North Side: the London House, Mister Kelly's, and Happy Medium. The London House was located across the Chicago River from the Wrigley Building at Michigan and Wacker Drive in the London Guarantee Building, which was also the historic site of the original Fort Dearborn. Mister Kelly's was at Bellevue and Rush Streets and is now the location of Gibson's Steakhouse, while the Happy Medium was at the northeast corner of Delaware and Rush, a couple of blocks from Mister Kelly's, on Rush. Mister Kelly's was named for a maitre'd that the brothers had hired to run the place but was let go before the opening.

As a boy, I would see my father go to work wearing impeccable suits and ties. After a day at the clubs, he would come home for dinner with the family and then return to the clubs at night. I wanted him to take me with him to work, and, when he did, I would play in his office with his old adding machines and help clean up. I always wanted to work at the clubs and be like him. I have great memories of working at Mister Kelly's during a summer when I was 19 or 20 years old for a few months. It was really a phenomenal place to work. I was handling the lighting and sound boards at the club. I would bring up the lights, make sure that the sound was all set and introduced the talent. I remember saying, "Here is the incredible sassy Sarah Vaughan!" Her voice was awe-inspiring. Ms. Vaughan clearly knew that she was the best. She was very beautiful, wore gorgeous gowns and very professional. The one problem I had with her performance was that when she began to launch into one of her songs we realized that I had forgot to turn on the switch for her microphone. She was livid about it and, probably if I was not the boss's son, I would have been out of a job.

I clearly recall working at Mister Kelly's when Lainie Kazan was performing. I was a young man and she was a sultry, gorgeous star. Simply put, I had a big crush on her. She was nice to me, and I was very disappointed when she left town without me. There were famous stand-up comics like Mort Sahl and Richard Pryor that were on the bill with these wonderful jazz singers.

There were actually two different Mister Kelly's,— the one before the fire, which opened in 1953, and the one that was built after the disastrous fire in 1966. I don't remember the original one very well, but I have strong memories of the second club that was a more modernistic-type building. I can still recall the leopard-skin tablecloths, the Naugahyde on the chairs, and the candles on the tables. The room was intimate and the stage was small, and there was always a jazz trio that played in between the acts. When I handled the lights, I was lucky enough to hang out after the shows even though I was too young to drink. The food was excellent because my father and uncle took great pride in having the best American food, the best steaks, the best chops, the

MISTER KELLY'S

MORT SAHL
DODO GREENE
MARTY RUBENSTEIN

CHARCO

mister
Kelly's
PROF. IRWIN COREY
AND
BILLY DANIELS
mister Kelly's

best seafood, and the Green Goddess salad that was very popular. And, the deserts were great, including the candy crunch cake, which they would bring out on tray to show to customers.

The London House featured classic jazz and the best piano players in the country. People went to the club often to celebrate special occasions. I can tell you that my father and uncle made certain that everyone, no matter their background or color, felt welcome. The club had brass chandeliers and fancy carpets, and there really isn't a restaurant that looks like it anymore. I recall that they served Oscar's steak, which was a sirloin cut like a fillet, pepper steak, and delicious coleslaw. I think that, looking back, the London House was considered to be a cultural center in Chicago. Many people came to the club who had just gotten married, were celebrating their anniversary, and after their high school proms. People in Chicago were proud that the London House was in their city.

As for why the London House and Mister Kelly's closed, my uncle had passed away 10 years before my father in 1963, and my father ran the clubs successfully after his death. He ended up selling the three venues to a larger corporation, the Arts and Leisure Corporation, in 1970. He agreed to stay to run the clubs but unfortunately he passed away in 1972. My dad saw the writing on the wall as talent became more expensive and downtown began to change. The London House and Mister Kelly's did stay open for a couple of years after my dad died, but all the clubs were closed by 1975.

ROSS KONIKOFF | MUSICIAN | NEW YORK

I played with the Buddy Rich Big Band from 1975–78 and needless to say, interesting stories abound. We pulled into Chicago to play Mister Kelly's with Buddy in the summer of 1976, and it was very exciting because the place was legendary. There were bouncers out front, real tough looking guys, one of whom turned out to be T. Laurence Tureaud, who became known professionally as Mr. T., the actor and eventually, a television personality. He also became identified as B. A. Baracus in the 1980s television series, *The A-Team*, and as boxer Clubber Lang in the 1982 film *Rocky III*. Nothing exceptional

happened but it's one of those instances that remain in your mind.

One time in Chicago, we played the Playboy Club and Hugh Hefner loved Buddy. He invited us to play at the Playboy Resort Hotel in Wisconsin later that winter, which we did. Hugh came for the gig and allowed us all to take out snowmobiles after the gig; to speed around the vast snow-covered grounds. Of course with 16 maniacs, the event turned into a virtual demolition derby, with guys limping back to the hotel with blood on many faces, arms and legs mangled, and returning with only half the number of snowmobiles we had started out with. Even Buddy crashed his. It was the last gig we ever did for Hefner.

Another time, we played Kelly's and Dizzy Gillespie's band was playing up the street at The Jazz Showcase. Buddy's ex bass player, Ben Brown, was touring with Diz so we went over to hear his last set and say hello. Afterwards, a few of us got into Dizzy's van and Dizzy whipped out a few joints, lit them and passed them around, telling his driver to just drive around. We got high and listened to Diz talk about a thousand different things from his past, who he played with, etc. An hour later he dropped us at our hotel and said goodnight. It was an amazing night for us.

In Chicago, we always stayed at the Maryland Hotel where it cost $6 a night and THAT was overpriced. The place was a dump with no locks on the doors, just hook and eye latches, tiny rooms with bathrooms up the hall, and broken mirrors, lamps, and beds full of critters. Buddy, of course, always stayed elsewhere, like the Hyatt Water Tower and we used to rush over and have breakfast with him where he'd order three eggs, scrambled in butter, toast, lightly browned, orange juice without the pulp. We were always impressed with that. Then one afternoon he was going out to buy a suit at some custom tailor so Dean Pratt and I went with him. After he was fitted, for a six hundred dollar suit (1976 price!), he turned to us, and then to the tailor and said, make one for these guys too! Of course Dean and I couldn't accept that incredibly generous offer but he meant it. That's only one of a thousand stories demonstrating his kindness.

I also toured with Liza Minnelli off and on during the 70s, 80s, 90s and until she retired in 2014. In 1983, the tour took us to Japan and we were to play Suntory Hall in Tokyo. We got in a few days early and to my astonishment, I saw that The Hi-Los, one of the greatest singing groups of all time, was going to perform for the first time in 20 years! Now, this was at the same hall at which we were to open on the following night. I bought a cassette recorder and crashed the concert sitting in an empty front row seat and listened to Gene Peurling and the boys sing with the Frankie Capp Trio, recording every note. The reason I mention this is because travelling with us at the time was guitarist Frank D'Rone, Chicago native, fabulous singer, and friend of Gene and Don Shelton, the tenor in the Hi Los. When we got back to the states, and back to the Chicago Theater for a Liza concert, Frank arranged a lunch for Gene, Don, and himself, inviting me along. I sat listening to the three of them talk about the old days, the new days, and everything else. I was thrilled to be sitting in the company of one of the greatest vocal arrangers ever!

CLARK WEBER | RADIO DISC JOCKEY AND PROGRAM DIRECTOR | WLS-AM

As the Program Director of WLS-AM in the mid '60s, I met all the famous singers of the time. One day in 1963, I had a call from Columbia record promoter Freddie Salem, who had a problem and needed a favor. It seems that Columbia had signed a relatively unknown singer to an album contract. She had just finished an appearance at Bon Soir, a small New York club, and based on that performance was booked at Mister Kelly's on Chicago's Rush Street. It was the early part of her career, and she may not have been well known to many Chicagoans. Consequently, she was drawing relatively small crowds to the club, and as could be expected, she was less than happy with the situation. I was told that the singer felt that there had been a lack of publicity about her appearances. Salem asked that my wife, Joan, and I join him for dinner at Mister Kelly's so that we could hear her sing and also to help fill up the place.

I should note that show business was not my wife's favorite thing, but, being a good sport, we showed up together for the Friday night show. It was a good thing we did because the place was almost empty. The singer, who would go on to be a superstar in her nightclub, recording, and acting career, definitely showed promise but, at that time, it was my judgment that she would need to improve her singing voice in order to become a star. Well that turned out to be an understatement. After the set was over, she joined us at our table to make small talk. She was complaining about the fact that the piano squeaked, her accommodations in Chicago were less than adequate, and Columbia Records was just not treating her well. Then, Joan, in an effort to get the young lady to focus on more positive issues. After the singer left to get ready for her next set, Joan announced that it was time for us to go home.

The following Monday, on a hot July day, Salem showed up at my WLS office with this singer in tow to present me with a copy of her first album. She was dressed in a style that I would describe as right out of the late '60s: short skirt, purple tights, thigh-high black boots, full cape, and deer stalker hat. But despite all initial appearances, she became, by far, one of the most popular singers of her generation and she would go on to earn $95 million in record sales and appearances in one year. Her name—Barbra Streisand!

PENNY LANE | BROADCAST PERSONALITY AND ENTERTAINMENT CONSULTANT

My background is in theater and radio. I graduated from the Goodman Theater School of Drama, which is now DePaul University's theater school. There was a radio station called WSDM—which stood for "We're Smack Dab In The Middle Of The Dial"—the station with the girls and all that jazz. They were looking for someone to fill a time slot, and I auditioned for the station and I got the gig. I stayed there for seven and a half years. Being a disc jockey gives you many opportunities. I got to see a lot of different artists for free, plus, I got to talk to them. I've always loved entertainment. I eventually went to work for

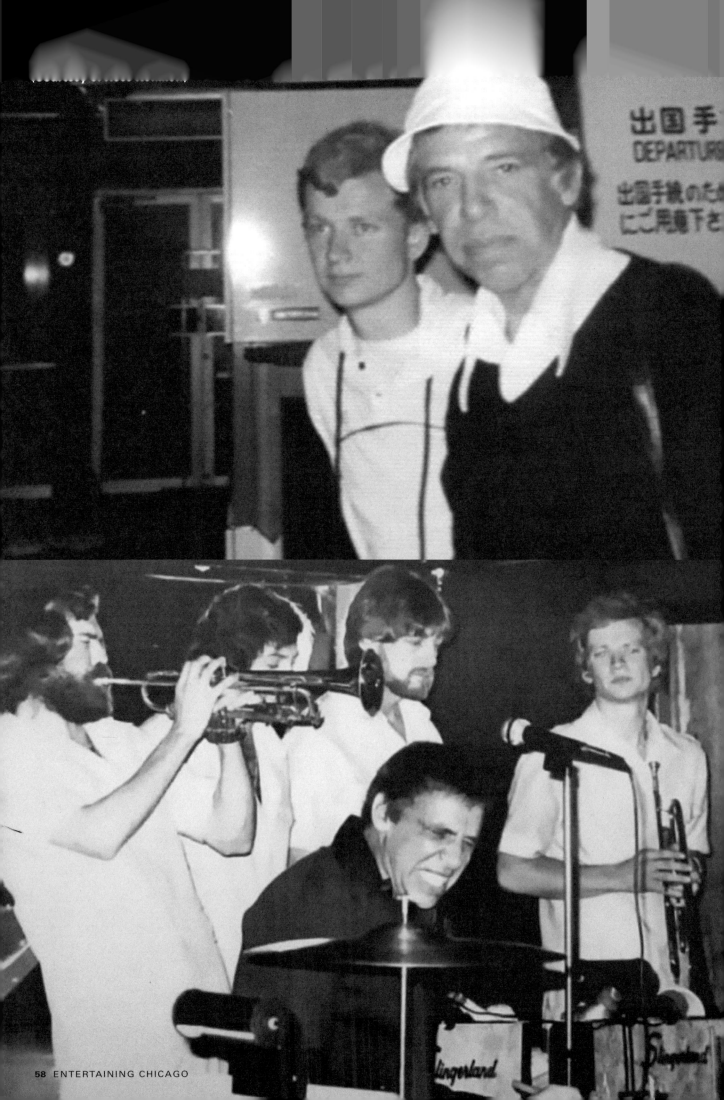

the Marienthal brothers (Oscar and George), who owned some of the best and biggest clubs in Chicago. I worked in the box office of one of their venues, The Happy Medium, in the evenings for various shows like *Jacques Brel Is Alive and Well and Living in Paris* and Oscar Brown, Jr.'s *Joy '66*. In addition to handling that, I danced downstairs at a little club they owned—a disco club called the Flower Pot, where everybody listened to the DJ; as well as dance to the music. I also danced, and in addition ran their club in Highland Park that was called The London House North. By working at the radio station during the day, I was able to work other creative entertainment jobs when I was off duty, so to speak.

When I was working at the radio station, we would have famous personalities do little introductions about the station. For example, we had Barbra Streisand say, "This is Barbra Streisand and I never listen to WSDM." Or, we had Mose Allison saying, "WSDM—what's that? Never heard of it." We would interject these little bits throughout the day. One of my favorite entertainers happened to be Mort Sahl. He was appearing at Mister Kelly's, and I asked my program director if I could go there and interview him and get him to cut one of these ID's, and he agreed. So, one of my friends and I went there with our recording gear and we were brought back to his dressing room. We went in, and he was sitting toward the back of the room reading a book. Again, we were kind of nervous because we were in front of this very famous person. I said, "Hi," and he said, "Hello." Now the book he was reading was *The Warren Report* — the book about the assassination of President Kennedy. I told him that I loved President Kennedy. He asked if I had read the report. I told him that I'd read part of it, but not the entire report. He said, "So, you loved him, but not enough to read the entire report?" I thought to myself, "Omigod, where is this going?" I went on to remark about the size of the book. He said, "Well, what do you read?" And I said that I try to read a little bit of everything. And he said, "OK. Well, I don't want to do an interview tonight. Why don't you

come back tomorrow night." And I told him that we would. So, the next night, we went back with our recording gear and the maître d' greeted us and said, "I'm sorry, Penny. Not only does he not want to talk to you, but he doesn't want you anywhere near the club." I was crushed; absolutely crushed. He didn't appreciate me not reading the whole *Warren Report*, so he was not going to do the Id's as he promised. I know that he's still around and if I could hear his opinions and views, I would listen. But that experience really cut me and I don't understand it at all.

MARC SCHULMAN | OWNER, ELI'S CHEESECAKE

My memories about places for entertainment are twofold: first of all would be when my father opened Eli's Stage Delicatessen in 1962 and then closed in 1968. That was the heyday of Rush Street and the great entertainers of the time, including Barbra Streisand, early in her career, Woody Allen or Shecky Greene, and a great amount of talent that would come over to the restaurant late at night or before the shows on the weekends. Eli's was a great meeting place for that generation. Phase 2 was when we moved to Eli's The Place for Steak on Chicago Avenue and then it was more of Sinatra, Sammy Davis, Jr., Dean Martin, and a lot the people that the *Chicago Sun-Times* columnist Irv Kupcinet would bring in to the restaurant.

My dad had a lot of great relationships with people like Sean Connery, Roger Moore, and Johnny Carson. We also have a great picture of Sinatra with my dad and Sammy Davis, Jr., and when Frank and Barbara Sinatra gave my dad the Cartier watch engraved in the year before my dad died in 1987. I think that my parents obviously had memories of the Chez Paree. But it was a great thrill for me to see the role that Eli's and my father had in Chicago history. I went to Mister Kelly's and London House and have memories of those places and just being pretty young and able to go there as a teenager. My memories are clearer of when those people came to our restaurants.

Shecky Greene was a dear friend of my father's and would spend a lot of time with us. It was an exciting time in Chicago, and I'd say that the role that live entertainment played and the role that these clubs had in Chicago have not been duplicated. Clearly, the Sinatra era and the big tours were very special.

JOE LEVINSON | MUSICIAN

The great Mister Kelly's on Rush at Elm. It was a wildly popular place to eat great chops and see and hear the greatest singers and comedians perform. Ella Fitzgerald, Sarah Vaughn, Victor Borge, Mort Sahl, Lenny Bruce, Shelley Berman, and dozens of other name acts worked the room during its years of operation. Standing room was the name of the game on weekends just to get in at Mister Kelly's. I played for several of the acts that worked there but never for Ella or Sarah; they came with their own well-rehearsed trios. On many occasions I found a little corner at the back of the room and stood there listening to and admiring Ella and Sarah's expertise—and learning! Many years later, in the 1970s, I played at Mister Kelly's in a trio backing Bette Midler. It was one of the funniest experiences of my life, and I wound up with stomach aches from laughing so hard as she did her act.

In 1963, Kaye Ballard, the singer-comedienne from New York, was featured at Mister Kelly's and I was in the backup trio with Marty Rubenstein and Jack Noren. We rehearsed her during the afternoon, but I was totally unprepared for her opening night entrance. We started a vamp and Marty got on his microphone and said, "And now, direct from the phone booth on the corner, here's Kaye Ballard!" Well, she trounced through the crowded tables to great applause, climbed onto the little stage and showed off an enormously long purple boa, wrapped around her shoulders. So, we kept up the vamp we were playing, waiting for her to start singing her first number. Well, she stood there grinning toothfully at the crowd who were gasping at the ridiculous boa that she wore. Finally, she said, "You like it? S&H Green Stamps bought it!" Then she threw it behind her and Marty

and Jack started playing her opener. But I couldn't play because the boa flew back and wound itself right around the neck of my bass, blocking my fingers from playing anything! The audience was roaring with laughter, and so were Marty and Jack. Finally, she turned around and saw what was happening—I was frantically trying to unwind the boa. "Stop the music!" she shouted, "Let's keep it in the act!" So, every night for her three-week run, she tried to replicate that opening-night boa toss, but each time it landed on the drums, the piano, out in the audience, everywhere but around the neck of my bass. She was absolutely a dynamite performer, and we all loved her.

BROOKE AMLING | IRVING, TX

My maiden name was Ludwig, and I am the daughter of William F. Ludwig II and my mother, Maggie. We've been in the percussion business for my whole life. My grandfather, William F. Ludwig, Sr., and his brother, Theobald, started the business in around 1909 working from a garage. They began making pedals for bass drums and timpani mechanisms—accessories like that. That was the beginning and the company just grew, becoming Ludwig Industries and making percussion instruments for many famous musicians and jazz drummers—snare drums and so forth. Then, in 1981, Dad sold the business to the Conn-Selmer Corporation and it continues to this day under the Ludwig Industries name. They also bought several other musical instrument companies, too. During that time, we used to frequent the London House to go hear different musicians. I remember the London House had a house trio that was led by Eddie Higgins. We also went to Mister Kelly's quite often. There was another place down in the Rush Street area that we would go to called The Jazz Showcase, and there were a lot of musicians we would go to hear that played there, too. I remember you had to go down some stairs to get into the club, and I really didn't like it because it was always so smoky. My former husband, Bill Crowden, had a drum shop at 218 S. Wabash called Drums Limited. Of course, many drummers and jazz musicians came to his shop, including Buddy Rich and Joe Morello.

Gene Krupa, Max Roach, and percussionists from the Chicago Symphony Orchestra and the Lyric Opera were also customers of his.

I have a favorite story about Buddy Rich. Bill had arranged a clinic for Buddy to play, and he invited friends and other musicians to come hear him. So, he got set up… did his clinic and afterwards, was his usual cantankerous kind of self. One of Bill's customers had brought his 10-year old son to watch the clinic as well. The little boy went up to Buddy Rich and said, "My daddy says that he plays just like you!" Buddy turned to the boy's father and said, "You really shouldn't bullshit your kid like that!" That was Buddy Rich, all right. He played Ludwig drums for a number of years and then he switched to Slingerland. He was kind of difficult. He would play a concert, and then he would either leave the drums or give them to a kid who admired him and then expect Ludwig to have a brand new set ready and waiting for him at the next gig. Louie Bellson was a neat guy, and his personality was quite different than that of Buddy's, although Buddy could be nice at times, too. But Louie was sweet and kind and nice to everybody all the time.

SHELLEY BERMAN | COMEDIAN AND ACTOR

One day I heard about a fellow named Mort Sahl. He was performing at a place called Mister Kelly's, so I went there to see this young man work. I saw the thrust of his efforts—he was working within certain limits, and he was improvising, finding his way, but he knew which way he was going each time—and the shows were always different. I saw this marvelous creativity taking place before me, and he didn't have to tell hard jokes. All he had to do was be bright and original—and he was.

I first performed at Mister Kelly's soon after I saw Mort. I wangled an audition and performed a few phone calls, and they hired me at $350 a week with an option for four weeks. My g-d, I was earning money! About a year later, since Mort and I were friends, he talked me into doing an album. He said that I should record my show with his record company. The album was called *Inside Shelly Berman*—and it was a phenomenal hit. That album became one of the biggest selling comedy albums ever and won me the first Grammy for a non-musical record. I wound up making six such albums, the last one with Jerry Stiller and Anne Meara.

Pretty soon I was working in all the places that you are supposed to work, including The Hungry I in San Francisco, the Blue Angel in New York—and Mister Kelly's. These were the key places for performers. When the record hit, all of a sudden, people I was opening for were now opening for me! It was exciting and splendid. Chicago was such a key part of my life. In the 1960s, after my acting and comedy career had already begun in Chicago, even though I wasn't living there during the decade, I still was able to get back to Rush Street as often as I could. The Marienthal brothers were happy to have me, and I was still performing at Mister Kelly's most of the time. Then, later on in the '60s, I tried performing at the Palmer House in the Empire Room, and although it was okay, I wasn't as happy with that as I was performing on Rush Street. I never was asked to perform at the Chez Paree, and although it was a very nice nightclub, I guess that I wasn't the kind of comedian, like a Danny Thomas, who they felt was right for their club.

TOM DREESEN | COMEDIAN

My first introduction to Mister Kelly's happened as a result of caddying for the owners of the club, Oscar and George Marienthal, who were members at Ravisloe Country Club where I caddied as a little boy. They also owned the London House and the Happy Medium. When I first went into show business, I started going downtown a lot. In those days, Mister Kelly's was the place where the big comedians and singers from all around the world would perform and whom you might see on the *Ed Sullivan Show*. Mister Kelly's was the ultimate place to perform for Chicagoans who wanted a career in show business. I also remember the Happy Medium and Punchinellos that were both on Rush Street. All the theater and show business people would eat at Punchinellos.

Oscar Brown, Jr., (Courtesy of Chicago Historical Society, ICHi-12244)

My career began to be shaped in the late '60s and early '70s, and I can recall all the hustle and bustle of being a new comedian and where the show business people met to have conversations. If you were lucky enough you might be able to begin your path to stardom on Rush Street.

If you go to that era when I came out of the military service in the 1960s, Mister Kelly's was at the apex of show business in Chicago. Although I wasn't in show business at that time, that club was where the big stars performed in those years and it was simply the premier nightclub where one wanted to work in Chicago if you were in show business. When I got into comedy, there were no comedy clubs in Chicago, or even in America at that time. There was the Improv in New York, but it wasn't a comedy club per se because it had singers, actors, and comics who could drop in and get up on stage at any time in the evening. The challenge as a stand-up comedian in those days was where you could perform and the fact is that you had to get up on stage somewhere in order to develop your act. So, in Chicago, you went around Old Town and areas like that. I was with Tim Reid at that time, and we were America's first black and white comedy team. There were places like The Earl of Old Town where you could try to get up on stage and do five minutes before or after the singer. In those days, most singers just sat on a stool with a guitar in those clubs.

When I went on stage with Tim Reid for the first time, I had never been on stage nor had he. So, when Tim and I started our comedy careers, Mister Kelly's was our goal. Of all the nightclubs in Chicago, we knew that if we made it to Mister Kelly's, we had made the big time and everybody in Chicago knew that to be the truth. When Barbra Streisand appeared at Mister Kelly's, it was the first big club she worked in Chicago. It was the apex, the place where you wanted to be performing. So, you worked toward that goal. But, that being said, every chance I got I would sneak into Mister Kelly's and try to stand over by the bar and catch what acts came in there...from Richard Pryor to Mort Sahl to George Carlin.

I've always told young comedians that if you want to be a comedian, study the masters...those who were on the stage that you hoped to be on one day. That is what I did. I remember one time, when I had become a stand-up comedian alone, I went to Mister Kelly's when Mort Sahl was appearing there and I snuck backstage to his dressing room. As you know, backstage was upstairs of what is now called Gibsons Restaurant. You would come downstairs to enter Mister Kelly's stage from the west end of the building and pass through the kitchen, and there was a side door that is still there. The north wall was where the stage was located. So, I snuck backstage and I knocked on Mort Sahl's door and I thought that his manager was going to answer. But, as it turned out, Mort opened the door and he was all alone. I said to Mr. Sahl, "My name is Tom Dreesen, and I'm a new comedian and I wonder if I can ask you a few questions?" I was real nervous, and he said, "Yeah, yeah, come on in." He was all by himself but he invited me to sit in the dressing room for almost two hours before his next show. He gave me advice and counsel, and it just was wonderful.

I remember one thing he asked me, "Do you write your own material?" I said, "Yes, I do." And, he responded, "Remember, they're wrong." I said, "Who?" And he said, "They." I said, "They?" He said, "Who are you writing about? They're wrong. The airlines are wrong. The government is wrong. Somebody has got to be wrong in the joke." I walked out of Mister Kelly's on a cold winter night and I said to myself, if I ever make it to the big time and a young comedian comes up to me and says, "Can I talk to you?," I am going to do it. I was on cloud nine because Mort took that much time with me and really helped me. And he talked to me not like an underling, even though I had only been in the business for four months. That happened around 1970.

The name of the maitre'd at Mister Kelly's was Monroe. I have to say that the owners, George and Oscar Marienthal, were terrific to work for. When Tim and I were performing at Mister Kelly's, we opened for Della Reese and Muddy Waters, and I opened for Fats Domino as a single after the comedy team broke up. The genius of the Marienthal brothers was that they would go around the country and they would find acts that they thought were going to become future stars. For example, they would go to New York to clubs like the Baths and see a young Bette Midler or a young Barbra Streisand who was making $250 a week at one of the clubs in New York. And, they would go to that person and say, "We want to hire you at Mister Kelly's. We are going to give you $750 a week, and that is three times what you are making now. And, we want a return contract that will double the $750 to $1,500." And, of course, the performers jumped on the offer. What the Marienthals would do is put them into the first week for $750 and then they would hold that contract until that person became a star. Everybody took the offer and the return engagement except for Barbra Streisand. She appeared for one week at Mister Kelly's, but when she became a star, she bought out her return contract for $15,000.

First of all, when you are making $250 a week and someone offers you $750 and they tell you that the next time you perform at Mister Kelly's the fee will double, that sounded like big money in those days. And, it was. The Marienthal Brothers were brilliant about that, and they were also brilliant about the issue of integration by bringing in black acts. The Civil Rights Act was passed in 1964, so when I worked at Mister Kelly's there were very few black people in the audience even though they were more than welcome at the club. Even in 1974, you would be going around the country and, even though it would be an all-white night club, it didn't mean that blacks weren't allowed, but just that blacks didn't go there. Even though Mister Kelly's welcomed African Americans, they just didn't go there that much. I performed at Mister Kelly's until it closed, and I was one of the last performers there. When the Marienthals decided to sell their clubs, Paul Wimmer bought all three venues: Mister Kelly's, London House and Happy Medium.

I toured with Frank Sinatra for 14 years in 45-50 cities a year. For two of those years, Buddy Rich toured with us in the big arenas where it would be Buddy Rich opening the show for us. Then, I would come out and do stand-up comedy, and, after an intermission, Frank would come out to perform. Buddy didn't particularly like that arrangement and he would say to Frank, "The kid should go on first." Frank insisted that comedy go before him and I loved that setup. Because with a 20,000-seat arena, having Buddy Rich go out and perform for 30 minutes meant that, when he got done with his incredible act, the audience was all in their seats and ready to go. However, when I would do a large arena, with just Frank alone, I had to go out and "get" the audience. With a 20,000-seat venue there were always 5,000 people who were still trying to find their seats. You've really got to have seasoning to know how to work that kind of arena, so it was always an interesting challenge. But, through the years I "got" them all ready for Frank to come out to perform.

As I said, when I started out with Tim Reid we were America's first, and as it turned out, last black/white comedy team. There were no comedy clubs, so it was a challenge for us to polish our craft. As a result, we would volunteer for every charity known to man because we needed stage time and we needed to develop our style. I coined a phrase— "We would play a phone booth if you promise to call us." All the black clubs in Chicago, like Lurleens, Lum's, Leek's, and Herman's on the South Side, would feature jazz players like Sonny Stitt, Gene Ammons, Eddie Harris, and the Jazz Crusaders, and they were places where we could go to them and say, "Do you mind, that when you finish your set could we go on stage to do a few minutes of our comedy?" And, those guys were real show business people, so they would say to the crowd, "Folks, this is our last number, but don't leave because we have a young comedy team that wants to regale you with some laughter until we get back. So stay in your seats."

Then, there were a lot of legitimate clubs that would hire us, like the High Chapparal. It later became called the Burning Spear. Also, there were other clubs where you could just walk in and get up and perform like The Guys and Gals and the Dating Club

Lounge which were black clubs on Chicago's South Side.

There was a distinct difference between Old Town and the North Side clubs and South Side clubs, because, when Tim Reid and I worked the South Side, I was usually the only white guy in those places. And, when we worked the North Side, Tim would be the only black guy, for the most part, in those clubs during that era. Black-owned, black-operated nightclubs were affectionately called the "Chitlin Circuit" by black people. When I used to tour with Sammy Davis, Jr., he used to tell me how he had worked the "Chitlin Circuit" in the early years of his career. When you worked the "Chitlin Circuit" in Chicago, it meant performing at the Burning Spear or the High Chapparal or Roberts 500 Club. In Boston , it was the Sugar Shack, and in Detroit, it was the 20 Grand. At the same time Motown Records had begun in Detroit, so all the black acts like Diana Ross and the Supremes, the Temptations, the O-Jays, Smokey Robinson, and all such acts worked in that city and they broke in their acts at the 20 Grand before they went to Las Vegas.

I am proud to say that I still come back to Chicago all the time, and I have a one-man show called *An Evening of Laughter and Stories of Sinatra*. I have done that show in Chicago several times, and they want me to do it again. I also sing *Take Me Out To The Ballgame* each year at Wrigley Field, and I have my golf tournament that I do every year in the Chicago area.

When Frank and I used to come to Chicago to perform together, we would hang out at Gibsons Restaurant on Rush Street (the original location of Mister Kelly's) and the Pump Room in the Ambassador East Hotel. Before my time, Chicago had been the hub for vaudeville because all the vaudeville acts would come through Chicago since all the cross-country trains stopped there. So, Chicago was a great place to work. At the Pump Room, a guy named Jack Eigen used to do a nationwide radio show live from Pump Room, and I did his show many times. When we were in town, Frank and I hung out in the Pump Room at Booth One

until dawn each night. Whenever Chicago came up in our discussions, Frank would tell me that Chicago was one of his favorite cities to perform and hang out. He also told me that it was ironic that everybody thought that he primarily worked in New York when he started out. In actuality, he performed in Chicago more than anywhere else.

He said to me, "This was a great city for me to perform in." And, he loved coming back to Chi-town. I remember that when he would perform in town at the Chicago Theater, and after my show, the spotlight would be on the microphone at center stage, and Frank would walk out on stage with no introduction, the audience would go wild with cheers, and he would pause, open up his arms, and sing…"This is my kind of town, Chicago is!" The room would just tremble in reaction because of their love and excitement to see Frank. It was funny to me that when I was growing up I used to shine shoes outside the Chicago Theater on State Street. And, here I was performing with Frank Sinatra at that very same place some 30 years later.

When we were in Chicago after the show, we would always eat at Gibsons. After that, we would go drink in the Pump Room until late at night, in fact, until dawn. Dave Colella was the manager of the Ambassador East, and he would tell the bartender to stay at the hotel's bar and he would close the place down at 2 a.m. and we would remain there until dawn every morning. And, of course the bartender wouldn't leave because Frank was such a great tipper. We always flew into Chicago on Frank's private jet. Frank only primarily stayed in three places in the country. In New York, the Waldorf Astoria was the place and we would satellite out of there to eastern cities. We would do Boston one night and Hartford, Connecticut one night. Sometimes we would helicopter to those cities, but most of the time we would fly on his jet to the different East Coast cities. If we were performing on the West Coast, we stayed at Frank's home and we satellited to Denver and all the western cities. When we went to the Midwest, we only stayed at the Ambassador East and Frank would do St. Louis one night, Detroit one night, Omaha one night, Lincoln,

Nebraska one night, and we would fly in and out and return to the Pump Room each night, and Steve Lombardo would keep Gibsons open late for Frank. Frank loved it and loved the food there. For those of us who worked the "Chitlin circuit," black or white, you worked your way downtown to finally get to Mister Kelly's.

TIM REID | COMEDIAN | TELEVISION PERSONALITY | PRODUCER

I was born in Norfolk and grew up in Chesapeake, Virgina. I ended up coming north to Chicago when I was working for DuPont, and I was the first black hired by that company out of college in a management training program. They were trying to find a place to send me. At that time, because of the racial segregation situation in America, they had a hard time finding a place to send me where DuPont had manufacturing or headquarters. So, the only three places available for me without them feeling that they were putting me in danger was Detroit, Chicago, and Los Angeles. In Detroit they figured that I would be in danger because of the auto worker situation. Thus, it was between Chicago and Los Angeles, and, when they said LA, someone said no, if you send him out there he will go into show business. So, they sent me to Chicago where three years later I went into show business. Tom Dreesen and I met in Chicago through our mutual involvement in the Junior Chamber of Commerce. My company, at that time, was very aggressive in terms of being socially involved in the community. So, it was almost expected for us to get involved in community organizations and I chose the Junior Chamber of Commerce (JCs). The Kiwanis wouldn't have us.

Ironically, I never had a desire to become a comedian and it was the furthest thing from my mind. Instead, my goal was to make a lot of money as a businessman. So, it was just happenstance that I became a comedian, and it occurred because a little girl said to Tom Dreesen and me, "You guys are funny, you ought to be a comedy team." That was when the "pilot light" was lit, and we have been funny ever since. Tom and I were the only successful black and white comedy team in American history. There were others who attempted to do that, but we were the only successful ones. We were out into the field for five years doing our comedy and taking the slings and arrows and the slight successes that we had, including writing our material, doing television, and performing in clubs. No one has attempted to do that since then with a professional approach that lasted more than a year or so.

I performed at several clubs in Chicago with Tom, including the Chicago Playboy Club, Mister Kelly's, Happy Medium at their basement bar, and at black clubs all across Chicago, including the Burning Spear that had been the High Chapparal all during the 1970s, as well as the Golden Horseshoe in Chicago Heights near the horse racing track.

Mister Kelly's was the "primo." It was one of, if not the finest club in America. Everybody and anybody who wanted to have a career in show business dreamed of working at Mister Kelly's. You name it... Barbra Streisand, the Smothers Brothers...you name them and they all worked to get there. Everybody wanted to be at Mister Kelly's. In my estimation, it was the finest night club outside of a Las Vegas or Atlantic City setting. Even clubs in New York. New York had that thing about itself, and the clubs there wanted you to feel privileged just for being in New York because it was the Big Apple. But, Mister Kelly's actually catered to the audience and to the entertainers and you could tell that the Marienthals loved show business. So, if somebody asked me what I would try to do in real life, I would tell them that I've both tried it in television series to build a bar or do a series at a bar. So, I've done two television series about a bar. In fact, my father actually owned a bar for a brief period before happenstance caused him to lose it. And, it is in my blood and I've always wanted to have a place where people could come and be entertained and I could hang out. Mister Kelly's would be my ideal place. If someone gave me money or the opportunity to build my own bar or entertainment center, it would be as close as I could get it to Mister Kelly's. I don't know how to explain it, but it clearly was the atmosphere there.

The first bug that I ever had about being in the entertainment business ironically occurred on New Year's Eve, 1968 when I went to Mister Kelly's. It happened because that afternoon, on my couch, December, 31, 1968, I was just looking at the paper and it said, "Richard Pryor at Mister Kelly's." Now, I am just a country boy from Virginia and I just assumed that you dress up, go downtown, and go into the club. As it happened, it was a very cold nine degrees outside that day. So, I told my wife, at that time, "We are going to see Richard Pryor." She said, "Okay. When do we leave?" I said, "We will just go downtown and catch the next show, I think, the second show, the one before New Year's Eve." She said, "Okay." Now, this is in the afternoon, New Year's Eve, nine degrees." So, we left the house around 8 p.m., and we drove down to Rush Street, and as I am approaching the place I saw this line around the block. But, it is nine degrees outside and I wasn't going to stand in a line in that temperature. And, every parking lot said, "Full." I said to her, "What is going on?" So, as I turned at the corner where Mister Kelly's was located, to make a right turn, go back down and circle back around, a guy came out of the parking lot and changed the sign in front of the garage from "Full" to "Vacant." So I just pulled right in. I mean, the timing couldn't have been better. The guy said to me, "One spot available!" I said, "Okay." I pulled in and paid him, although I was upset with how much money it cost me. Now, I was thinking that I was lucky because Mister Kelly's was located right across the street.

Instead of getting in that line, I walked up to the glass door of the club, and the maitre'd, Monroe, who, as it turned out would later become a friend, was standing there. I was banging on the door, but I was doing that while people were coming out from the earlier show. The door where people would go in was locked because the people in line were waiting to go in. The maitre'd looked at me, and I was gesturing like "Open the door!" But, he was looking at me like what was wrong with that person. Finally, he just turned away from me, but people were coming out, so I just opened the door and walked in. He said, "May I help you?" I said, "I would like to have a table for two. We would like to see Richard Pryor." He looked at me in total amazement and he said, "What? Do you have reservations?" I said, "No." I had never had reservations for anything in my life up to that point. He said, "Are you kidding me?" I said, "No." He could see that I was honest in my response. He said, "Where are you from?" I said, "From Virginia." He said, "Ahh. Stay right there for a minute." He said to me, "Young fellow, people out there in that line booked this thing a year or two ago and they have reservations. You don't come into a club the night of the event, and especially on New Year's Eve, with no reservations, and expect to get in. What is wrong with you?"

At that time, a fight broke out as they were letting people out of the earlier show. So, as Monroe was about to lecture me, people were coming out of the exit. I had to stand back against the wall so people could get out. He said to me, "Stay right there!" I waited because I was thinking that I was going to get in the club. After all of these people exited from the first show, the maitre'd walked over to me and he let people in. He said to me, "Young fellow, how long have you been in town?" I said, "I just moved here." At that time, another fight broke out at the bar between a woman and her husband. She threw a drink in his face, broke the glass, and stormed out of the building. The maitre'd turned to me and he said, "Take those two stools at the bar!" So, we had great seats, and out came Richard Pryor and I was blown away by the performer. I turned to my wife after Pryor performed, and I said to her, "I want to do that!" She said to me, "Well, it is good to have a dream." And we left.

Do you know, as it turned out I was the last comic to perform, as a solo, at Mister Kelly's in 1975 on New Year's Eve, right before they closed. That was how my dream happened and how I was part of the end of Mister Kelly's.

In truth, performing at Mister Kelly's was a dream come true. Even if the audiences were bad, you didn't blame the audience. You blamed yourself. And, even then, you felt good about being at Mister Kelly's.

London House, (As published in the
Chicago Sun-Times, Photographer– Gene Pesek.
Copyright, 1960 by *Chicago Sun-Times*, Inc,
Reprinted with permission)

London Ho se
THE PIANO
XIE
BARBARA CAR
OLL
WHITE WAY
NO PARKING ANY TIME
PRIME

Anybody in show business, even if you won awards during your career, you had that feeling that you had accomplished something. When you walked out on stage at Mister Kelly's, you felt that you were in show business and that you were really doing what you dreamed of doing and there was no better place on the planet. That atmosphere that was created there had to do with the people who owned the club and the people who ran it. In fact, the people who worked there really paid attention to the shows and the performers. I miss that now in the world that we live in and that sense of place. Las Vegas is a wonderful place, but nothing like Mister Kelly's exists today. We have trivialized everything, and the importance that things have in terms of the spiritual values found in the entertainment business and the spirit of performing and that feeling you get has all been trivialized. Everybody is a star today, but not like the true stars of the past and what it meant to be called a star. In the days of big movies, you weren't a star until your name came before the title. You didn't just get that the first time out. You had to earn it. When you hear people talking about a club like Mister Kelly's, they weren't just talking about a club. When you walked into that venue, it was like walking into an entertainment cathedral. You could feel the history and you could almost assume the greatness of the place and that you were a part of it. When I think back in my early career, there were only a few places that really exist in my heart that way: Mister Kelly's was one; the Playboy Clubs where we worked were others; and Lucky Pierre's in New Orleans, that no longer exists, was another. Even to this day, and you can talk to anybody, you say Mister Kelly's and if they've been there, they will go "Oh, Mister Kelly's!"

LONDON HOUSE

The London House, also owned by George and Oscar Marienthal, was a jazz club and restaurant that was renovated in 1946 and revamped in 1955. It was located at 360 North Michigan Avenue in the London Guarantee Building at the corner of Michigan and Wacker Drive, a building that was designed by Alfred S. Alschuler in 1923. The building also was the home of the very popular WLS-AM radio station. The London House was considered to be one of the foremost jazz clubs in the country, and the range of performers included Oscar Peterson, Bill Evans, George Shearing, Dave Brubeck, Dinah Washington, Cannonball Adderley, Nancy Wilson, Gene Krupa, Teddy Wilson, Billy Taylor, Ahmad Jamal, Bobby Short, and the Ramsey Lewis Trio which served as the club's house band for several years. At the 20th anniversary celebration in November 1966, Frank Sinatra, Jr. headlined the program. Later, as jazz began to wane in popularity to rock and roll, the London House closed in the 1970s.

JOE LEVINSON | MUSICIAN

One of the most popular downtown clubs was London House, located on the southwest corner of Michigan and Wacker, in the London Guarantee Building. The place served top-flight steaks and chops and had the world's greatest jazz players performing there. I saw Oscar Peterson's trio with Ray Brown on bass, George Shearing's quintet with Margie Hymes on vibes, Woody Herman's septet, Andre Previn's trio and, believe it or not, Spike Jones and the City Slickers played there. You name it—the best small bands in the world were booked at the London House. I actually played at the London House on what were known as "off nights," Sundays and Mondays, either when the featured acts were not working, or to alternate with them on stage when they were working. Performers on off nights included Audrey Morris and Judy Roberts, and the Ramsey Lewis Trio was the house band for many years. The long-running, off-night pianist in those years was Eddie Higgins, today regarded as one of the world's premiere jazz players.

Duke Ellington, Edward Kennedy Ellington II and Mercer Ellington, (Courtesy of Edward Kennedy Ellington II).

EDWARD KENNEDY ELLINGTON II (DUKE ELLINGTON'S GRANDSON) MANASQUAN, NEW JERSEY

After my grandfather passed away, Mercer Ellington, my father, took over the band. I was just finishing up at Berklee and I joined the orchestra. One of the more memorable gigs we did was playing at the London House. As I recall, we were the final act to appear there before the London House closed. Needless to say, this was a very historic venue. Anybody who was anybody played the London House, and it was a grand experience to be part of the legend. But, the one thing I remember about the London House and Chicago, in particular, was that in order to get to the London House, you had to go across this bridge, which was between where we were staying and the venue, itself. It was winter, and it was the coldest I'd ever been. You know, I'd been to Sweden; I'd been to Alaska. And having to cross that bridge was just frigid. I remember that a rope had been put in place for people to hang onto as they crossed so they wouldn't be blown over by the wind. Plus, we're carrying instruments in cases. God only knows what happened to the bass! When we got into the place, we literally had to sit down for 20 minutes just to catch out breaths and defrost. Then, of course, after the gig was over, we didn't want to leave and have to go out into that weather again. Thinking about that, it was always difficult for us to go to Chicago because planes wouldn't leave at 1 or 2 or 3 in the morning when we'd finished, so we were on the bus. There were literally times when we'd take the bus from Chicago to New York, after the show—not exactly a short road trip. But, that's what I remember about Chicago and playing the London House.

HAPPY MEDIUM THEATRE

JOE LEVINSON | MUSICIAN

I returned to the music scene in Chicago in 1963 after nearly four years in New York City, and I was happy to be back in my home town. I played bass and electric bass regularly with a variety of Chicago band leaders, working at weddings, country clubs, corporation parties, and political events. Several years later, in 1968, I was asked to join the instrumental quartet that would back up a play that was going to open in a few weeks at the Happy Medium Theater on Rush Street.

The play was *Jacques Brel is Alive and Well and Living in Paris*. It was created in New York in 1967–68 by Mort Shuman, Eric Blau, and Jacques Brel and staged off-Broadway at the Village Gate on Bleeker Street in Greenwich Village. The play ran there for four-and-a-half years, and, soon after it opened, there were spin-offs run in several U.S. cities, the first one being Chicago, and then in London. It was made into a film, shot in Paris in 1974, and released in the United States in 1975. It starred Jacques Brel himself, most of the New York cast, and one member of the Chicago cast. Columbia Records issued a two-disc LP album of the original cast.

Four musicians were signed to back the singers: Hans Wurman, piano, celesta, and conductor; Jack Ceccini, guitar (doubling on banjo and mandolin); Hal Russell, percussion (marimba, or orchestra bells, drum set, triangle, and other noisemakers); and me on bass violin (doubling on electric bass). Midway through the run of the show, Hal Russell left and was replaced by Shelly Elias. The show was comprised of 26 songs that were written by Jacques Brel, the Belgian-born singer-songwriter. The songs were a compendium of his compositions dealing with a wide range of human emotions reflecting the angst of the times, especially post-World War II remembrances and emotions related to the on-going Vietnam War.

Jacques Brel, who was born in 1929 in Belgium, became famous in Europe as a composer and singer and performed his songs in numerous French films and on nightclub stages around the world. Ironically, Brel had claimed that he never wrote a love song, but his works exhibited a wide range of joyful celebrations of wine, women, and song. He captured the strong feelings of people caught in war and fearful of old age, as well as cynical observations of drunks and people in bars, thoughts of religion, and of lust, false celebrity, rejection in love, and

The Happy Medium stood at the northeast corner of Rush and Delaware Streets. Directly across the street was the Hotel Maryland. (Sigmund J. Osty photo, courtesy of the Chicago History Museum, ICHi-52285).

fears of obscurity, deception, and death. He was a heavy smoker and died of lung cancer in 1978 on Hiva Oa Island in the Marquesas, French Polynesia. Brel was buried next to the great French artist, Paul Gauguin.

We four musicians, while rehearsing *Jacques Brel*, were playing music quite different from what many Americans were accustomed to hearing. Hans Wurman and Jack Ceccini were well trained in European classical music, and their training proved extremely valuable as we rehearsed the material. In addition, Hans Wurman was a gifted organist and concert pianist. The cast of the show included four singers, two men and two women. Some of the action on the stage used spoken dialogue as well as dancing and mime, and they performed nine times a week. I remember that during rehearsals at Mister Kelly's, the famous nightclub across the street from the Happy Medium, several of us felt that the show wouldn't last very long because we concluded that the critics would find it politically questionable. For years, Chicago critics had bad reputations with performers from across the country, and in those days, there were some artists who absolutely refused to perform in Chicago because of the city's newspaper critics.

After rehearsing without the cast at Mister Kelly's, we then rehearsed at the Happy Medium for a week with the entire cast and stage crew. Several preview performances came next, and they seemed to go well, but there was still some final fine turning necessary to prepare for opening night. We played the music while on stage with the cast during each performance, and although we could see the stage action, the audience was unable to see us, as we were behind a scrim.

Finally, it was opening night, Thursday, September 12, 1968. I still thought that it was going to be a short run, and I was curious about the audience's reaction to Brel's musical genre. However, to my surprise, the first show was rewarded by the audience with tumultuous applause, and that was followed the next day by rave reviews from Chicago's major critics, notably a glowing review from Sidney J. Harris of the *Chicago Daily News*. We immediately sold out for many months, and all of us in the orchestra were told to get alternate musicians in case we might be unable to play for any reason. I arranged to work one week on and one week off, alternating with an excellent bassist, Bob Surga. This allowed both of us to keep our connections alive in the city's busy freelance music scene.

That move also allowed me to retain my sanity because it soon became obvious to me that I'd wake up in the middle of the night hearing one or another of Brel's 26 songs and then try to get back to sleep. The ability to play a variety of other composers' music during the long run of *Jacques Brel* saved my sanity, although after the show finally closed, it took nearly a year for me to completely erase Jacques Brel's music from my brain.

Jacques Brel was so popular that people came to see it again and again. I remember leaving the stage one night, carrying my bass case, when someone from the audience spotted me in the lobby and told me how much he loved the show. "I've seen it 11 times," he said, "and I have tickets for several more performances." This happened many times over the show's run, and women would exit performances with mascara and tears running down their cheeks after the final, powerful song, *If We Only Have Love*. It was a powerful, emotional experience for many people, and, for me, each show was so physically demanding that I would leave the stage drenched in sweat.

In the end, I performed in 422 shows at the Happy Medium and double that for the total number of performances. Its long run in Chicago finally came to an end, although it did return for a few short weeks several years later in a different theater.

BOB CUNNIFF

Happy Medium was in business at the time, just off Rush Street, and after Oscar and George Marienthal opened that place, they brought in "Broadway-type" acts. The wonderful thing about it was that Anne

Meara and Jerry Stiller were doing an act, although I wouldn't classify it as a comedy routine. One day I suggested to them, "Why don't you two do an act like Nichols and May?" And, they started doing that, and their careers took off.

PLAYBOY CLUB
Hugh Hefner opened his first Playboy Club in Chicago on February 29, 1960 at 116 E. Walton Street. It led to the later opening of an international chain of nightclubs and resorts that featured the Playmates in their bunny costumes, a Living Room, a Playmate Bar, a Dining Room, and a Club Room. The Bunnies, some of whom were featured in *Playboy* Magazine, served food and drinks and top name entertainment was provided to guest members at the Playboy Clubs. Hefner also opened the Playboy Club in Lake Geneva, Wisconsin that became a popular resort.

HUGH HEFNER | JOURNALIST AND OWNER *PLAYBOY* MAGAZINE AND PLAYBOY CLUBS
I think that, particularly the '30s and the first half of the '40s, there was the Depression Era and War years, which were a very romantic time. The popular music of that time was very romantic, and the most popular music of that time was big band swing. It is a music that I related to and would play at the *Playboy* mansion when friends gathered there on the weekends. As for the Chicago jazz clubs, I did go there after I was grown up and away from home. Sometimes I would go up to the South Side to see the jazz groups, and I went to Club DeLisa. I grew up on jazz, and one of the things that I loved about the music was that it spoke to me in a special way because it was black music and there was something for me quite special about that and very American and I had strong feelings about integration. The jazz clubs on the South Side were the only place where you really saw mixed black and white audiences. I was a very liberal kid, and it was the very early beginnings of the Civil Rights movement, and I had

strong feelings about all of that. Even when I was in the Army, the men whom I served with were all white. There was no bigotry when I grew up in the neighborhood, but I became aware of it when I was in the Army.

The late 1930s and early 1940s were a special time for me before starting *Playboy* because once I began *Playboy* I began living in a world all my own that I created and nothing other than that. For me it is connected to dreams that came directly out of childhood, so it was the '30s and early '40s that were the most intensely romantic times for me at a time that I remember with the greatest fondness. And I was very fortunate in terms of the peer group that I grew up with, both in the neighborhood and then also when I was in high school. And, that was the fertile soil that my life grew out of.

During the '50s, I would work afternoons and evenings, and then, around midnight, I would go out on the town and hang out with friends, including Mort Sahl and Lenny Bruce. By the late '50s, in a very real sense and although I wasn't conscious of it at the time, I continued the reinvention of my life. I had been separated from my first wife since the mid '50s, but, in 1959, she met somebody and made plans to remarry. The divorce became final in 1959, and that set me free in a certain psychological sense. Also, in the space of the next few months, we celebrated the 5th anniversary of *Playboy* with the Jazz Festival at the Chicago Stadium in August 1959.

I started hosting a television show called *Playboy's Penthouse* in October 1959, but it didn't start airing until January 1960. We recorded the show at Red Quinlan's studios at WBKB-TV in Chicago and were on the air for two seasons. In the second season, we taped six shows at CBS. Thus, 1959 was a key year in my life as I started hosting the television show, and, in December that year, I purchased the Playboy Mansion at 1340 N. State Parkway. Before that, I had purchased some property on the Near North Side of Chicago on Bellevue Place where I was planning to build a townhouse, but instead, I decided to buy the Mansion. I started moving in there piecemeal in 1960, and when we would complete

Playboy headquartered in the Palmolive Building
(Courtesy of Playboy Enterprises)

The first Playboy Club,
(Courtesy of Playboy Enterprises)

taping of the television show, the whole cast would go to the Mansion and party there, even before it was furnished. The ballroom had nothing in it but a couch and a couple of chairs, and it took a year or so to get a permit from the city to build the swimming pool. The city gave us some problems, as often happened in Chicago, because of the connections between the Archdiocese and the mayor. However, after going to court we obtained the required permit to construct the pool.

When I moved into the Mansion, it had a dramatic influence on my life because I decided to spend so much time there rather than at my office. By the early '60s, I was literally working full-time at the Mansion. Throughout the decade, I lived, worked, and played there and weeks and months would go by without me even leaving the Mansion. My life had changed dramatically and forever, and I started living the life I was describing in the magazine and became "Mr. Playboy." Those years were among the most invigorating of my life. Thus, within the space of a year, I was hosting the television show, had bought the Mansion, and opened the first Playboy Club. Our plan for opening a series of Playboy Clubs was for them to represent the life described in the magazine. Indeed, initially, at a subconscious level, I wanted to have my own bar/café like the one Humphrey Bogart owned in the movie *Casablanca*.

In the middle '60s, we took a long-term lease on the Palmolive Building instead of buying it, and changed the name to the Playboy Building. The Playboy Clubs were successful beyond words, and immediately, the most successful became the one in Chicago. We opened the first Playboy Club on Walton Street, right off Michigan Avenue, on February 29, 1960. It was across the street from the Palmolive Building, as well as being within walking distance of the Mansion. The original notion was not to have a string of clubs, but to open up a club where one could hang out. The Gaslight Club was the model for the club and had been very popular in Chicago. My major reservation was that since the magazine created a kind of fantasy world,

could we live up to it with the Playboy Clubs? Instead, I discovered that the Key Holders brought the fantasy with them. The Chicago Playboy Club was as hugely popular as the magazine had become by then, and *Playboy* was the hottest magazine in America in the 1960s. We also opened a Playboy Club in New York, and it was successful despite the fact that the city of New York wouldn't give us an entertainment license. And, although the showrooms had no shows being presented in them, they still were packed because of the mystique of *Playboy* and the Bunnies.

Chicago didn't change very much during the '50s and the '60s, and the city of that time period and when I grew up on the Northwest Side were essentially the same. It was the period after Mayor Richard J. Daley had died in 1976 when Chicago became a different city. However, it has always been, in my mind and in my own experience, the "city that worked." It is a curious phenomenon because despite the dynamics that were related to Machine politics, the Mob, and the Catholic Church, the city operated efficiently and it was a wonderful city in which to work and live. I think it would have been very difficult to successfully start *Playboy* somewhere else.

In the early 1960s, the magazine experienced its greatest success when circulation climbed from 1 million copies a month at the beginning of the decade to 7 million by the early part of the 1970s. That growth was unprecedented for a magazine of such limited scope and high price. In 1962, I began writing the Playboy Philosophy and we started printing a monthly *Playboy Interview* in the magazine, as well as other non-fiction. In the '50s, the magazine had essentially been a lifestyle magazine but in the '60s, we added the other half of who I was, and that was really the non-fiction, the interviews, and a variety of concerns such a Civil Rights, changing the sex laws, gun control, capital punishment, and then, opposition to the Vietnam War. In 1965, I formed the Playboy Foundation to help support these causes and "put my money where my mouth was."

MORT SAHL | COMEDIAN

I lived at 25 E. Delaware, and, then, later on, Hef put the house together. At that time, he was living near Ohio Street where they put out *Popular Mechanics*. He had an apartment over there with suntan lamps over his bed and drawers for his shirts and socks that went one way to the bathroom and the other way into his bedroom. He used to work all day, and then I would meet him around 2 a.m. and we would go prowl at places like the Cloister Room in the Maryland Hotel. Hef was a very dapper dude, with suits and everything, and full of intellectual curiosity.

Later on, Hef got the house on State Street. I was the first person to stay there, and I was the first celebrity to write an article for *Playboy*. Everything was beginning to really brew then because we were on our way to the Kennedy convention in Los Angeles. Chicago really was the "first city," and not the "second city." It jumped all night and Hef and I used to go to Musket and Hendriksen drugstore that was open 24 hours. Finally, when he put in the club down there on Oak Street, everybody used to come by and get that steak sandwich with cheese at 5 o'clock in the morning. It went all night, and the Bunnies stayed at the house and they used to go out and ride their horses in Grant Park in the morning at sunrise. There was something going on all night, and it was really a wild time. Then, Kup started his television show and gave us an awful lot of help there.

When Hef moved into his house on State Street, I brought Frank Sinatra and Bob Hope there at Hef's request. We had a lot of good times, and Hef was staying up all night writing his Playboy Philosophy himself and he would be up four days at a time typing the column. Chicago was percolating. I knew Studs and I knew Garroway and Mike Royko and Dan Sorkin on the radio. We would stay up all night and then go over to the radio station and heckle Sorkin when he was on the air.

When I started performing in Chicago during the 1950s, I did those good, long engagements where I would get up and do my stuff about the Republicans. Jake Arvey was running Stevenson's campaign, and I think that Adlai Stevenson was the finest man whom I ever met. His son was a pretty great senator, too.

Chicago was anything but the "second city." It was the last American city, and it had a lot of gusto. Everyone was deep in the community, and you could do a lot of community jokes. I didn't do a general act, but, instead, I did stuff about the town. It was really popping in Chicago in those days. My memories of those years are wonderful. Hef said to me one day, "You know, it's not nostalgia. We knew it was great then."

PENNY LANE | BROADCAST PERSONALITY AND ENTERTAINMENT CONSULTANT

When I was on the air, I used to beg to be invited to the Playboy Mansion. People told me that the Mansion always had our station, WSDM, on and they listened to our programming. I did this constantly for weeks on end and one day, I got this elaborate invitation delivered to me. It was an envelope that was about 10 inches by 20 inches, and in it was an invitation to a party at the mansion. I asked one of my girlfriends from the station to go with me. And when we got there, we were just shaking with excitement. We were just a couple of young girls, working at a radio station going to the Playboy Mansion—Hugh Hefner's place! So, we got there, knocked on the door. The door opened and who's opening the door? Bill Cosby! Needless to say, we were stunned. And he said, "Welcome, ladies." And we walked in and it was just an amazing night.

TOM DREESEN | COMEDIAN

When I started out, I used to hear about how wonderful vaudeville was for entertainers because there was an actual circuit of showrooms all around the country. For Tim Reid Reid and me, The Playboy Clubs became our vaudeville. So, when we got on the Playboy circuit, we really honed our act because there were 17 Playboy Clubs in America and two resorts, Lake Geneva and Great Gorge. When you went on that circuit, you started in Chicago and then on to places like Kansas City, New York, Boston, Baltimore, Philadelphia, and every city that had a Playboy Club. You worked all the Eastern cities,

Tim Reid and Tom Dreesen, Mr. Kelly's, 1975
(Courtesy of Tom Dreesen)

Chez Paree Restaurant Nightclub, (Courtesy of Chicago Historical Society, HB-08380)

the Midwest and the South, and you did five or six shows a night. There were two showrooms in every Playboy Club: one was the Penthouse and one was the Playroom. You would go into the Playroom, the girl singer would go on, she would sing three or four songs, and then the comedian would come on. She would go upstairs to the Penthouse and wait until we had about five minutes to go downstairs, and she would start singing upstairs. Then they would clear that room and we would run upstairs and so you went upstairs and downstairs all night long. For Tim and me, our timing became impeccable. I have to emphasize that Hugh Hefner was way before his time in terms of his acceptance of the integration era and the role of entertainers.

TIM REID | COMEDIAN | TELEVISION PERSONALITY, PRODUCER

The Playboy Clubs were like performing in the NFL championship "games," and we played in seven or eight of them around the country. To travel that circuit, there were required qualifications and the way you had to perform. In fact, on a Saturday in the Boston Playboy Club you had to do five shows and four shows each night in all the other clubs. So it was work, but, also, it was a place where you could really hone your craft and you could really work the room and learn what you needed to learn about performing before an audience. There weren't many places like that. The concept was that a comic would come on and do 20 minutes, and then a singer or a musician would come out and do 30 minutes if they were a headline act.
It went on like that all night, three, four or five times a night for six days a week. You really could learn a lot about performing and about audiences doing that. I should emphasize that my comedy team partner, Tom Dreesen, was and is a great comic. In fact, he is one of the best comics on the circuit today. I was there when he was learning the basics for his career. While I just don't like doing stand-up comedy, I never did. I like performing and doing sketches, but I never liked the comedy part as much as Tom. He loves it. As it turned out

for us, the Playboy Clubs were the quintessential opportunity for young comics.

CHEZ PAREE
The Chez Paree was opened in 1932 by Mike Fritzel and Joe Jacobson but was sold to a group of new partners in 1949. A major Chicago nightclub that was located on the third floor of a loft building that had been designed in 1917, it was in operation from 1932 until 1960. It was located at 610 N. Fairbanks Court in the Streeterville neighborhood east of Michigan Avenue and was very popular during the middle part of the 20th Century. The club was known for its elaborate dance numbers and star entertainers who included musicians, singers, and comedians ranging from Louis Armstrong, Cab Calloway, Sammy Davis Jr., Billy Eckstine, Duke Ellington, Ella Fitzgerald, Eydie Gorme, Billie Holiday, Tony Martin, Louis Prima, Frank Sinatra, Sarah Vaughan, Dinah Washington, Milton Berle, Sid Caesar, Shecky Greene, Buddy Hackett, Alan King, Danny Thomas, Cyd Charisse, Mickey Rooney, and Sally Rand.

SHECKY GREENE | COMEDIAN

The famous Chez Paree nightclub was not a favorite of mine even though it was considered to be one of the top clubs in the country. But, as young performers, we were frightened of those places because we were all getting our start and it was the height of one's career to work in those clubs. My first job at the Chez Paree was with Ann Sothern, but I really didn't belong there because I had no act, and it was clear that Ann didn't appreciate me. I remember that the Chez Paree brought in the big stars of the day and it was the atypical nightclub, just like the Copacabana. As I became more popular, I began performing at the major nightclubs across the country and it became a measure of my popularity. Then, finally, Las Vegas opened and if you performed there it meant that you were beginning to make it. It is not that way anymore because, today, these kids

Sammy Davis, Jr. and Penny Lane

come out of comedy clubs, do seven minutes on a television show, and they immediately become stars. I guess that is the way it should be since I don't believe that the new performers should have to go through that same tortuous route of nightclubs I was forced to endure, and, besides, the average person today can no longer afford the cost of going to nightclubs.

The Chez Paree was one of the top clubs in the country at that time and so was the Copacabana in New York, but we were frightened of them because we were all getting our start and it was the epitome to work those places. Either you worked London House or you worked Mister Kelly's, and, besides, the London House only had musical acts, so my comedy career really started on Rush Street.

JOE LEVINSON | MUSICIAN
One of Chicago's most famous clubs was the Chez Paree, east of Michigan Avenue on Fairbanks, near where Northwestern Hospital is located. Sophie Tucker practically lived there, and Jack Eigen used to do his radio show from the back of the club. Many of the biggest stars performed at the Chez Paree, including Frank Sinatra, Sammy Davis, Jr., Tony Martin, Jerry Lewis, Nat "King" Cole, Louis Prima, and Keely Smith.

PENNY LANE | BROADCAST PERSONALITY AND ENTERTAINMENT CONSULTANT
When I was a teenager in high school, I begged my mom to take me to the Chez Paree in Chicago. The Chez Paree booked big-name talent. On this one occasion, Sammy Davis, Jr. was appearing there and I really wanted to go see him. I had met him once before, and I never knew that one person could have so much talent. Now, my experiences with African Americans were rather limited. I had gone to mostly white, mostly Jewish grammar and high schools. And when I found out that he was black, I was astounded that he could imitate so many people so well and sound just like them and they were all white! He could sing and he could dance and he could play all kinds of instruments. I thought, I've got to go meet him.

So, I went to the Chez Paree with my girlfriends and my mother and we bought him a set of cufflinks with a Jewish star on them. He sent a note back to our table through the maître d' that said we should meet him in the lounge after the show. We were dying! So, we sat down with him—my two girlfriends and me. It was between shows. Towards the end of the conversation, I said to him, "Is there any possible way I could work for you?" I was so taken with him. I offered to do publicity or book hotel reservations for him whenever he came to Chicago—anything! After all he was the most talented man I'd ever seen and I thought there would never be anyone like him again! And he turned his body towards me and took my hand in his and said, "There is one thing you can do for me… stay in school, because I never had a formal education and it's bothered me all my life. You have the opportunity. Stay in school." I was so choked up. I just stared at him and then we took a picture. That night changed my life because my high school didn't have any theater classes, very few speech classes; nothing that I knew I would use later on. I went back to school the next day, knowing I was going to finish high school. I went on to college. Went to a theater school and took classes at Second City. I even went to Northwestern as recently as 12 years ago to take some classes. But really, that night changed my life. I never thought of education as being a privilege. I just took it for granted. What an eye opener!

JOEL ZIMBEROFF
My parents used to go to the Chez Paree on McClurg Court and Ohio on a regular basis, and I would go with them on some occasions. I remember seeing the Chez Paree Adorables, and you would take the elevator up to the club. I saw stars there like Joel Grey, Jimmy Durante, Dean Martin and Jerry Lewis, and many others, and I went there during my years in grammar school.

GASLIGHT CLUB

In 1953, Burton Browne and a few friends re-created the "Good Old Days" of the early 1900s in one small room in the city's Gold Coast complete with Dixieland jazz, Gaslight girls, and a "speakeasy." That would lead to the creation of Gaslight Clubs around the country, including New York, Washington, and Paris. In 1973 a club was opened at O'Hare Airport. After Browne's death in 1976, Robert Fredericks took control of the clubs until 1984 and then Jim Roberts took the reins.

JOE LEVINSON | MUSICIAN

There were also many clubs north of the Loop, on the Near North Side, like the Gaslight Club, which opened in 1952. It featured "hot" Dixieland bands and became a gathering spot for young people who were seeking a sophisticated good time. The club had a line of women who dressed like frontier dance hall girls in the Old West, and the Dixieland band dressed like barrel house band players and accompanied them in their routines. The club was housed in a multi-story house that had numerous rooms for small groups of guests, with paintings of scantilly-clad women on the walls.

JIMMY RITTENBERG | OWNER OF FACES

During the mid '60s, Rush Street and Old Town became the center of my activities. We would have a couple of beers at Mister Kelly's, stop at the old River Shannon, go either to Old Town or Butch McGuires, and then walk around the corner to Rush Street. The place where I used to work was originally the Gate of Horn, and that was where Lenny Bruce got removed from the stage by the police and the club was shut down. When it got closed, three young guys bought it and transformed it into The Store, a post-college bar. By that time, State and Division had become the location of several college bars, whereas Rush Street still remained the place for the "Boys," including entertainment, the Whiskey A-Go-Go, the Candy Store, the strip joints, and the "dress-up" joints. So, the city's Near North Side was like three different cultures: Old Town, Rush Street, and State and Division. I worked in Old Town and tended bar at Chances R, and I was very fortunate because I had the opportunity to hear Steve Goodman, Bonnie Koloc, Johnny Prine, and many others.

I went to the college bars on a regular basis in the '60s and later became a mainstay at Mr. Kelly's, so I became known to performers like Jackie Mason, Shelley Berman, Joel Grey, Chad Mitchell, Bill Cosby, and Tom Jones. London House didn't have the big acts in the late '60s, but Happy Medium, Mister Kelly's, and the Empire Room all had major entertainers in those years. The clubs began to lose their clientele because of television and the fact that you could see the comedy acts on television every night. Then, the bands started hitting big, and they couldn't fit into the little clubs.

SHECKY GREENE | COMEDIAN

I grew up in Rogers Park and went to Field School and Sullivan High School. I got my big break in show business when I appeared on Rush Street at the Club Alabam that was just a few blocks west of Michigan Avenue. Mort Sahl performed there just a little bit after I did. The first place he was performing in Chicago was at the Black Orchid. He wasn't doing well, and came up to me asking and he said, "Shecky, could I borrow your tape recorder?" And, he began to tape all of his shows. They wanted to fire Mort but I went over to see Al Greenfield, the owner of the Black Orchid, who was one of my best friends, and Benny Dunn, Al's right-hand man. I begged them to keep Mort on because the college kids would come to see him. Eventually they did and he was a big success. As a matter of fact, I did such a good job of promoting Mort that my shows were empty. Shelley Berman was also performing around that same time and he was working all over Rush Street. Gibsons was originally Mister Kelly's and the Esquire Theater was there and the Gate of Horn was right around the corner. Rush Street had some magnificent restaurants, including the Singapore that was world-famous.

FICKLE PICKLE

The Fickle Pickle was a small Chicago blues and folk club on Rush Street in the 1960s that was founded by musician Mike Bloomfield. Bloomfield also recorded with the Paul Butterfield Blues Band.

BOB DAUBER | AUTHOR
DICK GREGORY AND THE FICKLE PICKLE

In 1959, I performed playing saxophone and/or bongos with a pianist, between sets of the headliners, at a coffee house located on North State Street. It was called the Fickle Pickle and was a favorite hang for underage folks, in particular, because it was a non-alcoholic club setting. One night, the main act was a Calypso singer who went by the name of Sir James. He announced he was bringing in a special guest performer who had just completed a run at Roberts Show Lounge. The performer was a comedian that, virtually, no one had ever heard of—Dick Gregory! Well, he stunned everyone with his brand of humor, which, at the time, was very self-deprecating in terms of racial material. As they say in the business, "He killed." Word quickly got around and each night he did his thing, more and more people came to the coffeehouse. After a couple of weeks, Alex Drier, who at the time was the local ABC-TV news anchor, came in and was immediately bowled over by Gregory's material. He took Gregory under his wing and brought him to the attention of Hugh Hefner. As a result, Dick Gregory made the giant leap from the obscurity of the Fickle Pickle to the Playboy Club circuit!

Dick Gregory at Mr. Kelly's

FOLK CLUBS

GATE OF HORN

The Gate of Horn folk-singing club was first located in the basement of the Rice Hotel at 755 N. Dearborn Street at the corner of Chicago Avenue. The club existed in the 1950s and 1960s as a 100-seat venue before moving to larger quarters west of Rush Street near Oak. It was opened by journalist Les Brown and Albert Grossman in 1956, and among the famous performers who appeared at the Gate of Horn were Bob Gibson, Bob Camp, Roger McGuinn, Odetta, Oscar Brown Jr., Sonny Terry, the Clancy Brothers, Judy Collins, and Joan Baez. The frequent master of ceremonies at the club was Bob Gibson, who along with Bob Camp, recorded a very famous album, _Bob Gibson and Bob Camp at the Gate of Horn_. The club became notorious when comedian Lenny Bruce played there in December 1962 and was arrested by Chicago police on a charge of obscenity.

Selective liner notes written by Shel Silverstein from the album _Bob Gibson & Bob Camp At The Gate of Horn_. (reproduced with permission of Elizabeth Myers, Shel Silverstein Archives, Meridian Green, Bob Gibson Family, LLC, and Gene Lee, Rhino Records)

I'll tell you a little bit about the old Gate of Horn. It was in a basement. I don''t mean a basement club, I mean it was just in a basement. Chicago is full of places like that. Leroy Neiman, the artist, was living around the corner in another basement and it wasn't just a basement apartment—he was living in a basement. The Gate of Horn was sort of the same. It was sort of chiseled out. It was on North Dearborn Street, and there was a door that said "Gate of Horn" and some steps that led downstairs and then when you got down there, it had a sign on the door that said "use the other door." So you had to climb up and go around the other side and there was another door that went down and you were in a crowded little ante room, or whatever the hell it was.

The bar was off to the right. That's where you would find everybody mostly between sets. Either there or in the backroom—it was really more like backrooms plural and it was all like carved out of rock with bricks showing through and ash cans sitting around the further in you got, the more like catacombs it was. And any minute you expected to trip over the dusty bones of some medieval folk singer, and there was one bright light and you had to sit on the ash cans or lean against the icebox and that is where you would see Gibson and Camp tuning up to go on stage or combing their hair or going over some arrangement or complaining about some chick who didn't show up the night before. Herb Brown was back there, too, doing something great with his bass but I never heard him say anything.

The waitresses used those catacombs as a short cut from the bar to the main room. There it was dark and hot and crowded and great. They would come in from the back of the club—that's where the entertainers came on, too. Gibson would come out of the back with Brown and they would do a few numbers and then he would introduce Camp and, when Camp came on, the whole thing would start to jell and swing and Brown's bass would be going like hell and Gibson would be up there cool and cocky, playing the 12-string and singing, and Camp would be like a little rooster with his head back screaming and bouncing up and down and it was really something.

After a while, I think that Gibson and Camp even started to look alike. They must have weighed about 45 pounds together, and they sat and they whispered and they looked like two crooked English jockeys fixing a race. And they wore those thin grey suits.

I'll tell you some more about the old Gate of Horn, though. The final night there was really a blast. Everybody was wearing carnations and there were more people high than I would care to mention and it was a full house...Del Close did one of the wildest, funniest bits.

Alan Ribback has a new Gate of Horn now over on Rush Street, and it is very fancy and there are carpets and velvet ropes at the door and everybody wears dark suits and ties and there are two floors

Gate of Horn, (Courtesy of Chicago Historical Society, ICHi-116010)

with a bar downstairs and a beautiful showroom upstairs and they say the acoustics are great. They have a lot of people to seat you, and the waitresses have sort of costumes and they say it is greater and better, more beautiful than ever. They say it is better to work in, better to run and everything and maybe they're right. But you should have seen the old Gate of Horn.

JOE LEVINSON | MUSICIAN

The Gate of Horn, on Rush Street, became one of the country's most famous folk music showcases. I remember seeing the Kingston Trio there as well as Odetta. Also on Rush was the Hotel Maryland, which had the Cloister Inn Lounge in the lower level of the hotel. This dimly lit lounge featured a piano bar where Dick Marx and Johnny Frigo played, backed by the great singer Lurlean Hunter, one of Chicago's greatest jazz vocalists. Many other small groups also worked there for years, including one led by the late, great Sandy Mosse, a fabulous tenor sax player and sublime wit.

PENNY LANE | BROADCAST PERSONALITY AND ENTERTAINMENT CONSULTANT

The night before Lenny Bruce was arrested at the famous Gate of Horn, friends of mine said, "Look, we've got a bunch of fake IDs—let's go in to see him." So, we did and he was about 10 minutes into his act they began leaving left and right. I don't know what they expected to hear, but I sat there enthralled. He was a very, very different kind of performer. Very cutting edge. Rather amazing. Personally, I was thrilled to have been there and his blue material did not bother me at all.

BILL BENJAMIN | ASHEVILLE, NC

I think it was 1962, and Lenny Bruce had been appearing at the old Gate of Horn. A buddy of mine and our girlfriends were going to see Lenny at the venue. So, we drove down there, went through the hassle of parking the car and of course, paying for it. We had to walk about two or three blocks to get to the club and when we walked up to it, there was a big sign on the door that said the night's performance had been canceled by the Chicago Police Department. Lenny Bruce had gotten arrested the night before for using obscenities in his routines at the club. We were crestfallen in that here we had been anticipating seeing him only to discover that the police had shut down him and the club! Modern comedy started with Lenny Bruce. Without him, there would have been no George Carlin, no Richard Pryor, no Robin Williams, and so forth. As people say, "Way ahead of his time."

MARC DAVIS | AUTHOR AND FREELANCE WRITER

Lord Buckley, the legendary stand-up comedian, was described by the The New York Times as, "an unlikely person ... part English royalty, part Dizzy Gillespie."

Born Richard Myrle Buckley, he adopted the "Lord Buckley" appellation as a capper to his shtick as a fictional, street-smart British nobleman. For his act, Buckley affected an aristocratic hauteur and spoke like a whacked out, well-educated hipster in a vaguely British accent.

One night in 1965, I was at the Gate of Horn where Buckley was performing. We were there for his late set, in a not too crowded house. As Buckley did his classic bit, "The Naz," a satire on Jesus and his New Testament deeds and miracles, movie actress Linda Darnell, a great star in her day, and a stunning beauty, walked in, without an escort. Buckley immediately stopped his act, bowed deeply, and true to his bogus aristocratic character, he said, "Good evening, M'lady. I'm honored by your presence."

I expected Ms. Darnell to courteously acknowledge his greeting and take a seat in the audience and that Buckley would then resume the bit. Instead, Ms. Darnell stood at the entrance to the room and started talking at length about her love of Buckley and his work and various other unrelated subjects. I won't libel Ms. Darnell to say she seemed to be drunk, but in my opinion, in her maunderings, she did sound a bit lubricated. But perhaps it was only my compromised perception of what she said, filtered through my own state of drunkenness, in which even a sober, cogent remark seemed half-cocked.

Odetta, (Courtesy of Chicago Historical Society, ICHi-140877)

Bonnie Koloc
(Courtesy of Bonnie Koloc)

Bill Goldman and Dickie Smothers
(Courtesy of Bill Goldman)

Buckley's forbearance was extraordinary as Ms. Darnell continued to talk. The comedian listened patiently, respectfully, and when her monologue had concluded, he thanked her graciously for coming to his show and for her insightful remarks. He then resumed his bit and completed it to much laughter and applause.

Tragically, just a few short weeks later, Ms. Darnell was burned over 80 percent of her body in an accidental residential fire in Glenview, Illinois. She died soon after in Cook County Hospital, on April 10, 1965, at a much too young 41.

BILL GOLDMAN | LINCOLNSHIRE, IL

One of the places we used to frequent a lot was the Gate of Horn. There, we would be treated to the likes of Bob Gibson, Bonnie Koloc, Odetta, and so many others. The original Gate of Horn was a tiny joint, which, as I recall, was in the basement of a flophouse hotel on Chicago Avenue. Later on, they moved into the Rush Street area after which "The Gate" became a high-end folk venue.

While I'm not certain, I think I may have seen the Smothers Brothers there, but here's an interesting story: I have a place up near Lake Geneva, and I spend a lot of time there during the summer months. There is a driving range that I go to and a couple of years ago, I was hitting balls and there were only two of us there, another guy and me. The guy started talking about a short swing that he had developed and that it was really helping his game. While this was going on, I kept looking at the guy, thinking he looked familiar. After a while, I introduced myself. "I'm Bill," and he said, "I'm Dickie." So then I said, "Well, I'm Billy." Then, he asked me for my last name and I said, "Goldman." Then he said, "mine is Smothers." So, there we were hitting balls together at a driving range. He had a hat on, but I'll tell you that he looked exactly as he did years ago and how I had remembered him. So, we started talking about our lives and it was a really fascinating conversation. Over time, we would bump into each other at the range and I even have a picture of the two of us together.

EARL OF OLD TOWN

The Earl of Old Town, named for its founder, Earl J. J. Pionke, was a saloon and folk-singing venue located at 1615 N. Wells Street in the Old Town neighborhood. Among the many folk singing stars who performed there were Bonnie Koloc, Steve Goodman, John Prine, Ed Holstein, Jim Post, and Jim Tullio. In 1964, Pionke opened the club in Old Town.

OLD TOWN SCHOOL OF FOLK MUSIC

A teaching and performing institution, the Old Town School of Folk Music opened in December 1957 at its first home at 333 North Avenue. Students attending there took banjo and guitar lessons, as well as participating in folk dancing and sing-alongs on a weekly basis. In the 1950s, concerts were offered by such stars at Mahalia Jackson, Pete Seeger, Big Bill Broonzy, Josh White, and Jimmy Driftwood, and then, in the 1960s, as the school continued to grow, other performers would include Bob Gibson, John Prine, Bonnie Koloc, and Steve Goodman. In 1968, the School purchased and moved to a new location at 909 W. Armitage Avenue. By 1975, more than 650 students were attending the School. In the 1990s, after a decline in enrollment, the Old Town School of Folk Music moved to another new location on North Lincoln Avenue.

BONNIE KOLOC | FOLK SINGER | ACTRESS

I was born and raised in Waterloo, Iowa and attended college at the University of Northern Iowa. I attended there on and off for six years, starting as a drama major then switching to be an art major, then started making my living playing the guitar and singing traditional folk music. I performed in the Waterloo area for about five years while I was in school.

In the spring of 1968, I came to Chicago. In that first week I was introduced to the Old Town School of Folk Music where I met a lot of the Chicago folk singers, including Fred Holstein, Eddie Holstein,

Ginny Clemmons, and Steve Goodman, who was 19 years old at the time. Later, all of these performers and I myself would work together at the Earl of Old Town. Steve Goodman would introduce me to John Prine within a few years who, at that time, was a postman in Melrose Park and taking lessons at the Old Town School of Folk Music. My first performances were at the old Quiet Knight on Wells Street owned by Richard Harding. I walked in and auditioned on a Sunday afternoon, and Richard hired me for the summer. In the fall, I had heard that Earl Pionke wanted to hire me at the Earl of Old Town and I started singing there in the winter of 1969. Folk music remained popular in Chicago, I believe, partly because of the Old Town School of Folk Music. Win Strake and a few other people started the Old Town School of Folk Music approaching folk music as an art form of the people.

Earl of Old Town was owned by Earl Pionke, a native Chicagoan. Jimmy Johnson was behind the bar, and Gus Johns was the doorman. They had known each other all their lives. The Earl of Old Town was right across from where Second City was on Wells. The room was long and narrow with a stage that was six inches off the floor. It had old brick walls and beautiful old windows in the front. The place was very smoky, but it was magical in the fact that they had wood burning fireplaces on each side of the stage. When I first started, there I would do five shows a night. The music was transitioning from pure folk music to original songs by writers like Steve Goodman, Ed Holstein, John Prine, and Michael Smith. I was the first one to record Eddie Holstein's song *Jazzman* and Steve Goodman's first song, *Song For David*.

In terms of recording, when I first came to Chicago, the major record companies like RCA were leaving and going out to the West Coast. So, I signed with a small record company from Chicago, Ovation Records, and did three or four records with them. After my initial record did come out in 1971, I opened at Mister Kelly's

on March 14 for the first time when I opened for Tim Reid and Tom Dreesen and they were great guys. I played at Mr. Kelly's two or three times. It was wonderful and Mr. Marienthal was a sweetheart. I was still with Ovation when I finally had a hit single, *You're Gonna Love Yourself in the Morning*, that was written by Kris Kristofferson's piano player Donnie Fritts, but, unfortunately it fell off the charts because of lack of distribution. That was a huge thing for me. After that, I recorded two more albums for Epic Records.

Then, in 1982, I decided to go to New York. I was living in an illegal sublet and I was living on $10 a day. I got into a show with Joseph Papp at the Public Theater which ran for 13 weeks. It was called *The Human Comedy*. It went to the Royale Theater and it ran one week. On Monday, I was at a cast party at Sardi's, and the following Saturday morning I was in Queens in the unemployment line.

I won a couple of awards in New York, including a Drama Critics Award nomination for Best Actress in a Musical, and I won the Theatre World Bronze Award for Outstanding New Talent on Broadway in 1984. I came back to Chicago because I wanted to finish my degree in art. I continued to sing, but I did complete the degree. I took one class at the Art Institute of Chicago, and then I took other classes at the University of Illinois-Chicago, but I got my degree in Art from the University of Northern Iowa because I had started there.

I came back to Chicago because it was home to me, so I was happy to be back there. When I go back to Chicago I feel like I am home. All of the great musicians that I have worked with are in Chicago, including Howard Levy, Don Stille, Elliott Delman, John Bany, Phil Grateau, and Steve Eisen, Chris Siebold, and Al Ehrich. Overall, my music and my art are my passion. I love what I do and I love to relate to people through my art. And, I love and I am grateful to the beautiful city of Chicago that has been so good to me.

MOTHER BLUES

A large and successful folk club located in Old Town at 1305 N. Wells Street that featured such artists as Odetta, Jose Feliciano, Josh White, Oscar Brown, Jr., Chad Mitchell, George Carlin, Sergio Mendes and Brasil '66, and The Jefferson Airplane.

MARC DAVIS | AUTHOR AND FREELANCE WRITER

A major Chicago-based performing artist of the mid to late 20th century was Robert B. Connelly—singer, cornetist, guitarist, pianist, composer, author, and an artist in many other idiom.

Bob founded and was the lead singer of the New Wine Singers, one of the most popular and highly acclaimed folk groups of the 1960s and beyond. He owned a club in Chicago's Old Town in the 1300 block of Wells Street called The Rising Moon and later, after a disastrous fire, it was rebuilt and renamed Mother Blues. He performed at Chicago's premier clubs and all over the country for more than a decade and earned rave reviews from *Variety, Billboard,* and other media.

Beyond his musical accomplishments was his expertise in silent film. He was a serious scholar of motion pictures and authored a definitive book on this subject called *The Silents*, which included reviews and commentary on the most notable films of the silent era. Bob also worked in broadcasting and advertising, producing, writing copy, composing music, and creating visuals for major corporate clients, including radio superstar Earl Nightingale.

Later on, Bob was hired as a screenwriter for MGM. As a singer, Bob could bring tears to your eyes with his version of *Danny Boy* and evoke hilarious laughter with his humorous song lyrics, risqué poetry, and from the cartoon panels he drew and captioned. One of the most engaging of raconteurs, Bob held his listeners in thrall as he recounted stories of celebrated and ordinary people he had known and various events in his extraordinary life. For many

decades, Bob and his wife, Linda, regularly hosted parties for local and visiting performing artists, writers, painters, others in the arts as well as a legion of interesting people in almost every category of human endeavor.

Bob's father was a top aide to President Harry S. Truman. So, as a young boy, Bob grew up in the White House, swam in the president's pool, and played on the lawn. As a result of his childhood exposure to the highest level of Democratic government and politics, he became a principled liberal and activist and performed at countless fundraisers for liberal politicians and causes. Robert Connelly's recordings are produced by Folkways and are available from Amazon.

NO EXIT CAFE

The small, but popular, cafe operated from 1958 to 1999 on the city's Far North Side at 6970 N. Glenwood in East Rogers Park. It was a coffeehouse and a venue for presentations of poetry and folk music. The last owner of the cafe was Brian Kozin who was the fifth person to own the place which was located over the years in three North Side locations, with the original site in Evanston when it first opened. No Exit was popular with such famous Chicagoans as singer Steve Goodman, author Saul Bellow, writer Michael McCarthy, and actor Tracy Letts. One of the best known performers at No Exit over the years was the late folk singer Art Thieme who was also active at the Old Town School of Folk Music.

AMUSEMENT PARKS

RIVERVIEW AMUSEMENT PARK

An amusement park in Chicago that operated from 1904 to 1967, it was located on the city's North Side bounded on the south by Belmont Avenue, on the east by Western Avenue, on the north by Lane Technical High School, and on the west by the North Branch of the Chicago River. Riverview had numerous famous attractions from The Bobs roller coaster, The Silver Flash, The Fireball, Aladdin's Castle, a classic fun house, Tilt-a-Whirl, Wild Mouse, Shoot the Chutes, and the Tunnel of Love. There were approximately 120 rides in the park.

JIM O'CONNOR | FORMER CHAIRMAN OF THE BOARD, COMMONWEALTH EDISON

Riverview Amusement Park was very big in everybody's life, and you had to go at least once or twice a year. You would normally try to go there on "two-cent day" which was Wednesday and Friday where you could ride everything but the Bobs for two cents. That was a big opportunity in the summertime. You normally didn't hitchhike there, but, instead, you would take the streetcar down Western Avenue all the way from 79th Street to Belmont Avenue.

JOEL WEISMAN | LAWYER | JOURNALIST | TELEVISION PERSONALITY

I went to Riverview a lot. My sister had tuberculosis, and my mother used to take us on the streetcar to a public health clinic that she had to go to check in at, and we had to take the Western Avenue streetcar. So, every time we would come back from the clinic, we would go to Riverview. I knew every single ride, including the roller coasters, the Bobs, the Silver Flash, the Blue Flash, the Greyhound, and the Comet. I remember the Shoot The Chutes, Aladdin's Castle, the freak show, the Caterpillar, the Whip, and the Tunnel of Love, as well as the Merry Go Round.

CHUCK SCHADEN | RADIO PERSONALITY ON *OLD TIME RADIO*

Riverview was a playground for the city's Northwest Side residents and a must place to go to every year or a couple of times, at least. I remember all the rides, Aladdin's Castle, the Midway, the Chute-the-Chutes, the Bobs, the Blue Streak, the Silver Streak, the Spook House, and the Arcades. It was just a great place to be. They had two-cent days and five-cent nights for admission, but you almost always received a free pass from some politician or alderman who would give out free passes to Riverview as if they were water. But, you paid for every ride, on the spot, because it was not a single-ticket amusement park. It was magic. The big symbols of Riverview included the big face on Aladdin's Castle, and that was what so many people remember as well as the thrill of riding the Bobs.

HOWARD ROSEN

In June 1943, I have a very clear memory of when I graduated from grammar school and we celebrated with a couple of friends by going to Riverview Park. Riverview was a major part of the lives of kids of my era and their growing up. My father could afford to take us there because they used to have two-cent day when you could go on just about any ride for $.02. I remember that the big deal was The Bobs and the Blue Streak, but The Bobs was the favorite, and I did something with my friends that my father would never allow me to do, and that was to go on the parachute ride. You would sit down, and they would harness you in, and it would go way up in the air, it would hit something at the top to release the parachute, and you would have a sense that you were freefalling. Apparently it was a very safe ride. I remember that in 1943.

HOWARD CARL

I started working at Riverview Park when I was 15 years old, in 1946, and, at that time they didn't check to confirm your birth date. I went to work there as an extra, and that meant that I would wait in front of the park, a guy would call out your name, and then you

would be assigned to a different ride each day. At the end of the week, you would go and collect your little envelope that had cash in it because you didn't get paid by check. So, I worked on various rides, and eventually worked on almost every single ride in the park as an extra, and I was lucky enough to work at the park every time I got there. I worked at Riverview Park during the years when I was in high school. One summer I worked there as a boatman and would take the boats down the Chutes. The Chute and I would steer the boats from the back by controlling the rudder and leaning on my weight. I steered a little, but it was a rudder, and the water would splash me when the boat hit the water at the bottom of the ride. It was a fun ride. On Thursdays, we used to test the ride for an hour, so they would give us $.50 extra. I did that for a whole summer.

I always liked playing basketball. So, on my breaks, I would go over to the basketball concession and shoot baskets. I became very friendly with the guys who operated that concession. The following year, after working at the park for about three years on the rides, I worked at the basketball concession and, eventually, in the early 1950s, I took over the concession. By taking over, I didn't own it, but managed it. I went to the University of Iowa for one year on a basketball scholarship, but I broke my foot. My brother, Howie "Hershie" Carl, who was a great basketball player, also worked with me at the basketball concession.

On Mondays, Wednesdays, and Fridays, Riverview Park was two-cent day. So you could get into the park for $.02, and many of the rides cost $.02, while others were $.05, during the daytime. They were $.05 or $.10 at night. And, on Tuesdays and Thursdays, it was nickel day. It was a very busy place with a lot of big crowds. Riverview Park was supposedly the world's largest amusement park and it had picnic groves. The biggest and fastest roller coaster was the Bobs, and when I was an extra, I worked on the roller coasters. I would just take tickets and help people off the roller coaster. As an extra, you would get a uniform that you would put on over your street clothes. The park opened in 1904 and closed in 1967.

Interestingly, on the South Side, a long time ago, there was a very popular amusement park called White City, but it had burned down by the 1940s.

WHITE CITY

White City Amusement Park was located on the city's South Side at 63rd Street and South Park Avenue (now Martin Luther King Drive) in the Greater Grand Crossing and Woodlawn community areas and operated from 1905 until the 1940s. When it opened on May 26, 1905, it was claimed to be the largest park of its type in the United States. The Goodyear Blimp was introduced to the public at White City. In its early days, the park featured a Wild Animals show, Flying Airships, Scenic Railway, Trip to Mars, and the Chutes, along with a small Ferris Wheel. It suffered several fires, and the onset of the Great Depression led to its eventual demise.

HOTELS

PALMER HOUSE

Potter Palmer, a dry goods merchant, opened a store on Lake Street in 1852. In 1871, he married Bertha Honore, the daughter of a leading Chicago businessman, Henry Honore. Potter made plans to build a 225-room hotel on State Street as a gift to his new bride. However, in October 1871, the Great Chicago Fire destroyed the new hotel. Within the year, he began to build the second Palmer House which opened in July 1873. In the 1920s, a third Palmer House was built which included the Empire Room, the hotel's principal dining room. It became one of the city's most popular supper clubs and hosted such stars as Maurice Chevalier, Frank Sinatra, Tony Bennett, Ella Fitzgerald, Harry Belafonte, Eartha Kitt, Sid Caesar, George Burns, Jimmy Durante, and Bob Newhart. The hotel hired Liberace to play cocktail music in the Empire Room. Eddie Duchin also performed there along with the Merriel Abbot Dancers.

JO MINOW

One drawing card in the Loop was the Empire Room at the Palmer House where leading performers of stage and screen and radio made appearances. I will never forget being t-h-i-s close to Jack Benny, and watching the Merriel Abbott Dancers was always a delight, especially since some of my schoolmates were taking classes with her and, perhaps, one day, they might appear on the Empire Room stage. I remember going to the Chicago Theater from time to time to see the latest movie and the bonus, a glorious live stage show.

RANDY WALDMAN | COMPOSER | PIANIST | GRAMMY AWARD WINNER

I think it was in the mid-70s. I was doing the Empire Room thing, and Sinatra was on tour in the Midwest. Now, I don't know the reason for this, but he decided to have Bill Miller, who was his pianist for decades, be the musical director but not play piano for his concerts. To this day, I don't know why. I got a call from a music contractor who asked if I would be available to go on tour with Frank Sinatra. This is the same contractor who used to hire me for bands he'd put together for weddings and parties and so forth. But, he was the one who got the call to put the orchestra together for Sinatra, including a pianist. Certainly, I knew who he was, but I wasn't all that familiar with his music and he really wasn't on my radar. I mentioned it to a friend of mine who said, "Are you kidding?" He had a huge collection of Sinatra's albums and he loaned them to me and said, "Listen to these—over and over. Learn them!" So, I did and when the time came, I played the piano with the full orchestra. We did like a full rehearsal with Miller directing. Another interesting thing—I'd never seen Sinatra. I'd never met him and he wasn't at the rehearsal! At one point, someone brought a phone to Miller and he held it up while we played. When we stopped, he said, "That was Frank on the phone. He thinks you sound great." And, we were ready to go!

So, I started doing concerts with him. I was around 19 or 20, and we would do these shows in arenas. The band would play an overture—a kind of medley of the songs to be performed. And then, Frank would walk on stage and for the most part, all of the songs would begin with the piano and him singing and then the orchestra would kick in and that's how it was done. I didn't know if it was good or bad or what. Halfway through the show, Sinatra walked over to the guitar player and there was some whispering going on. I don't know what was said, but then Frank walked to middle of the stage, with microphone in hand and said, "Ladies and gentlemen, that song was beautifully played on the piano by Randy Waldman!" From that point on, he would announce my name. I feel very fortunate to have worked with him and down the road to have worked with him with Nelson Riddle conducting. Obviously, it turned out to be the most incredible music experience of my life.

RANDY WALDMAN | LOS ANGELES, CA
PIANIST | ARRANGER | COMPOSER |
CONDUCTOR | MULTI-GRAMMY AWARD
RECIPIENT

When I was still in high school, I wanted to quit and just pursue being a musician. My parents were bound and determined to see me graduate. One of the reasons that I wanted to quit was that all of the good musicians there had graduated. In reality, I had no interest in any of my regular school classes other than anything that was concerning music and the different ensembles. My parents talked with some higher-ups at Northwestern University and they struck a deal with the school. It was this: If I went to Northwestern, played in their big band, and took classes in theory, they would make credits applicable to put towards my ultimately getting my diploma from high school. So, that's what I did. In fact, Rufus Reid, a fabulous jazz bass player who is now in New York, was the director of the big band and he would pick me up at my high school and take me to Northwestern for my classes there. You might say I was destined towards a life of music. I was the house pianist at the Empire Room at the Palmer House—part of a 16-piece orchestra. We would play as back-up to whoever was performing in the room. One of the first singers that I remember playing for was Barbara Eden. I remember that she'd had a very bad cold and she tried to perform, even though she was feeling terrible. I remember her crying backstage because she felt so bad.

The next act that I played with was a group I think you might remember—The Lettermen. They were self-contained, but we'd play between their acts. I became friendly with their guitar player, who'd been hurt in a motorcycle accident and his mouth was wired shut. We were able to communicate and about three weeks after they left Chicago, he called me from their being out on the road and asked me if I'd like to become part of the Lettermen tour. Of course, I was thrilled to do that. I toured with them for about a month—just long enough to get me to Los Angeles.

I should mention that one of the other acts that I worked with at the Empire Room was Diahann

Carroll, and her conductor at the time was a guy named Ernie Freeman. Ernie had done arrangements for Frank Sinatra and other people. In fact, he won a Grammy for his arrangement of *Strangers in the Night* for Sinatra.

When I got to LA, I really didn't know many people other than Ernie Freeman and a man by the name of Bill Miller, who did a lot of conducting as well as being the pianist for Frank Sinatra. Here's an interesting side note: I'd met Bill Miller when I played a concert with Frank Sinatra at the Arie Crown Theater. It was a benefit for a policemen's association of some sort, and my mom and dad called the police station and found the person in charge of the event and said, "Our son is going to be playing the piano for the concert that Frank Sinatra is doing, and we would love to be able to see the event." The person who took the call actually not only arranged for my parents to attend, but they had front row center seats at the Arie Crown Theater to watch the concert. That was a very cool thing.

So when I got to LA, I called Ernie Freeman, Bill Miller, and I had also gotten to know Barbara Eden's conductor and I called him, too. Those were my only LA contacts. After being there for only about a week, Ernie Freeman called me and said that he had a lot of record sessions to do and asked if I would be available to work them. Of course, I was and after having done them, the contractor who actually did the hiring told me how great he thought I was and that was my introduction into the music scene in Los Angeles.

DRAKE HOTEL

The Drake Hotel was built in the 1920s at the southeast corner of Oak Street, North Michigan Avenue, and Lake Shore Drive on the city's Near North Side. On top of the Drake, radio programs were broadcast, including "Amos and Andy." The Gold Coast Room was the hotel's main dining room and home to many big band performances and the Camelia House was a dance spot.

JOHNNY FRIGO | MUSICIAN

The reason that I think I started playing jazz was because I didn't have enough formal training to be a concert violinist. So, I just started playing. In 1940

Empire Room at Palmer House, (Courtesy of Chicago Historical Society, HB-03386-c)

Randy Waldman, Barbra Streisand's pianist for 35+ years, (Courtesy of Randy Waldman)

I was with a group called the Four Californians, and we played at the Morrison Hotel and at the Drake Hotel. What was good about that was because at the Drake Hotel we would play in the lobby and I played bass. Curtis Junior High School at 115th and State Street or Prairie Avenue didn't have an orchestra and they only had a band. And, the only instrument that nobody wanted to play was a tuba. So, I got stuck with the tuba. When I got into high school, the obvious thing to play was the string bass. I made 95% of my living playing string bass for the next half century, because of that situation. If they had an orchestra, I would probably have played the violin. So, for the next 50 years, I hardly played my violin. I played here and there, so everybody knew me as a bass player.

At the Drake Hotel, we played at the lobby and that was when the Chicago Cubs were truly hot. The Cubs had Hack Wilson, Kiki Cuyler, and Riggs Stephenson, and I knew all the averages of every ballplayer. I would walk five blocks to get a picture of a Cub. So, the minute the ballgame was over, WGN Radio would cut in and broadcast our quartet from the Drake Hotel, right in the lobby. Then, what was interesting was that we played there at night, too, in the Gold Coast Room. During the summer, they would decorate the columns in silver and call it the Silver Coral Room. We alternated with different bands, including Fred Waring and the Pennsylvanians, a whole orchestra with three women singing, and they had the glee club in white, Eton jackets. The room was filled with people, all dressed up, six nights a week.

IRA BERKOW | SPORTS JOURNALIST | *NEW YORK TIMES*

Between undergraduate and graduate school, I had a job with the Israel Bonds organization. I was hired as the Assistant Public Relations Director on a two-man staff. One of my jobs was to pick up various celebrities and deliver them to locations for their speaking engagements. Sometime in 1963, I was assigned to pick up the former Miss America from 1958, Marilyn Van Derbur, at the Palmer House Hotel, where she was staying and bring her to the Drake Hotel, where she was scheduled to speak at an Israel Bonds event. I met her in the lobby, and she was dazzling. I drove her to the location, which was a couple of miles away and I dropped her off and left her there. It was a Saturday night and I met some friends down in the Rush Street area where we, unsuccessfully, attempted to meet some girls. The following Monday, I came into work and was told that the top guy of the organization wanted to see me. He said, "Saturday night, you picked up Miss America to take her to the speaking engagement." "That's right " I said. "And then you dropped her off." "Yes. That's what I was supposed to do." He then added, "Your job was also to take her back to the Palmer House when she was finished with the speaking engagement."

As I looked back on the event, I'm thinking I was single, just 22 years old, and she was about the same age, and she was Miss America. She was staying alone, and I didn't even think about picking her up to bring her back to the Palmer House. What was I thinking? Obviously, I wasn't.

Years later, after the Miss America gaffe, I'd become a sports columnist for the *New York Times*. I wrote a column about how every year, Bear Bryant, the legendary football coach for the University of Alabama, would read an inspirational column to his football team that was written by Ann Landers. She contacted me about it, and we became friends. I would come to Chicago and she and I would visit. She lived right down the street from the Drake Hotel on East Outer Drive. At the Drake, there was a private dining room and she was a member of that exclusive restaurant, and she would take me there and we would talk into the night. It was fascinating. Sometimes, she would call me on a Saturday night just to chat. I can't recall how this happened but I had written that Babe Ruth held the record for strikeouts by a batter, and I think she might have made reference to it in a column. Why she was writing about Babe Ruth, I don't know, but someone had contacted her with a correction—that it was Reggie Jackson who was the all-time leader for strikeouts by a batter. She wrote me a note that read, "Help! Help!"

NEIL HARTIGAN | FORMER ALDERMAN | ILLINOIS ATTORNEY GENERAL AND ILLINOIS LIEUTENANT GOVERNOR

My uncle was Frank "Tweet" Hogan who had been a bandleader and talent agent. He was a very good athlete and he had a great band. He opened the Drake Hotel when he was only 20 years old, and, over the years, all sorts of people were in his band. To this day, I have people come up to me and ask, "Are you Tweet Hogan's nephew?" When I was married in Lake Geneva, we got married to the music provided by his band. Up in the Lake Geneva and Lake Delavan area, he was the hottest band in those days, and the same thing was true in Chicago. My aunt Monica was one of the three Skelly sisters and her brother, Hal Skelly, was one of the truly big stars of the silent movie era. The three Skelly sisters were in vaudeville, played the Palace, and they were really good. The arrangement was that they both had to come off the road to take care of the family, so Frank became an agent instead of a band leader. In fact, as an agent, he was really a central figure who helped create the so-called "Chicago School of Comedy." Those comedians included George Gobel, Shelley Berman, Bob Newhart, and all of them were, at one time or another, managed by my uncle. The great Danny Thomas also played on the city's North Side at the 5200 Club on Broadway. I remember one time when we were celebrating the 100th Anniversary of Loyola University, I invited club members to lead the parade down Sheridan Road to celebrate the event. Of course, Danny's daughter, Marlo, went on to a big career and was the chairman of the effort to pass the Equal Rights Amendment.

KNICKERBOCKER HOTEL

The Knickerbocker Hotel opened its doors in 1927 at 163 E. Walton Place on the city's Near North Side along North Michigan Avenue. The 14-story gothic-inspired building was designed by architects Rissman and Hirschfield and was constructed in less than one year. During the 1970s it was known as the Playboy Towers and, earlier, the Lindbergh Beacon sat on top of the building. The hotel was known for its illuminated glass dance floor, and it has 306 guest rooms and suites.

JOE LEVINSON | MUSICIAN

Many of the city's downtown hotels had nightclubs and ballrooms in the '50s, including the Knickerbocker Hotel on Walton Street, right across from the Drake Hotel. On the hotel's first floor was a large ballroom that featured a glass dance floor with built-in colored lighting. For years, this room was a public nightclub as well as a place for high school proms. The glass floor still exists today, and the room is now used for private parties.

MORRISON HOTEL

Located at Madison and Clark, this high-rise hotel was designed by the famous architectural firm of Holabird and Roche in 1925. The hotel was named for Orsemus Morrison, Chicago's first coroner, who bought the site in 1838. The hotel that later opened on that site had 650 rooms in 1918, but was later expanded in 1931 to include 1,800 rooms and a fourth tower was built so that the hotel would have 2,210 rooms. In 1936, the Terrace Casino opened with Sophie Tucker as the performer. The hotel was torn down in 1965.

AMBASSADOR EAST AND AMBASSADOR WEST HOTELS

The famous restaurant, The Pump Room, was established on October 1, 1938 by Ernie Byfield and closed in 2017. It was located in the Ambassador East Hotel in the city's Gold Coast neighborhood at the corner of State Parkway and Goethe Street. Arturo Petterino was the maitre'd of the restaurants, and famous people from around the world would be seated in Booth One. Guests ranged from Frank Sinatra, John Barrymore, Marilyn Monroe, Bette Davis, Natalie Wood, and Humphrey Bogart. The Ambassador East was sold in 2010, closed for remodeling in 2011, reopened in 2011, resold again in 2017, and the Pump Room was renamed by Lettuce Entertain You Enterprises as Booth One.

JOE LEVINSON | MUSICIAN

The Pump Room at the Ambassador East Hotel was a very popular venue during the war years and after. The John Kirby Sextet played in the back of the room where they had a dance floor and bandstand. One of the local radio stations broadcast the Kirby Sextet live from there at night, and I think they were one of the finest little jazz groups that ever happened—their arrangements were spectacular. Charlie Shaver, the trumpet player and the arranger, used to take classical music pieces and modernize the arrangements. The dance floor would be filled with people in those years—they loved to dance to that little band! Eventually, the great Stanley Paul would come to the Pump Room.

Across the street, at the Ambassador West Hotel, they had a small room located off the lobby called the Buttery. It was a very intimate bar that featured, among many things, a magician who did tabletop magic tricks for the guests. There was also a little four-piece band in there that was led by a pianist with the amazing name of Romeo Meltz. They played mostly Latin music, and a lot of people came to the Buttery to hear them. The club was also very popular with salesmen because of the call girls who frequented the club. Of course, you wouldn't even know what was going on there unless you were there every night—or you worked in the band!

CONRAD HILTON HOTEL

Formerly the Stevens Hotel, construction began in 1925 and opened in 1927. It is located on South Michigan Avenue across from Grant Park. Conrad Hilton purchased the hotel and renamed it on November 19, 1951 and it was the largest hotel in the world with 3,000 rooms.

The Stevens was popular with many stars, including Frank Sinatra, Bing Crosby, and Bob Hope. After it was renamed by Hilton, luminaries such as Bette Davis, Lauren Bacall, President Dwight Eisenhower, Senator John F. Kennedy, and even Queen Elizabeth II and Princess Diana of England stayed at the hotel. The hotel was also the site of the riots in 1968 during the Democratic National Convention that was held in Chicago. Its Boulevard Room was a supper club that even offered the Ice Frolics ice shows to visitors.

SHERMAN HOUSE/COLLEGE INN

The Sherman House, originally named the City Hotel when built in 1837, was located on the north side of Randolph Street between Clark and LaSalle. The first structure was destroyed by the Great Chicago Fire in 1871, but Mayor Francis Cornwall Sherman, quickly rebuilt the hotel and the new eight-story hotel had 300 rooms when completed in 1873. As the hotel deteriorated, a new owner, Joseph Beifeld, an emigre from Hungary, bought the property. Beifeld restored the hotel to its original glory by 1904, and he opened a new restaurant, the College Inn, which became famous for its chicken ala king and chicken broth. In 1911, Beifeld decided to tear down the hotel and build a new 15-story structure with 757 rooms. In 1925 he expanded the hotel with a 23-story tower, and the College Inn restaurant became one of the city's premier jazz venues. One of the rooms in the hotel, the Panther Room, was known for the music played there. The Dome was located downtown in front of the Sherman Hotel situated out on the sidewalk. They had great groups there playing jazz, and the drummer named Barrett Deems used to play at that venue. He had a popular group and he also played with Louis Armstrong and Woody Herman. In 1973, the Sherman House was razed to make way for the new James R. Thompson Center.

Conrad Hilton, (Courtesy of Chicago Historical Society, ICHi 3954-167)

Hotel Sherman, College Inn
(Courtesy of Chicago Historical Society,
Photo by Paul Facuna, 1973, ICHi-18383)

PHIL HOLDMAN

I went to the Panther Room at the College Inn of the Sherman Hotel many times. I took my girl, Alberta, there and she later became my wife. There was no cover charge at the Panther Room and a beer was $.50 a bottle and I didn't even drink and she didn't drink, so we just sipped it like we were drinking beer, and most of the time we would go up on the dance floor. Charlie Barnet would play and we would sway just like we were listening to the band and we had a great time. The whole night cost me a dollar, and then she took me home in her mother's 1938 black Ford. It was a great date, a great time, and it was cheap.

RON KAPLAN | MUSICIAN | DALLAS, TX

When I was 17 and about to graduate from high school, I wasn't certain that I wanted to attend college. In fact, I got this wild idea in my head that it would be fun to go on the road with the 5th Dimension and tour with them as their drummer. I knew all of their music, and I used to practice to all of their tunes for hours on end. They were playing in Chicago at the College Inn at the Sherman House Hotel—this would be 1968. Now, they didn't know me and I didn't know them, but a group of friends and I were going to prom and planned to see them perform afterwards. They were staying at the hotel and I wanted to talk to them, so I called and asked to speak to one of the members of the 5th Dimension and of course, I was told that I could not. I had their recordings and so I looked at the jackets and found the names of the members of the group. One of them was Billy Davis, Jr. So, I called the hotel again and asked to be connected to the room of Billy Davis, Jr. And they put me right through! He got on the phone. I told him that I was a drummer and wanted to know if they needed one to go on the road with them. I must have been insane! But you know what? He was the nicest guy and we talked on the phone for about 20 minutes. He told me that I was probably a little too young for such a venture and that they had a regular, permanent drummer. But, he wanted to know if I had any plans to come down to see their show. I told him that we had tickets for after the prom, and he told me to be sure to come to the side of the stage after the show and ask for him and someone would come to get me. Of course, I told my friends and they didn't believe a word of it. So, I followed his instructions and did what I was told and after a bit, out came Billy Davis, Jr. and a couple of other members of the group and they hung out with us for a while. I was a hero! I still have the autograph that they signed. It's a postcard with their picture on it.

There's a follow-up to this story.

I had been taking drum lessons from Roy Knapp, who became known as the Dean of American Percussion Teachers. I was now graduating from college and Roy asked me what I was going to do? I told him that what I really wanted to do was to become a studio session drummer; that I wanted to go out to California and study with Hal Blaine.* He said, "You mean Harold Belsky?" I corrected him and reiterated Blaine's name. Again, he said, "You mean Harold Belsky?" I thought he was losing it, but he went on to tell me that Hal Blaine had been a student of his in Chicago and his name was Harold Belsky. Roy Knapp had the first percussion school in the United States and he taught Gene Krupa, Louie Bellson, Ed Shaugnessy and Hal Blaine, among others. So, Roy offered to write a letter of introduction for me and off to California I went. Mind you, this was 1972 and there was no email in those days.

When I got there, I called the number for Hal Blaine that Roy had given me and of course, I got an answering service. Everyone in Hollywood had an answering service. So, I left a message for Hal and guess what? A short time later, I got a call from Hal Blaine. I told him my story and why I'd come out to California and he invited me to come to his house. Of course, I had to ask for directions—there was no such thing as a GPS in those days. I went to his house and he welcomed me in and we talked for the longest time. Then, his wife asked if I'd like to stay for dinner and of course, I said I'd be pleased. We had meat loaf in case you're interested. After dinner, he asked what I was doing that night and I told him I had no plans. So, he told me to come with him. We got in his car and drove to a studio, and I went in with him and watched him record a session with Andy Williams. After that, he handed me a piece of paper with an address on it and he told me it was another studio and that I should come there in the morning. So, I get there and guess who he's recording with? The 5th Dimension. I went in and he introduced me to the players in the band, and then one of the members of the 5th Dimension said to me, "You look awfully familiar to me." And I said to him, "Do you remember playing the College Inn in Chicago about four years ago and there was this kid who wanted to play drums for your group?" Then the singer said, "You're that kid! What are you doing here?" I explained to him that I had come out to California in the hopes of furthering my education. It was a pretty amazing twist on an interesting situation.

Hal Blaine was one of the most successful studio musicians in the history of the music industry. He was reported to have done 35,000 studio sessions for everyone from Frank Sinatra to Simon and Garfunkel to the 5th Dimension and Barbra Streisand.

JUDY NEUHAUSER | MORTON GROVE, IL
"THE GOOD OLD DAYS"

When I graduated high school, many senior proms were held at four distinct places. I graduated from Von Steuben and mine was at the Sherman House. We had gotten tickets for afterwards to the College Inn at the Sherman House where the headliners were O.C. Smith and Professor Irwin Corey. This was right when O.C. Smith had his big hit with *Little Green Apples*. Other popular places were the Camellia Room at the Drake, the Boulevard Room at the Conrad Hilton, and the Empire Room at the Palmer House. It was interesting that these popular prom venues and nightclubs were

all at first-class hotels in downtown Chicago. Thinking back, one of the most remarkable memories I have is the cost for our event: including a steak dinner, the entertainment, tax and tip was $25.00 per couple. We thought that was absolutely outrageous! This was in 1969. Think about that compared to today's prices.

EDGEWATER BEACH HOTEL

It was a resort hotel complex located at 5301-5355 N. Sheridan Road along Lake Michigan in the Edgewater neighborhood on Chicago's Far North Side. The hotel was designed by Benjamin H. Marshall and Charles E. Fox with the first section of hotel opening in 1916. An adjacent south tower was added in 1924, and the Edgewater Beach Apartments were completed in 1928. The Edgewater Beach Hotel quickly became a very popular destination since it had a 1,200-foot private beach and it offered seaplane service to downtown Chicago. Many famous guests stayed at the hotel, including Marilyn Monroe, Judy Garland, Frank Sinatra, Bette Davis, Charlie Chaplin, Lena Horne, and Nat King Cole. In fact, U.S. Presidents Franklin Delano Roosevelt and Dwight D. Eisenhower were guests over the years. The Edgewater Beach was also nationally known because of radio broadcasts of big bands like Benny Goodman, Tommy Dorsey, Glenn Miller, and Artie Shaw on the hotel's own radio station WEBH. There was a famous beach walk and the Yacht Club. The future of the hotel was directly affected when Chicago decided to extend North Lake Shore Drive from Foster Avenue, to the south of the hotel, further north to the new Hollywood Boulevard in the early 1950s. That construction eventually led to the closing of the Edgewater Beach Hotel on December 21, 1967, and final demolition of the buildings, except for the apartment building to the north of the hotel in 1971.

LEE STERN | OWNER | CHICAGO STING, PART OWNER | CHICAGO WHITE SOX | BROKER, CHICAGO BOARD OF TRADE

The pier at the Edgewater Beach Hotel extended out into the lake, like a small Navy Pier, and they would have speedboats out there. The beach walk was a place to walk along the lake and go dancing. I remember going there and hearing Xavier Cugat and all the big stars of the day. As a kid, I would walk around the fence and sneak in and I remember drinking mint juleps at the Edgewater Beach. There was always a tennis club next to the hotel at the Edgewater Beach Tennis Club, and Bobby Riggs was the professional tennis player there.

IRA BERKOW | SPORTS JOURNALIST
NEW YORK TIMES

In 1949, I was a little boy, but already following the Chicago Cubs and an incident took place at the Edgewater Beach Hotel. The Philadelphia Phillies were in town and staying at the hotel. Another hotel guest, Ruth Ann Steinhagen, had become infatuated with the Phillies first baseman, Eddie Waitkus. She paid a bellhop to deliver a note to Waitkus' room saying that she wanted him to come to her room. He got the note and called her room and said that he'd come there. Upon his walking into the room, he took a seat in a chair. She went to a closet and produced a .22 rifle she had purchased and preceded to shoot him. The wound was not fatal and later, she was charged with assault and intent to murder. Three weeks later, a judge declared her insane and had her committed to a psychiatric hospital where she stayed for three years. Turned out that she was obsessed with him and thought that if she couldn't have him, nobody else could, either.

I was only nine years old at the time, but the event was very impactful because I came away from it knowing that athletes are human beings and vulnerable, too. He was on his deathbed, but survived. The next year, 1950, the Phillies went to the World Series and Eddie Waitkus played in every game for the Phillies that year.

Years later, I became a sportswriter for the New York Times and I wrote a column about the incident. After it was published, I was contacted by Eddie Waitkus, Jr. Turns out that his father, Eddie Waitkus, Sr. went to Florida to a rehab facility to recover from the shooting. While there, he fell in love with his nurse and they eventually married. Thus, Eddie Waitkus, Jr.

NEIL HARTIGAN | FORMER ALDERMAN | ILLINOIS ATTORNEY GENERAL AND ILLINOIS LIEUTENANT GOVERNOR

The Edgewater Beach Hotel was one of the truly great hotels in America. It had its boardwalk and provided big band jazz in the dining room and which could be heard outside. Today, part of Lake Shore Drive southward from Hollywood was built to block off access at the hotel to Lake Michigan all the way to Foster. That is where the boardwalk was located and where the jazz was heard. The Edgewater Beach was also a place to hear big band music, as well as the Blackhawk Restaurant downtown, and both places had nationwide radio broadcasts. The Edgewater Beach Hotel went all the way out to the water of Lake Michigan, and it had a great boardwalk. And, the boardwalk had terrific entertainment on summer nights.

BOB CUNNIFF

I had a sister who got married at the Edgewater Beach Hotel, and there used to be a place there called the Yacht Club. After the War, that was a good evening for a date and you could go to the Yacht Club and get "sloshed." I don't remember dancing there at all, but they had the Yacht Club and they had a little, wobbly gangway where you would go in, and in between, there were the marvelous grounds of the hotel.

Edgewater Beach Hotel, (Courtesy of Chicago Historical Society, ICHi-021458)

BLUES CLUBS

SOUTH SIDE

PEPPER'S LOUNGE

Opened by Johnny Peppers in 1956 at 503 East 43rd Street in Bronzeville, it quickly became one of the city's legendary blues bars. It was nothing fancy, just a bare-bones nightclub with a small stage and featuring great blues musicians, including Muddy Waters, Howlin' Wolf, Shakey Jake, Otis Rush, Junior Wells, and Buddy Guy. Waters was a mainstay at Peppers in the 1960s, and, in 1971, the club moved to 1321 S. Michigan Avenue.

CHECKERBOARD LOUNGE

An historic blues nightclub, it was located on the city's South Side at 423 E. 43rd Street. Opened by Buddy Guy and L.C. Thurman in 1972, Guy decided to leave the club and open his own venue in 1985. In danger of closing because of structural issues, the Checkerboard Lounge moved to a new site at 5201 S. Harper in Hyde Park, but with declining attendance the decision was made by Thurman in 2015 to close the club. During the Lounge's existence, such performers as Guy, Muddy Waters, Junior Wells, Chuck Berry, Stevie Ray Vaughan, Magic Slim, and Eric Clapton there.

BUDDY GUY'S LEGENDS

Buddy Guy is a Rock and Roll Hall of Fame inductee, a legendary bluesman, and the son of a Louisiana sharecropper who arrived in Chicago in 1957. His first blues club, the Checkerboard Lounge, opened in the 1970s, and he began his current club in the city in 1989 in the South Loop at 700 S. Wabash Avenue. Buddy Guy's Legends features top-notch blues music, and the club has hosted such big-name entertainment as Eric Clapton, the Rolling Stones, and Koko Taylor.

DAVE SPECTER | PROFESSIONAL BLUES MUSICIAN AND CLUB OWNER

Looking back, two of my greatest guitar idols have been Buddy Guy and Otis Rush. It was around 1993; I was playing at Buddy Guy's Legends club. Now, when Buddy wasn't on tour, he would hang around at his club. One particular night, I was playing and the next thing I knew, Buddy came up on stage with his guitar. At the time, the club also had a couple of pool tables and Otis Rush was shooting pool. So, Buddy took to the microphone and called out to Otis and invited him to come onstage, too. So, the next thing I knew, I'm playing at the club, flanked by Buddy Guy and Otis Rush—two of my all-time idols. I got so emotional about what was happening, I was almost crying from the joy of being part of this event. Fortunately, a friend of mine was there with a camera and he captured images of what took place on the stage.

So, it's safe to say that I fulfilled my goal of becoming a blues musician and I've been doing it in Chicago for more than 35 years.

THERESA'S LOUNGE

One of Chicago's earliest blues clubs was opened by Theresa McLaurin Needham on the city's South Side in her basement at 4801 S. Indiana Avenue. She was able to attract such top blues talent as Junior Wells, Buddy Guy, Otis Rush, Earl Hooker, and Howlin' Wolf. The club closed in 1986, and Theresa died in 1992.

NORTH SIDE

WISE FOOLS PUB

In the 1970s, this was a blues club located at 2270 N. Lincoln Avenue on the city's North Side. Performers at the club included Muddy Waters, Howlin' Wolf, and Mighty Joe Young. After being sold twice, the club now is more likely to host local alt-rock and cover bands than blues performers.

Otis Rush at Peppers Lounge, (Courtesy of Chicago Historical Society, ICHi-139113)

Dave Specter's band with Buddy Guy and Jimmy Johnson at Buddy Guy's Legends in Chicago. (Photo courtesy of Edward Spinelli)

Junior Wells and Little Walter at Theresa's, (Courtesy of Chicago Historical Society, ICHi-133606)

LES HOOPER | PROFESSIONAL MUSICIAN AND COMPOSER | LOS ANGELES, CA

I often played with Dave Remington's big band at the Wise Fools Pub on Lincoln Avenue. I also did a lot of arrangements for him as well. So, a funny thing happened there. One night, I wasn't playing and I decided to leave after a couple of tunes and Harriet Choice, who was a jazz critic for the *Chicago Tribune* at the time, was there and asked Bobby Lewis, the lead trumpet player, "Where's Les Hooper?" He proceeded to tell her that I'd gone home. She told Bobby that she'd been wanting to meet me after listening to the charts I'd done but that I was never there.

When she finally hooked up with me, she said that she wanted to book me to play a concert at the Chicago Museum of Contemporary Art. In addition to the music, she wanted me to address the audience and that kind of freaked me out because I was never very good at that sort of thing. I've always regarded myself as a musician and not an entertainer, and I'd never been comfortable in that kind of role. So, in preparation for the gig, I came up with a couple of little tricks that would help to take the focus of attention off of me and center more on the band. For example, I put a chart in front of the band that they'd never seen before. I did tell the audience how amazing these musicians were—that they could just take a chart that they weren't the least bit familiar with and just take off playing it, without any rehearsal. Appropriately, it was called *First Time Ever*. Later on, she told me that she'd been waiting to interview me, but that I was never around. But, when we did finally talk, she wrote a column for the *Arts & Entertainment* section and titled it, *The Phantom Takes The Lead*. That, apparently, was me. In it she said, having heard my music, she really wanted to talk with me. This is what led up to the booking at the museum. It was a valuable lesson for me, too, in that it helped me to understand that I couldn't just be a young jerk musician—that I had to learn to work with people, as well.

DAVE SPECTER | PROFESSIONAL BLUES MUSICIAN AND CLUB OWNER

I started my own band and we had a gig—every Wednesday night—at the Wise Fools Pub. This was after my playing as a sideman for four years, but I had a vision of having my own band. I hired an African American blues singer from the West Side, Barkin' Bill Smith, who had this big baritone voice, kind of reminiscent of Joe Williams who sang with Count Basie for so many years. Barkin' Bill and I signed a deal with Delmark Records in 1990. I also played with Sun Seals there and Lonnie Brooks, and Albert Collins would appear there from time to time.

While it's not the same, Chicago still has a thriving blues scene. I think there are more places to play than any other city in the world, including places in the suburbs—even more than Memphis. I would say that the Chicago area has rooms that book more blues and blues musicians per capita than anywhere else. Of course, the music has changed. Really, the 50s and 60s—maybe even the 70s, were the Golden Age of the blues in Chicago. I was fortunate enough to have heard it and learned it because most of the people from that era are gone. Some of the younger musicians are playing it; some very well and some not so very well. A lot of the quality and innovation are missing from the current music. Black people began to alienate themselves from the music, but black people were the pioneers and developers of blues, jazz, R&B, soul and gospel. They were not exclusive, but they certainly played a major role in the genesis of these genres and in my opinion and the opinions of many others, they created the best of these styles. It's not a matter of race, but it is where this music came from and as the elders have left us, the younger musicians are into other kinds of music.

Another thing that's happened is that bars and clubs have 27 television screens in them. Old Town has gone through that transformation, where it once was the mecca for blues and other live music styles. I wish I could have lived through the 60s there. I wish I could have lived through the 60s in London.

B.L.U.E.S.

The club is across the street from Kingston Mines at 2519 N. Halsted. It was opened in April 1979 by Rob Hecko and Bill Gillmore and has featured such musicians as Sunnyland Slim, Otis Clay, Bonnie Lee, Otis Clay, Eddie Shaw, Jimmy Burns, and Nicholas Barron. B.L.U.E.S. has predominantly featured local bluesmen and attracts an old-school blues crowd.

KINGSTON MINES

Located at 2548 N. Halsted Street on the city's North Side, Kingston Mines is one of Chicago's oldest, largest, and most infamous blues joints. It began as a coffeehouse before it adapted to an all Chicago-style blues format in the Lincoln Park neighborhood. The club features a Southern menu of New Orleans-style food. The club predominantly features local bands including such performers as Magic Slim, Jimmy Johnson, Hoochie Man, and Kid Dynamite. It has also attracted such visiting performers as Bob Dylan, Mick Jagger, and Robert Plant.

HOUSE OF BLUES

The House of Blues Chicago is located in Marina Towers at 329 N. Dearborn Street and opened on October 1, 1996. It includes a concert hall, restaurant, and bar, all housed in a shed-like building. The music at the House of Blues covers blues as well as rock, jazz, and gospel. The original House of Blues Hotel is now the Hotel Sax. The music venue is owned by Dan Ackroyd and Jim Belushi.

ALICE'S REVISITED | CLUB 950 LUCKY NUMBER

During the late 1960s and early 1970s, there was a hippie juice bar called Alice's Revisited. Upstairs of the club was the underground newspaper, *The Seed*, that advertised selling spots of pot dealers. The club regularly featured such range of performers as Styx, Howlin' Wolf, Muddy Waters, Otis Rush, Junior Wells, the

Woody Herman 19-piece big band, and Buddy Guy. The Club 950 Lucky Number was one of the premiere alternative clubs in the city in the 1990s offering punk, alternative, goth, and raver music. It was located just off the corner of Lincoln Avenue, Sheffield, and Wrightwood. It closed in 2000 but reemerged in 2007.

BEN HOLLIS

There was another place that is worth noting because of what it was and who was there. It was called Alice's Revisited and it was at 950 Wrightwood. It later became called Club 950 Lucky Number. Upstairs was the office of *The Seed*—the hippie newspaper. Alice's was a juice bar—they didn't serve liquor—only juice. But, they had entertainment and it was there that I got to see the likes of Corky Siegel and Styx, all for $3 on a Tuesday night. And because they didn't serve alcohol, anybody could walk in and it was great. I was about 14 as I recall. I also saw Muddy Waters and another local band that did well for a short time—Wilderness Road. That whole thing was transformative for me because I could walk in and just be myself, dance around by myself. That was a significant thing for an adolescent to be able to do. It was very important to me.

CORKY SIEGEL | SIEGEL-SCHWALL BAND

Jim Schwall is best known as the co-founder with Corky Siegel of the Siegel-Schwall Band, a blues duo that was formed in 1964 and played at several Chicago bars and clubs. They performed regularly at such clubs as Pepper's Lounge and Big John's. a small club in Old Town. The performers at both clubs included Muddy Waters, Howlin' Wolf and Willie Dixon. The Siegel-Schwall duo expanded to a quartet and Schwall would use an amplified Gibson B-25 acoustic guitar. The band became quite popular and, by 1967 they were touring nationally. They also collaborated with the famous orchestra leader Seiji Ozawa combining blues with classical music. Big John's Blues Club provided what would be called classic Chicago blues music.

Corky (and harmonica) Bill Russo Composer of Three Pieces for Blues Band and Symphony Orchestra, and Maestro Seiji Ozawa at Ravinia, July 1968.

House of Blues

DAVE SPECTER | PROFESSIONAL BLUES MUSICIAN AND CLUB OWNER

I have been on the Chicago music scene starting around 1984-85. I grew up on the North Side of Chicago in Hollywood Park. I decided that I wanted to become a professional blues musician. I came from a very musical family. My older brother, specifically, used to tell me stories about seeing Muddy Waters and Howlin' Wolf and buying peppermint schnapps for Howlin' Wolf at Alice's Revisited and hanging out with Junior Wells and Koko Taylor. He turned me on to a lot of that music, and I started playing guitar when I was 18. I discovered blues guitar and blues music, and it moved me like no other music ever had.

Two of the first places I ever worked were for Bob Koester at the Jazz Record Mart and Delmark Records in Chicago. I worked as a shipping clerk at Delmark Records and at the store at Jazz Record Mart. The first job I got at any venue was as a doorman at B.L.U.E.S. on Halsted in Lincoln Park. This was when Wise Fools was also still happening. I was working the door at B.L.U.E.S. on Halsted for a couple of years in my early 20s and I got to hear great music every night. In addition to learning the music, I got to meet the musicians. Some of the amazing nights that occurred there were during one of the Chicago Blues Festivals. Every Sunday night, Sunnyland Slim, a legendary blues pianist, played there. He helped Muddy Waters get signed to a record deal—first with Aristocrat and then with Chess. Sunnyland was like one of the patriarchs on the Chicago blues scene. This was when Chicago Blues piano was like a living art form and you could hear people like Blind John Davis, Pinetop Perkins, Jimmy Walker, and Sunnyland. I remember a night during a Chicago Blues Fest, and Sunnyland's band was playing and Eddie Boyd and Willie Dixon walked in and they all got onstage and took turns singing, playing, and telling stories. There was a night when Jimmy Page and Robert Plant from Led Zeppelin came into B.L.U.E.S. On Halsted. I also recall a specific night when Hubert Sumlin, the great guitar player for Howlin' Wolf, was playing. It was a warm summer night, and I was standing out front collecting the cover charge money and John Forgerty (Credence Clearwater Revival) walked up and looked at me a bit skeptically and said, "Hubert Sumlin? He's playing here tonight?" I told him he was and he said, "I can't believe this," and he walked in. Didn't want to be "comped." He paid the cover charge. I have other memories of Boz Scaggs and people like that coming to Blues on Halsted.

On a personal level, one of the first gigs I got was with playing with the band of Sam Lay. He, of course, was known as the original drummer with the Paul Butterfield Blues Band and he also played with Bob Dylan when he went electric. I remember going on a two-week tour to Canada with Sam that turned out to be a three-week tour in the middle of winter. About a week before the tour, he called and said, "Dave, I'm thinking about adding another guitar player along for the tour." Of course, I said, "Sam, it's your band. You do whatever you feel you need to do that's best. I'm just honored to be playing with you." He went on to say, "I'm going to bring Hubert Sumlin along with us." Well, I about dropped the phone. I was thrilled, scared and excited all at once! It was two weeks in Calgary and then we drove north to Red Deer, where for the entire time, the temperature did not get above zero. But, I was in my early 20s, playing with Sam and Hubert every night and making 50-bucks a night and just loving it. This all came about because of my exposure at Blues on Halsted. I started playing gigs as a sideman with other musicians like Big Time Sarah, Jimmy Johnson, who is 90 years old and who I still play with. Steve Freund, who was Sunnyland's guitar player. These are all people who took me under their wing and encouraged me. I guess Sam Lay had heard about me because I knew members of his band. I also played with Sun Seals for about a year and a half; this was back in the late 80s. I also did a European tour with Jimmy Rogers, who was part of Muddy Waters rhythm section and one of the premiere blues guitarists in Chicago.

BALLROOMS

SOUTH SIDE

SAVOY BALLROOM

The Savoy Ballroom opened on November 23, 1927 at 4733 South Parkway on Chicago's South Side and although most of its patrons were African Americans, white patrons also visited the ballroom. Originally, the venue featured jazz artists such as Louis Armstrong, Count Basie, Duke Ellington, Earl "Fatha" Hines, Stan Kenton, Dizzie Gillespie, Billie Holiday, Ella Fitzgerald, Gene Krupa, and Woody Herman. In addition, the Savoy hosted boxing, figure skating, and basketball exhibitions, including ones by the original Savoy Big Five that would later change its name to the Harlem Globetrotters when the group was managed by Abe Saperstein. From 1927 to 1940, the Savoy would have continuous music that was provided by two bands each night. The ballroom closed in 1948, and the building was demolished in the early 1970s.

TRIANON BALLROOM

The Trianon Ballroom was a name that had been given to several ballrooms on Chicago's South Side. The first such ballroom opened in 1922 during the big-band era in the Woodlawn neighborhood at 6201 Cottage Grove Avenue. It was designed by the theater architects Rapp and Rapp and owned and operated by William and Andrew Karzas, who also opened the Aragon Ballroom. Like the Aragon, music was broadcast in Chicago on WGN radio. The 60 x 180 foot ballroom had famous bands headed up by Benny Goodman, Glenn Miller, and Tommy and Jimmy Dorsey.

JACK HOGAN

As for the Trianon, when I got released from military service I used to go to the Trianon quite a bit, and Lawrence Welk played there. He was one of the resident bands there. Ironically, all the time that I went to listen to Lawrence Welk, I never knew that he had an accent. He never talked, and if he did it was very brief. I didn't know that he had an accent until I saw him later when he performed on television.

NORTH SIDE

ARAGON BALLROOM

Built in 1926, the Aragon was designed in a Moorish architectural style and had a ceiling that looked like the sky as clouds moved across the stars. It was located on Chicago's North Side at 1106 W. Lawrence Avenue in the Uptown neighborhood. The ballroom was an immediate success and continued to be a very popular attraction throughout the 1940s. It was built near the "L" tracks and that gave patrons easy access. A very large building, it could handle up to 18,000 patrons each of the six nights it was open during the week. Radio station WGN broadcast an hour-long program from the Aragon across the United States and Canada. A fire in 1958 forced closure of the ballroom for a few months, but, after reopening soon after, it offered a popular location for dancing until finally closing for regular dancing in 1964.

SHELLEY HOWARD | UNOFFICIAL MAYOR OF RUSH STREET

In May of 1983 I was asked to DJ for U2 at the Aragon Ballroom. I was doing this regularly. I loved when I was able to do my video *ShelleyVision* show as well, but this was a big gig for the band and being able to spin records for a few hours before they went on was still great. The *War* album had just been released and it contained such future classics as *New Year's Day* and *Sunday Bloody Sunday*, and I was playing both those songs in the clubs.

I set up my portable DJ case on the sound booth that was located in the middle of the arena, elevated above the crowd. They told me I could have a sound check after the band performed theirs. So around 6 p.m., before the doors opened, they came out, and indeed performed *Sunday Bloody Sunday*. After they wrapped, the sound tech pointed at me, and said "OK, let's get some levels. One song." Hmm, which song? A no-brainer. The big tune in my world was *Revenge by Ministry*. We all hung out with Al Jourgensen, and the band and this was their

Jackie Wilson at Trianon, (Courtesy of
Chicago Historical Society, ICHi-106482)

Aragon Ballroom, (Courtesy of Chicago Historical Society, ICHi-038968)

signature song at that time. I plopped my 12"
single on my Technics record player and let it rip.
It sounded GREAT; loud as it should in an empty
Aragon. No sooner than I finished, Bono comes
running up to the booth. OK. He shouts to me,
"What is that song? It's fantastic!" So I tell him about
Ministry and how proud we are in Chicago of the
band and our hopes for the success of the single.

Bono asks where he can get the record. No problem.
I give him my copy, and he walks away happy. But
now I had no copy of the record to play that night.
It was about 45 minutes until the doors opened.
So I did the only thing a conscientious DJ would do.
I hopped in my car and drove to like a madman to
Wax Trax. Double parking on Lincoln, I ran in, told
Jim Nash the story, and he just did a "Wow" and
gave me another copy. Fortunately, I was able to
get back to the Aragon just before the doors opened.
I played my two-hour set and had the whole joint
bobbing up and down. And of course, you know
what I spun just before U2 came on, right?

The next day, I called Al to recount the story. His
response was less than lukewarm. Later I learned
that he had disowned the song and the album,
complaining that his label, Arista, had pushed him in
synth-pop direction, when he was trying to take
Ministry down a harder path. But that was Al for
you. For Bono and me, "Revenge" was sweet music.

JACK HOGAN

When you talked about music, the Aragon Ballroom
and the Trianon Ballroom were the places to go.
Even though I was a South Sider, I didn't really
frequent the Trianon that was at 62nd and Cottage,
as much as I did the Aragon, probably because
of my desire to hear the Dick Jergen Orchestra.
Then, they would bring in different bands like
Kai Kaiser and Glenn Miller and Eddy Duchin. The
'40s was a great time for sports and a great time
for music. We had a place called the Village up on
78th and Ashland, and the Rose Bowl was on
79th Street, near Racine. These places were just ice
cream meccas, and most people of our age in
the 1940s circulated around the ice cream parlors.

In 1942, there was a place that was going to open
called the Rainbow Gardens at Clark and Montrose
or Lawrence. This place was supposed to be open
and geared for young people. There wasn't going to
be any hard liquor, just Cokes and sandwiches
and ice cream. The night that it was supposed to
open, the featured performers were the Charlie Spivak
Orchestra and Dinah Shore. I remember that we
went up to opening night, and all kinds of people
were mingling around. However, they never opened
because they didn't have the proper licenses.
So we ended up going over to the Aragon Ballroom
which was not that far away. A singer named
Harry Cool was a vocalist for the band leader Dick
Jergens. It was customary in those days that if
it was a big name band, a lot of people used to hang
around the bandstand and listen to the music
and watch the musicians, as opposed to dancing.
That's what I was doing that particular night.
All of a sudden, Harry Cool came down off the
bandstand and was trying to make out with the girl
I was dating. I remember that so well.

PHIL HOLDMAN

The Aragon and the Trianon were the most
beautiful ballrooms in the city. I went to the Aragon
more than the Trianon, and I was only at the
Trianon once; I think that we saw Wayne King.
The Trianon was on 63rd and Cottage Grove.
The Aragon we went to many times and it was
closer to us. We liked Dick Jergens and he was
featured a lot there with Eddie Howard, and
they were very popular at the Aragon. It was located at Lawrence and Broadway, and it was one of
the most beautiful ballrooms. I think that the place
opened in 1923, and the first band that played
there was Paul Whiteman. At that time, only the
society people went there to hear Paul Whiteman
and carriage horses used to take them there
because there weren't too many cars. It was near
the Edgewater Beach Hotel, and I went there many
times too to hear the dance bands and shows.
But, the Aragon was one of the most popular
ballrooms in the country.

Bobby Bland at Trianon, (Courtesy of Chicago Historical Society, ICHi-138947)

BB King, (Courtesy of Chicago
Historical Society, ICHi-134339)

BEN HOLLIS | THE CHICAGO POP FESTIVAL AT THE ARAGON BALLROOM

It was 1969 and of course, that was the year of Woodstock. I think it was also the year of Monterrey Pop. So, this event kind of coincided with those two events in terms of timeframe. I think I was about 15, but I was intrigued by what was about to happen and so I went. I was introduced to the haunting aroma of what I had guessed was marijuana. I don't know if I got a contact high, but the whole experience was intoxicating. There was a band onstage that was really outstanding and just as I got into listening to them, they announced they were taking a break and the crowd went nuts. They didn't want them to stop. I didn't know who they were, but found out they were called MC5 and they were from Detroit. Another act from the Detroit area was Bob Seeger. At that time, his band was called the *Bob Seeger System.* Next up was the legendary blues singer, Howlin' Wolf, and he was absolutely electrifying with that big voice of his. What a performer! Another one of the groups that played this event was *Rotary Connection,* and their lead singer was Minnie Riperton. And Phil Upchurch was the guitar player who became a real luminary in the guitar world. Alice Cooper was on that bill, too, although I didn't see him. It was then and there that I discovered the total power of live music!

ROCK AND ROLL CLUBS

THE QUIET KNIGHT

A popular club that featured rock, jazz, and reggae, it was opened by Richard Harding in 1969 and lasted until 1979. Later located at 953 W. Belmont on the city's North Side in a 400-seat concert venue, it featured some of the biggest names in entertainment, including Herbie Hancock, Muddy Waters, Corky Siegel and the Siegel-Schwall Band, Bonnie Koloc, Linda Ronstadt, Chuck Mangione, Bruce Springsteen and the E Street Band, Bob Marley, Jimmy Buffett, and Arlo Guthrie. Harding had owned the first Quiet Knight at 1311 N. Wells and Poor Richard's at 1363 N. Sedgwick.

KINETIC PLAYGROUND

It was considered to be Chicago's principal stop for rock and roll music in the 1960s. Opened on April 3, 1968 at 4812 N. Clark Street, The Kinetic Playground, first called the Electric Theater, was established by Brooklyn-born promoter, 24-year old Aaron Russo. The site had been Rainbow Gardens, an entertainment center. The club only lasted a short time as a nightclub that offered rock and roll music. Among the performers at the club were The Doors, The Jimi Hendrix Experience, Led Zeppelin, Pink Floyd, The Byrds, The Who, Janis Joplin, Eric Burdon, Jethro Tull, Buffy Saint Marie, Jefferson Airplane, and Fleetwood Mac. In November 1969, there was a fire at the club, and although the Kinetic Playground reopened in December, 1972, it finally closed in 1975 and later went out of business. The building was demolished in 2003.

THE CELLAR

The Cellar was located in Arlington Heights, Illinois and was a teen dance club that provided its customers with live musical entertainment in the 1960s, both rock and roll and blues. It was founded by Paul Sampson in 1964 and became notable for presenting such groups as The Buckinghams, the Ides of March, Ted Nugent, The Amboy Dukes, The Who, The Cream, The Byrds, Buffalo Springfield, Three Dog Night, and The Steve Miller Band.

GASPAR'S | SCHUBAS TAVERN

Originally Gaspar's (also Bavarian Inn), it is now Schubas Tavern and is located at 3159 N. Southport Avenue near Belmont Avenue in Chicago. The tavern was originally erected by Schlitz Brewery in 1900. Renovated in 1988, Chris and Mike Schuba opened the bar in 1989. It is considered to be a classic neighborhood corner bar and draws crowds that range from 50 to 150 patrons. It has hosted such popular folk and country acts as Robbie Fulks and John Wesley Harding, as well as numerous rock acts.

RALPH COVERT | PROFESSIONAL MUSICIAN | LEADER OF THE BAD EXAMPLES | CHICAGO, IL

One of the first, so to speak, top-shelf clubs to put The Bad Examples in on a regular basis was a venue called Gaspar's (now known as Shubas). It was/is located at the corner of Belmont and Southport. Gaspar's was owned and run by a guy named Dean Karabatsos. Behind the bar at this club was a stairway that went down to where all of the alcohol was stored in the beer cage, a padlocked area with kind of chain link walls where all the kegs and bottles of alcohol were stored. Also inside the cage, Dean kept two large, ferocious Dobermans. After my first show, Dean and I have a beer, and then he says it's time to get paid. He leads me down the dark stairs to this musty basement, and of course the dogs begin throwing themselves again the fence barking frantically! It scared the shit out of me. Dean calmly pulls out the money for me to count. I do my best to ignore the dogs crashing against the fence inches away from me and do my best to count the money—all $100 of it! It turns out this was Dean's running joke and how he'd pay bands at the end of the night.

The dogs would be going wild because a stranger was down there with their master, and it cracked him up! Dean said that sometimes out-of-town musicians would be so freaked out at this set-up, they'd just take the money without counting and split, just to escape from the scene. I think he kind of considered it a rite of passage for the first-timers to see how they responded to tense situations. He was a good guy and was pretty much the first club owner to give The Bad Examples some nicely placed opening slots at his club and ultimately came to making us the headliners for the weekends, too. Dean closed the club in August of 1988, and he chose our band to be one of the featured performers for the closing. It was an amazing night—packed to the gills, hot and sweaty, and a great night of rocking. This may sound funny, but this was one of many times we were so honored to be the performing bands for clubs that were shutting their doors. In reality, because of the friendships we developed with a number of club owners, it was not uncommon for them to call us to play on their closing nights. I guess you could have called us a requiem band.

P. J. FLAHERTY'S

Another popular venue for music was P. J. Flaherty's located in Evergreen Park at 95th and Western. It was quite popular in the 1980s and early 1990s and hosted such bands as Robin Trower and Blue Oyster Cult.

RALPH COVERT | PROFESSIONAL MUSICIAN | LEADER OF THE BAD EXAMPLES | CHICAGO, IL

Pat (P.J.) was another club owner who championed us early on in our existence. What was interesting was that we were a North Side band that became really popular on the South Side; so popular that we were named the most popular band of the year by the *Southside Economist*. As a norm, the North Side bands didn't play South Side clubs and vice versa. But we were a mainstay at P.J. Flaherty's.

There was an incident at our first show that sort of cemented our friendship, though at the time it occurred, it seemed like it would be our last show. My bass player at the time, Greg Balk, thought it would be a good idea to smuggle his underage, younger sister into the club to hear us play. He brought her in through the kitchen, and one of the staff people noticed her and brought it to the attention of Pat Flaherty, P.J., himself. Now I was in the back room, tuning my guitar when one of my guys came to me and said, "Ralph, you've got to get into the kitchen. All hell is breaking loose." When I arrived in the kitchen, Pat and Greg were nose to nose, screaming at each other, about to come to blows. Pat was a six-foot five Irishman; a firefighter who had a couple of side businesses, the club being one of them. He was not to be messed with. Greg had a temper, and he was about to lose control. I, on the other hand, am not much of a fighter, but I got in between the two of them and pushed Greg away, told him I'd deal with him later. Then Pat and I went toe-to-toe, F bombs flying! He was furious that Greg had snuck his sister in, we were fired, we were idiots; I yelled back that Greg was my problem, but that I had a job to do and a show to play, and he yelled that I'd better play my show then and I yelled back that as soon he stopped yelling at me I would! He stormed off, and I tracked down Greg. He was hopping mad about his sister getting thrown out— I told him we had a show to play, and we'd deal with it later. A funny sidebar is that Greg always said he played best when he was angry, so needless to say, he was on fire, and we did an outstanding opening set. Afterwards, I went to Pat's office, to collect our money and fully expecting him to rip me a new one and tell me it was the last time we'd play at his club. Instead, he grabbed my hand with one of his huge paws and shook it rather firmly and said, "I like working with you. You're solid people. You put on a great freaking show!" When I apologized for Greg, he said, "What an asshole. Whatever." And from that moment on, we had a great relationship. He always took my calls. He always booked us to play on great shows. He paid us fair, and I never had any problems with him. We'd always hang out and have a laugh in his office after our shows. Years later, he hired us to play the last night the club was open.

Another happening that took place there involved a Southside Irish family—regulars at the bar. These were big folks—firemen, policemen, nurses—you know, a bunch of large people. There were many brothers and sisters, including a P.J. of their own and one of the girls, whose name was Colleen. P.J. was one of these people who, if you had just met him, seemed a couple of bricks shy of a full-load, a real "dems and dose" kind of guy. Well, we were performing and suddenly, P.J. threw a punch at some guy who was dancing. Next thing you knew, it had broken into a full-blown melee of fisticuffs on the dance floor; a good old-fashioned South Side brawl. Bodies and bar stools flying everywhere. What a mess. The next time we played there, there was a knock at the back-stage door. It was Colleen with P.J. in tow. She's kind of tugging him by the elbow and she says, "Tell him. Go ahead and tell him." So, he said rather sheepishly, "Ralph. I'm really sorry about the fight last time. Really sorry about the fight." I asked him what happened? He says, "I'm so sorry, man, but I love the words to your songs so much… when those people started dancing, it just made me so mad they weren't listening to your words! I felt like I needed to defend your honor." I told him, "P.J., it's okay. Some people, like you, enjoy listening to the words and others like dancing. Both things are okay." And he said, "Really??? Oh, man! I'm so sorry. I was just so mad that they weren't listening to your words and I couldn't control myself." Good old P.J. Farrell—I've played many shows since then when I could have used his true blue South Side loyalty to knock some sense into the people in the audience who were not listening to the words!

We would play all over the Chicago area, from the South Side and all the way up to the North Shore. And each area had their own scene—their own kind of music for the most part. For example, the western suburbs had clubs like McGregors and The Thirsty Whale that featured heavy metal cover bands. The South Side clubs were more blues-oriented and also had bands performing like Stevie Starlight that did a kind of music you might have called "Porn Rock." They would do parodies of popular songs and make them as rude and crude as they could—and they were a big hit in that area. Note: A *Chicago Tribune* review of Starlight's Band read, "His bawdy songs and stage patter have invited comparisons to the comedians Lenny Bruce (whom Starlite admires) and Andrew Dice Clay (whom he doesn't)."

When we would play around the area, we knew that we couldn't leave our gear in the van we traveled with, so we would store everything the basement of our bass player's home—"Pickles" Piekarski, a block off Belmont—drums, amps, and everything. One night, we were loading out into Pickle's basement after a show, and the next thing you know, we were surrounded by cop cars. Someone had phoned in that a burglary was in progress. On one hand, it was reasonable—a bunch of longhaired guys hauling stuff in an alley with a beat-up van. Pickles had lost his license and couldn't prove he lived there. To make things worse, the van had only recently been purchased after our motor home broke down in South Dakota. The plates and the registration for the van still showed the South Dakota owner. Then the cops frisked us and our lead guitarist John had a bag of pot on him. It looked like they were going to book us. Things were getting pretty hairy, but we finally said, "Look, what kind of incompetent burglars would we have to be to load broken down gear like this INTO a house? Isn't it obvious we're a band?" And Pickles was like, "I have a key, I have a dog inside—I'll show you my apartment!" Finally, the police decided that we were on the up and up, and that it wasn't worth the paperwork to book us when they had real crime to deal with. They told us we could hit the road, but as they turned to go, John said, "Hey, if you're not going to arrest us, can I have my shit back?" The cop with John's pot scowled, but he gave it back to him as the other cops laughed. Another night, another gig!

HOGHEAD MCDUNNAS

**Hoghead McDunnas is located
at 1503-07 W. Fullerton in Chicago.**

**RALPH COVERT | PROFESSIONAL
MUSICIAN | LEADER OF
THE BAD EXAMPLES | CHICAGO, IL**

I had a spare guitar that I would carry as a backup when we toured. It was an old Washburn with a rosewood top—beautiful guitar. I would carry it with me just in case I broke a string, I'd have another guitar ready to go. At this point, we now had a garage space to store our gear—no more stashing it in Pickles' basement. We were playing one night at a place called Hoghead McDunna's, over on Fullerton. It's no longer there. It was over near where the Gene Siskel Film Center is located now. I had brought the guitar in because I had a hunch that I was going to break a string that night. As it turned out I didn't break a string after all, and didn't need it. Now, that guitar would either live under the back seat in the van or it would live down at my studio, or sometimes, I would stash it in a storage loft above my bed. At some point in time, I thought it would be a good idea to put a new set of strings on it. So, I looked for it under the seat in the van and it wasn't there. Then, I thought that perhaps I had left it in my studio and the next time I was there, a couple months later, I looked for it. And guess what? It wasn't there either. I assumed that I must have left it with the pile of guitars in the loft over my bed. The next time I had time to dig through them, I looked, and again—couldn't find it. This went on for quite a while, but I was busy touring, and I forgot about it the rest of the time. I couldn't remember if I'd loaned the guitar to someone or if I'd put it in the van and forgotten about it. It was a mystery. After about a year to the day that we'd played the gig at Hoghead McDunna's, we got booked to play there again. The club had a bar in the room on the east side, and the stage and music shows were in the west room. The front had windows that looked out on Fullerton, and the back faced an alley. The stage was on the alley side, and you loaded in and out through a door to the alley that was unlocked most of the time. The door to the alley was next to the stage by the far southwest corner of the place. After the gig, we were carrying our gear out to the van, which was parked in the alley. I noticed a guitar case leaning up against the stage. I thought to myself that perhaps one of the guys had placed one of their guitars against the stage as they were loading out from the gig. It looked vaguely familiar, but was nothing I'd brought with me. So, I picked it up, put it on the stage and opened the latches. There it was! My old Washburn! I had brought it into Hoghead McDunna's a year before and apparently left it standing leaning against the stage. Hundreds of bands had played there since. Nobody had touched it. Obviously, nobody stole it. Amazing that after a whole year, it was still there. But that incident really gives a good impression of what the scene was like back in the day. There was a tremendous spirit of camaraderie back then and while you didn't see the other bands perform, unless you were co-billed with them, everybody knew everybody who was playing those places and we all kind celebrated our successes from a distance. And there was a sense of loyalty and old-fashioned honesty among the musicians, as embodied by the guitar. Everyone knew it had to be someone's, so they didn't take it.

LOUNGE AX

Lounge Ax was a music venue that was located in the Lincoln Park neighborhood across from Wax Trax. The club was a key place for live rock music. Opened in 1987, Jennifer Fischer and Julia Adams were joined in September 1989 by Sue Miller who had previously been the booker for West End and Cubby Bear. The famous band, Phish, performed for the first time in Illinois at Lounge Ax in 1990. The venue was featured prominently in the popular John Cusack movie, *High Fidelity*. Lounge Ax closed on January 15, 2000.

The Beatles at Comiskey Park, August 1965
(Courtesy of Clark Weber)

RALPH COVERT | PROFESSIONAL MUSICIAN | LEADER OF THE BAD EXAMPLES | CHICAGO, IL

The Bad Examples were booked into the Lounge Ax on Lincoln Avenue. The club opened in the late 80s and was originally owned by Jennifer Fischer and Julia Adams. It was a very popular venue, and they booked a lot of amazing up and coming bands there. It was really a great scene. Lounge Ax had kind of become our home base in the early 90s and we'd developed a big following. We were playing one night and it was a packed house. No one was leaving. We played our first set and then a second one. Then we played an encore and the time was approaching 3 a.m. and still, no one was leaving. It was now closing time and they turned off the PA and turned on the house lights and the crowd was "lovingly pissed." They wanted more. Jennifer came up to me and said, "You've got to stop. If the cops come in and the place is this packed, I'll be toast. Get on the mic and let them know we're done, it's time to go." The crowd was having none of it. They wanted more. I said to Jennifer, "Tell you what. I'll make a deal with the audience. One last song and they promise to go." She said, "OK. Just one." I turned to the crowd and I said, "Here's the deal. We're going to do one last song, and then I'm going to lead all of you out the front door so we don't get Jennifer and Julia in trouble for being open after hours. So, they turned the PA back on, and we did a song of ours called, *I Don't Want To Be God Anymore*. The chorus to the song is a crowd sing-along. We performed the song, and for the last chorus I unplugged my guitar, came off of the stage and went through the audience. I led them out the front door, all 250 of them, following me and singing the chorus, "I don't want to be God anymore, I just want to be with you." Out onto Lincoln Avenue went the parade, and we blocked traffic right across the street from the Biograph Theater where John Dillinger was shot, with the crowd just singing away under the streetlights. And, Jennifer and Julia were able to close the doors and not get in trouble with the police. I remember standing in the middle of the sea of people, everyone happily singing my song and celebrating life. It was a great Chicago moment.

MILL RUN THEATER/ PLAYHOUSE | NILES

The Mill Run Theater was a 1,600-seat theater in the round located in Niles, a northwest suburb of Chicago. Built in 1965 on the grounds of the Golf Mill Shopping Center, it was demolished in August 1984 with Lou Rawls as the last performer that year. It was originally a venue for off-Broadway shows and the first act to perform was Chicagoan Shecky Greene in early 1970.

MICHAEL RABIN | DEERFIELD, IL

Years ago, I took my son and a friend to see the Jackson 5 at the Mill Run Theater. Now, I knew someone who did food catering for the entertainers at Mill Run and so on occasion, I would help out and was able to go back stage to meet the performers as they would dine after the shows. My friend would take me back stage and on one occasion, I met Tom Jones. Another time I met Ella Fitzgerald. After the show was over, I went to my friend and asked if we could go back there and meet the Jackson 5. He told me they had already left. So, I asked my friend if he knew where they were staying and he told me the name of the hotel. At the time, I think it was the Hilton that was at Skokie Highway and Golf Road. So, we drove over to the hotel and went in. When we got there, we walked over to the elevators and there were a couple of big guys standing there—bodyguards, I guess. And I just asked, "What floor are the Jackson 5 staying on?" And they told me they were on the top floor; that they had the entire top floor. They didn't stop us, and we took the elevator to the top floor. The doors opened and we walked in. In the first room we saw the Jacksons' mother and all the kids and they were already in their pajamas! They were sitting on a bed and talking. I'm sure

Janet was there and LaToya and of course, Michael. At first, they just looked at us, but then they welcomed us and invited us to sit down. So, we did. We talked with them and they signed our programs and of course, it was a big thrill for the boys. That was the quality of acts that we would often see at Mill Run.

RONNIE RICE | ROCK AND ROLL SINGER

My parents were from Germany, and I was born in Haifa, Israel on March 30, 1944. They had left Germany and went to Israel because of the Nazis, and my family's real name is Schlotsover. When they came to America, there were people here by the name of Reiss and they were helping all of my family who came over from Europe. So, when my family came to the United States, they took the name of Rice. I was raised in Evanston from the time I was 13 years old, while, prior to that, I lived on the North Side in Lincoln Park and West Rogers Park. I went to Clinton Elementary School, and then I went to Nichols Junior High School.

In 1959, I started at Evanston High School, and it was actually okay. I didn't dread going to school, and for the most part, I enjoyed the kids there. I hung with a bunch of good people, but I couldn't make up my mind to be a "greaser" or a "dooper" so I was both. We used the term "dooper" for the collegiate kids. Actually, I didn't use grease on my hair, but used water to make my hair into a pompadour. I would also wear button-down shirts to look Ivy-league. I had friends in both groups, and that worked out well for me. In 1959, I met a local disk jockey named Bob Greenberg, and he was working on a radio station in Evanston, WEAW-AM. That was the first time I ever heard myself on the radio when he played a demo of mine that was just me singing and playing a guitar.

I met Dick Biondi when I was 16 years old. I knocked on his door one day when I found out that he lived in Evanston, and I had brought that same demo to Biondi's house: he was the hottest disc jockey on WLS in 1961. He was the guy who got me started and introduced me to his next door neighbor, Gene Taylor, the program director at WLS.

Later, Gene introduced me to a guy named Pete Wright, who along with Howard Bedno, were two of the biggest record producers in the city of Chicago.

Wright and Bedno said to me, "Okay, bring a tune with you and come on into the studio." So, I brought these guys to back me up, and we recorded on a Chicago label called IRC (International Recording Company). Pete became my manager, and I decided to take the song *Runaway* with me. I went in there, listened to the playback, and said, "No way! That isn't going to work." I wanted to do it again, but it was one of those things—don't call us, we'll call you. Then, after that, IRC gave me a little local record contract; I had my first record come out when I was only 16 years old. It was pretty thrilling. WLS would play the records I made for IRC, and because Pete Wright and Howard Bedno had connections with WLS, they were able to get my songs on the air. Pete and Howard owned Twilight/Twinight Record Company and were affiliated with Don Carone and his orchestra.

When I graduated from Evanston High School, I went to Columbia College for about 10 minutes, and I realized that I wasn't interested in college. For my whole life, the only thing I ever cared about was music, from the first day I listened to radio. When I was just a little kid and we went on vacation, we listened to a guy named Randy Blake who played country-type music. That was before I became interested in rock and roll. Later on, I would get into Top 40 music, and I think that it gave me an appreciation for a variety of music. I am the type of person who kind of jumps around anyway, and it is difficult to keep my interest on any one thing. Around the age of 13, I asked for a guitar, but, before that, I wasn't either singing or playing a musical instrument. So, once I had the guitar, I took lessons for a year. My influences at the time were blues singer, Jimmy Reed, and I liked the honky-tonk, "Chuck Berry-feel" to my music. I also had a strong affinity for ballads.

As the years went by, I never had a big hit record nationally although I was getting plenty of air play in

Chicago. Nothing happened to my career from my first recordings, so I graduated high school, went briefly to Columbia College, and got all of these other jobs, like working at Marshall Field's and Goldblatt's. I didn't have jobs for long periods of time because I was only interested in getting a record out.

At Columbia College, I met these guys who were in a band called The New Colony Six. They had never had a hit record, and all these kids had gone to St. Patrick's High School. They were familiar with me because they had heard my records on the radio. So, they asked me to join the band. Prior to that, I went to see them record a song called *I Confess*, which was their first single in Chicago. The kids' fathers owned a record label called Centaur Records, and *I Confess* came out on that label. Because of Wright and Bedno, who had promoted the tune after I introduced them to The New Colony, the record became the number two song in Chicago. However, at that time, I had not been asked to join the band. I recorded my first single, *Over the Mountain*, at Sound Studios in Chicago where The New Colony Six recorded their hit song. Later on, after *I Confess* came out, and they had established themselves by the next year, they released another song, *I Lie Awake*. That was also a Top 10 song in Chicago, but didn't do anything nationally. Then, they asked me if I wanted to join their group because they wanted to get rid of their keyboard player.

So, although The New Colony Six came out in 1965, I didn't join them until late '66 or in 1967. I played on their record, *I Love You So Much*, that came out in 1967. It was actually their third Top 10 recording in Chicago, but, once again, it wasn't a national hit. In 1967, I did one of the vocal parts for *I Love You So Much*. Then, it just turned into a situation where I wound up singing whatever I wrote. I hooked up with Les Kummel, a friend of mine in Chicago, and, later, he joined the New Colony Six as a bassist. He wasn't yet part of the band, but he and I sat down one day and we both wrote *I'll Always Think About You* and *Things I Like to Say*. So, now, at the age of 22 or 23, I was part of a successful recording group with hit records.

The New Colony Six was the first big rock and roll band out of Chicago. I wrote a song called *Treat Her Groovy*, but it didn't do well. In the New Colony days, there was a guy named Ron Malo at the Chess recording studios, and he gave us the opportunity to record our songs there. He was great, and he had recorded all the top Chicago groups, including the Buckinghams and American Breed. The guy who did all the arrangements for our band and for American Breed (*Bend Me Shape Me* and *Kind of a Drag*) was Eddie Higgins. Higgins used to play at the London House all the time. He did very, very good work, including *I Will Always Think About You*, which I wrote with Les Kummel after *Treat Her Groovy*. Wright and Bedno thought that would be a hit record. We recorded it, and a week later after it was released, one afternoon I heard it being played on WCFL (the big rival of WLS at the time). They were playing their Top Ten countdown every evening with new records that had just been premiered that day. I didn't hear the song and thought it had done nothing. As it turned out, it was the number one song requested that evening. A week later, it was number one in Louisville, Kentucky, and we realized the song was really hot and going to be our biggest record up to that time. It was a national Top 20 record for us and number one in Chicago. We were elated and excited.

Then, *Things I'd Like To Say*, recorded on Mercury Records, came out in late 1968, originally as the "B" side. Larry Lujack pushed the record on WLS-AM, and although *People and Me* was the "A" side, Lujack felt that the "B" side was better, and he told Pete and Howard to promote *Things I'd Like To Say*. He felt it was a hit record and he was right on. We traveled all over the country to promote our biggest hit, *Things I'd Like To Say*. That song became a Top 5 in all the major markets, but not Top 10 in the country, only for one reason: it was not promoted everywhere at the same time.

The '60s were the height of my early career. I got started in 1961, met the New Colony Six in 1963 or 1964, and was invited to join the New Colony Six in 1965. I think that if it weren't for the right timing, me meeting Ray Graffia and New Colony Six, and being invited into the band and the fact that they were already established, who knows if I would ever have had a hit record in my life. So, the combination of the timing of my getting with those guys and them getting airplay in the mid- to late-'60s, if it wouldn't have happened for them, it wouldn't have happened for me. It was just pure luck.

CLARK WEBER | RADIO DISC JOCKEY AND PROGRAM MANAGER, WLS-AM

In 1964, the success of the Beatles' *Hard Day's Night* didn't escape the notice of executives in the record industry. By 1965, Capitol Records decided on a Beatles' nationwide concert tour, including Chicago. To honor the four moptops, Capitol held a luncheon on August 20, 1965 for WLS DJs and the Beatles at the Saddle and Cycle Club on North Lake Shore Drive. That night there would be a concert for the Fab Four at Comiskey Park. It was a sold-out show with over 33,000 screaming kids shelling out $4.50 each to see the Beatles. DJs Bernie Allen, Dex Card and I stepped onto the stage that night to introduce the group and we could feel the sound of those thousands of screaming kids through our fingers. When the Beatles came out on stage to perform I can admit that we never heard a single note of their singing during the 45-minute show.

BROOKE AMLING | IRVING, TX

I'll tell you about the Beatles movie, *A Hard Day's Night*, and I think that was in February of 1964. The Beatles were booked in to play the now defunct Chicago Amphitheater. We were invited to the press conference before their performance because my dad had made this special gold-plated snare drum to present to Ringo Starr. So, we were there and the Beatles were seated at a table and they were delightful and funny and cute. Then it came time for a group photo to be taken and the Beatles were standing against a wall, surrounded by a group of Chicago's finest with their arms linked to prevent intruders from walking into the picture and of course

to keep the Beatles from being mobbed. So my dad had the drum and he was allowed to pass though the police line and then they closed ranks just as I was about to enter the picture. I tapped a policeman on the shoulder and said, "That's my dad, and I'm supposed to be in the picture," and the policeman said, "Yeah, sure, kid." Well, Ringo saw this and reached across the police line, grabbed my arm and said, "Come along, love," and pulled me through the police line and I got into the picture and snap-snap. So, that was pretty neat. We would stay in touch and we enjoy his music. Ringo still has the drum, by the way, and it was on display at the Metropolitan Museum of Modern Art in New York for about a year.

Of course, growing up, we always had drummers coming and going into the house. Joe Morello would come and Ed Shaughnessy, who was Johnny Carson's drummer for so many years on the *Tonight Show*. One time, we were at my parents' house and my daughter was a little girl. Ed Shaughnessy was there and Ed always wore this huge turquoise medallion around his neck. When he went to greet her, he bent over and this medallion swung and smacked her right on the forehead and he felt really bad about it. But it was a funny thing that happened. He also had a booming voice and she said to me, "Mommy... I think Uncle Ed is too loud!"

(Photo courtesy of Brooke Amling)

RESTAURANTS

DON ROTH'S
BLACKHAWK RESTAURANT

ANN ROTH | WIFE OF OWNER OF BLACKHAWK RESTAURANT

Don Roth's Blackhawk Restaurant was opened in 1920 by Don's father, Otto Roth. We are uncertain why he chose that location on Wabash for the restaurant. It may have been because that particular real estate was available. The restaurant business was a risky proposition in the 1920s and got even riskier by the 1930s and the Great Depression. The location of Marshall Field's just west of the restaurant may have been a factor in the selection of the site. It was just a hotbed and a very busy commercial area on Wabash and Randolph, just a block from the Chicago Theater. There was music being played at the Blackhawk before they had jazz orchestras, including string orchestras playing music upstairs.

In fact, they played music there for the first New Year's Eve celebration they had at the Blackhawk. It included a cover charge, dinner and dancing until 2 a.m. and the cost was $1.50 a person. Musical groups were traveling the country in the 1920s and the Blackhawk was one of the locales where it was performed. At that time, Chicago had the Trianon and Aragon Ballrooms where people could go to hear music and dance. The Blackhawk was one of the earliest restaurants to combine food with broadcast music.

I married Don in 1920 and he was very creative when he operated the Blackhawk Restaurant. He had a van to take people to the legitimate theaters and to the opera. There was always a military connection with the Blackhawk because Chicago was a big USO hub. As a result of that, a lot of the sailors and other military personnel who came to the city on their leaves, ate at the Blackhawk. Don was one of the first restaurateurs in this city to have art exhibits which were changed every two or three months. He would get art from galleries in the city, and they were hung in the restaurant on a beautiful backdrop in the main dining room. It helped create a beautiful atmosphere in the restaurant. It was his father who first had music broadcast, nationwide, from the Blackhawk.

PHIL HOLDMAN

I went to the Blackhawk on Wabash Avenue many times, and it was great. It was probably the most famous club because they would put bands on the radio and they were heard all over the country. It started in 1922 and Don Roth owned it and then his son took over when he died. The Blackhawk was a great restaurant and they had the famous Spinning Wheel salad.

JOE LEVINSON | MUSICIAN

The Blackhawk Restaurant on Wabash was right across from Marshall Field's. My mother and father loved to go to good restaurants, and I must have been around 11 years old when I first ate at the Blackhawk. It was a very, very good restaurant. They had the spinning salad bowl, but during the '40s they had jazz bands performing there. I remember that Bob Crosby played there a lot with the Bobcats and when I went there it was the first time that I heard live jazz.

Blackhawk Restaurant, (Courtesy of Ann Roth)

BLACKHAWK

RESTAURANT

"LAUGH IT OFF"
N.Y. YORK MUSICAL COMEDY
BRANDON & ORCHESTRA
LUNCHEON SERVED DAILY

INJUNBAR

BLACKHAWK
INDIAN ROOM

EASTMAN Kodak STORES

Cine Kodaks   Kodaks

Pump Room, (Courtesy of Marc Schulman)

Eli's Stage Delicatessen, Eli Schulman
(Courtesy of Marc Schulman)

MOVIE THEATERS

The largest and most beautiful chain of movie theaters in Chicago history were those owned and operated by the Balaban and Katz Theater Corporation. The Balabans began in the movie theater business in 1908, and, in 1916 they joined with family friends, Sam and Morris Katz to create the B&K Theater Corporation that would come to include such palaces as the Chicago Theater, State-Lake Theater, Oriental Theater, Woods Theater, Roosevelt Theater, and several others throughout downtown Chicago. In addition, there were B&K theaters in the neighborhoods, including the Uptown, Riviera, Granada, Southtown, Howard, and Norshore Theaters among many others across the city and suburbs. The theaters not only offered patrons first-run movies, but also included live stage shows from such entertainers as Benny Goodman, Louis Armstrong, Bob Hope, and Roy Rogers and Trigger. The theaters became Chicago landmarks for top-flight entertainment. In addition to the Balaban and Katz palaces, there were many other neighborhood theaters that were very popular and quite numerous during the 20th century as Chicagoans frequented those entertainment centers sometimes several times a week. In the 1920s, 1930s, and 1940s, the movie houses would present not only movies but short features, newsreels, and cartoons as well as offering free dishes and other gifts as inducements to increase attendance.

CHICAGO THEATER

BOB DAUBER | AUTHOR

Among my other memories of downtown Chicago, of course there was the Chicago Theater. When I started going there, you could go for around $.75 at the same time it cost $.25 at the Granada on Sheridan and Devon. But for $.75, you could go into the Chicago Theater, and who didn't you see there. You'd see a movie and then stage shows by some of the great stars of the day like Martin and Lewis, Bob Hope, Danny Thomas, Spike Jones, Cab Calloway, and an endless procession of jugglers and gymnasts and the folks who used to appear on the *Ed Sullivan Show* on Sunday nights. The stage show followed a single feature at the Chicago Theater, and, quite often, the stars who were in the movie also appeared on stage. Strangely enough, I was at the last stage show at the Chicago Theater in the late '50s and one of the performers was Eydie Gorme. I think that one of the last shows at the Chez Paree was also done by her.

MARC DAVIS | AUTHOR AND FREELANCE WRITER

When Louis Armstrong and his All Stars played the Chicago Theater in the mid-1950s, the huge theater was nearly full. Many in the audience were there to see the movie. But a great many of the crowd were there to see Armstrong and his great quintet of New Orleans-style musicians. The band included Jack Teagarden on trombone; Big Sid Catlett, drums; Bobby Haggart, bass; Dick Cary, piano.

In those long-ago days, the movie and stage show ran continuously and the theater was not cleared after every performance. Consequently, lovers of Louis Armstrong and his musicians remained for show after show, starting with the mid-morning performance. I was among them, a teenager fan of jazz and I lingered through the day, as did so many others.

The highlight of this day for me was the third show, in the afternoon. I had moved up to the first row to hear Louis. Louis must have seen me looking at him during *Basin Street Blues*, he turned toward me and raised his eyebrows.

I read that small gesture of Satchmo's as his way of saying *hello*. I was in my mid-teens and I idolized Armstrong. Thus, his brief, small acknowledgment of my existence was the best part of that day for me almost 70 years ago.

ERFIELD 8"
ZABETH
AYLOR
DIE FISHER
ERFIELD 8
LAURENCE
HOWARD
SUBWAY
WACKER-WABASH

State Street, (Courtesy of the *Chicago Sun-Times*, Inc.),
Copyright 1960, reprinted with permission.

LEGITIMATE THEATERS

AUDITORIUM THEATRE

The Auditorium Theatre opened in 1889 and was designed by Louis Sullivan and Dankmar Adler. Located at 50 E. Congress Parkway, the theatre offered Broadway hit plays, international and local dance and rock concerts. It is now the Chicago home of the Alvin Ailey American Dance Theater and American Ballet Theater as well as the Joffrey Ballet.

RON KAPLAN | MUSICIAN | DALLAS, TX
Michael Silva was Sammy Davis's drummer for many years. I knew of his work, and when Sammy Davis, Jr. began doing *Golden Boy* on Broadway, he made it a point to include his sidemen in the show orchestra so that they could keep working while Sammy did the show. Well, *Golden Boy* came to Chicago and it was playing at the Auditorium Theater in downtown Chicago on Congress. This was before it became the Ida B. Wells Drive. I remember going to see the show with my parents and I think I must have been at least 16 because I was driving. Anyway, after the performance, I went over to the pit area and Michael Silva was packing up his gear. I introduced myself and we talked for a while. Then, I asked what the possibility would be of my sitting next to him in the pit and watching a performance from there. He said that I could do that, just let him know what night would be good for me, and that he would leave my name and I could sit with him for the show. I don't know why, but he took an interest in me and I also found out a little later, that Sammy Davis, Jr. was beginning to move in a different direction with his music. More towards the rock type sound.

Michael Silva was a great jazz drummer, but really didn't know his way around the rock world. We became friendly and I invited him to our home for dinner. Now, I was pretty much into rock music and he asked me if it would be possible for me to lay down some rock beats on a reel-to-reel recorder for him to listen and practice to. He always traveled with a reel-to-reel recorder. So I did that for him. I saw *Golden Boy* several times during that period and, quite often, we would go to the Artists Showcase coffee shop around the corner from the theater. And there would be Sammy Davis, Jr. sitting with Michael Silva, me and about six or eight other people. I have a picture of Michael Silva standing in the doorway to my house and an autographed program from *Golden Boy* signed by Sammy Davis, Jr. Over the years, when Michael would come to town, he'd always come to visit. Obviously a treasured memory for me.

GOODMAN THEATRE

The Goodman is Chicago's oldest currently active nonprofit theater organization. Located in the Loop at 170 N. Dearborn in the city's theater district since 2000, the theater has two modern auditoriums, The Goodman has been awarded a Regional Theatre Tony Award as well as many Joseph Jefferson awards. Originally founded in 1925, the theater was located east of the Art Institute of Chicago before moving to its current location. In 1978 the Goodman School of Drama was taken over by DePaul University.

BLACKSTONE THEATER

(renamed Merle Reskin Theatre)
The theater is a performing arts venue located at 60 E. Balbo Drive in downtown Chicago. Owned by DePaul University, it was founded in 1910 and designed by Marshall and Fox. The theatre has a long history of live performances. It was developed by the owners of the nearby Blackstone Hotel, Tracy and John Drake who also were the proprietors of the famous Drake Hotel on North Michigan Avenue and Lake Michigan. The 1,400-seat theater has featured plays with such actors as Ethel Barrymore, Helen Hayes, Ruth Gordon, and Spencer Tracy. One of the most famous plays to be shown at the Blackstone was Lorraine Hansberry's *A Raisin In The Sun* done in 1959.

SHUBERT THEATER

(now known as the CIBC Theatre)
It is located at 18 W. Monroe Street in downtown Chicago. Operated by the Nederlander Organization, it was originally opened in 1906

SHUBERT

DAVID MERRICK PRESENTS AMERICA'S GREATEST MUSICAL CAROL CHANNING IN HELLO, DOLLY! DIRECTED AND CHOREOGRAPHED BY GOWER CHAMPION

as the Majestic Theatre. Currently seating 1,800 patrons, it presents Broadway plays, although in its early years it was a site for vaudeville celebrity acts. In the 1940s, it became part of the Shubert Organization and was renamed the LaSalle Bank, then Bank of America Theatre, and now CIBC Theatre. Stars who have performed on the site include Al Jolson, Harry Houdini, and Fanny Brice, and, more recently it was the location of *Jersey Boys*, *Kinky Boots, Book of Mormon*, and *Hamilton*.

MARC DAVIS | AUTHOR AND FREELANCE WRITER

We saw Jerry Seinfeld at the Shubert. Not once did he utter an obscenity, an unusual omission since so many standups these days use four letter words as the adjectives and nouns necessary to punch up their material.

Seinfeld asked his audience lots of questions as lead-ins to his bits: Did you ever notice? Have you ever wondered why? Why does it seem like? He was very funny that night, with a PG-Rated act, an increasing rarity these days.

We also saw Jackie Mason at the Shubert. He was in fine form that night, stalking back and forth across the stage, delivering his lines in a Jewish-New York accent and punctuating his gags with a repertoire of hand gestures. We were lucky that night because Mason regaled us with two of his classic bits, which in subsequent years he abandoned for new material.

The first uproariously funny bit was his imitation of Ed Sullivan, the cadaverous TV host of yesteryear who hosted a sort of televised vaudeville show, with jugglers, ventriloquists, singers and comedians. Mason's second dose of shtick, another classic equally hilarious, was his long take on the difference between Gentiles and Jews. This one brought down the house.

STUDEBAKER THEATER

The theater was created in 1898 in The Fine Arts Building on South Michigan Avenue. It was originally built to showcase vaudeville, but productions were expanded in the 1920s and, over the years, such stars as Bob Hope, Peter O'Toole, and Vincent Price performed at the Studebaker. In the 1970s, the theater was converted into four separate movie theaters before closing in 2000. The theater, which holds 740 seats, would reopen for live performances in 2016.

HULL HOUSE THEATER

The Hull House Theater was located on the city's Near West Side at 800 S. Halsted Street. It was established as an amateur theater in 1899. Later in the 1900s, Hull House Theater in the Jane Addams Center at 3212 North Broadway on the North Side became a venue for road tours of Broadway plays as guided by Robert Sickinger.

ERLANGER THEATER

The theater opened on April 1, 1912 as the Palace Music Hall and was located at 127 N. Clark Street in downtown Chicago. In January 1926, Abraham Erlanger acquired the lease to the building and, after remodeling the theater, renamed it the Erlanger Theater. It reopened on October 10, 1926 and was primarily a legitimate theater house although, over the years, it did show a few movies. The theater closed on March 10, 1962, with a stage production of *Bye Bye Birdie*, and the building was demolished soon after. Today it is the site of the Richard J. Daley Civic Center.

HARRIS AND SELWYN THEATERS

These twin theaters, now part of the redesigned Goodman Theater, at 180-190 N. Dearborn Street, were built by Sam H. Harris and Archie and Edgar Selwyn. In the 1950s, the theaters were purchased by producer Michael Todd, converted into movie theaters, and renamed the Michael Todd Theater and Michael Todd's

Victory Gardens Theater,(Courtesy of the *Chicago Sun-Times,* Inc.), photographer–Gene Pesek, Copyright, 1974, reprinted with permission.

Cinestage. Eventually, the Harris would show live performances such as *Two For The Seesaw* starring Ruth Roman. However, both theaters were closed in the 1980s, briefly re-opened in 1986 as the Dearborn Cinemas, but by 2000 they were completely gutted and rebuilt as part of the new Goodman Theater.

IVANHOE THEATER

The theater was located on Wellington, between Clark and Halsted on the city's North Side in the Lakeview neighborhood, and was in operation from the 1970s until the 1990s. The Tennessee Williams play *Out Cry* premiered at the Ivanhoe in 1971, and such stars as Jessica Tandy, Joan Fontaine, Piper Laurie, Christopher Walken, Sandy Dennis, Rita Moreno, Luther Adler, and Bruce Boxleitner appeared at the Ivanhoe when it was a theater-in-the-round.

RICHARD CHRISTIANSEN | DRAMA CRITIC

I held the title of critic-at-large and chief critic, but never had the title of the drama critic. I first started reviewing plays and theater in Chicago around the early '60s, but didn't take over the Panorama section in the *Chicago Daily News* until 1965. In the '50s and up until the early '60s, most of the theater in Chicago included shows that were brought in from New York with touring companies. The plays were seen downtown at theaters like the Shubert, Blackstone, Erlanger, Harris, and Selwyn. There was not much Chicago-based theater at the time, and, in the late '50s, things were in a rather sorry state among the touring companies. The great stars of the past were no longer touring since the lure of movies and television had taken the bloom off the desire of Broadway stars to travel around the country doing plays. They wanted to perform in New York, and then go into movies and television and make some money right away. Chicago didn't get many first-run Broadway shows, and, instead, we would get sort of smudged carbon copies of the Broadway productions, with only a few exceptions. One example of a different approach was the pre-Broadway production

of *Raisin In The Sun*, which played at the Blackstone on its way to New York. You would get things like that occasionally but, on the whole, the touring companies were not first quality.

The Chicago scene began to change when The Second City opened in December 1959. It was a very significant date because here was a home-grown resident company made up of Chicago talent which caught on and was an immediate success. It justified the fact that you could put on a very good evening in the theater, albeit a cabaret theater, without the inclusion of former television or movie stars. Compass Players had been a predecessor to Second City, but I have to confess that I never saw the Compass Players when they performed in Chicago. They were a brilliant group, and included people like Shelley Berman, Mike Nichols, Elaine May, and Eugene Troobnick who were incredibly talented. Then, when Second City came along in '59, there had also been the Studebaker Theater Company in the old Studebaker Theater on South Michigan Avenue. It had been started by Bernie Sahlins in an effort have a resident theater company, but it only lasted two seasons during the mid '50s and closed because they had no real funding base. Despite those previous failures, Second City caught on. The cabaret format worked very well for it, the talent was there, and the time was right. People like Barbara Harris and Alan Arkin came in very early, and were supported by a great local cast of people who were incredibly brilliant doing political and social satire.

One of the great turning points in local theater came in 1963 when Hull House Theater opened in the old Jane Addams Center, at Belmont and Broadway, directed by Bob Sickinger. As far as I am concerned, it was Sickinger who really made an exclamation point statement that Chicago could produce good theater on its own. He used such great actors as Mike Nussbaum, who was working in the pest exterminator business when Sickinger came along, and was a part time actor. Mike became a stalwart of the Sickinger theater company when they performed at Hull House. Bob had an amazing work ethic, and he brought to Chicago plays by Pinter and Beckett and Albee for the first time. Hull House was a little theater that only had about 110 seats, but the impact was tremendous among people who went to the theater.

It was a revelation you could have casts with people whose names you had never heard of, and yet, they were quite wonderful. Sickinger did productions of *The Three Penny Opera*, the Chicago premiere of Albee's *Tiny Alice*, Kenneth Brown's *The Brig*, and a lot of off-Broadway and European avant-garde plays that were superbly done by this cast of primarily non-Equity actors. It expanded for a while up to the Hull House on Beacon Street on the North Side, and added musicals there. For about five or six years, Sickinger's flame was very, very bright in Chicago, and, then, Bob sort of burned out. He had a falling out with the trustees of the Hull House Theater and left town with some bitterness. But, he had absolutely made the point that you could produce very, very exciting and rewarding resident theater in Chicago.

In 1969, when the Sickinger explosion had taken place, at long last, John Reich, who was the head of the Goodman Theater at the time, was able to turn the Goodman from a student into a professional operation. It had been working since the Depression as a place where student plays were produced. Reich, with the aid of Danny Newman, the publicist and subscription maestro, brought in professional guest artists to work with the students. Then, by the '60s, the mood was right for it to become completely professional. In 1969, it became a professional resident company, still under the aegis of the Art Institute. But, it wasn't really until David Mamet came along in the mid-'70s that the Goodman acquired its luster. It had experienced successes as a professional theater, but Mamet and Greg Mosher, the director, gave it a kind of pizzazz and flash that it had not had before. Then, when Mosher took over as artistic director of the Goodman in 1978, it was right in tune with the march of resident theater in Chicago.

I think that it was a gradual dawning for New York to recognize that Chicago regional theater was important. Of course, it didn't hurt when we had a playwright in our midst named David Mamet. David had his first full-length play, *Sexual Perversity in Chicago*, produced by Organic Theater in 1974, and he was certainly recognized by 1975 when *American Buffalo* was written and produced, first at the Goodman Stage Two, and then transferred to David's own St. Nicholas Theater on Halsted Street. When that came along, and *A Life In The Theater* was produced, it was obvious that he was a playwright of great talent. He won the New York Drama Critics' Prize for the best new American play of the season in 1975-76.

At that time, there was a small theater movement beginning to form in Chicago. The Chicago City Players began in a little church on Wellington Avenue. Their plays were produced by June Pyskacek, who, in turn, founded the Kingston Mines Theater on Lincoln Avenue. The group did wonderful productions of the off-Broadway plays of the time, and launched the world premiere of a little show called *Grease* in 1971. That again was an important breakthrough because it showed that a Chicago show had potential to go beyond the borders of the city and to become an important force in the theater business. Once *Grease* had left Chicago and was transplanted to the commercial marketplace of New York, for a while it was the longest running show in Broadway history, later eclipsed by other shows. That was important because it demonstrated the fact that you could produce something of local value with national importance.

I became aware of Gary Sinise and Steppenwolf when they started in 1975 at a church in Highland Park on Deerfield Road. That was another significant move forward for resident theater in Chicago because it was a phenomenal instance of a group of talent coming together in a really incredible way. You would go up there and see Terry Kinney, Gary Sinise, Joan Allen, Laurie Metcalf, and John Malkovich performing together, and it was an exciting mix of talented actors. They did the kind of very intense productions that Gary would loosely call "rock and roll" theater. It was a physical and emotionally tight theater with brilliant ensemble work from those

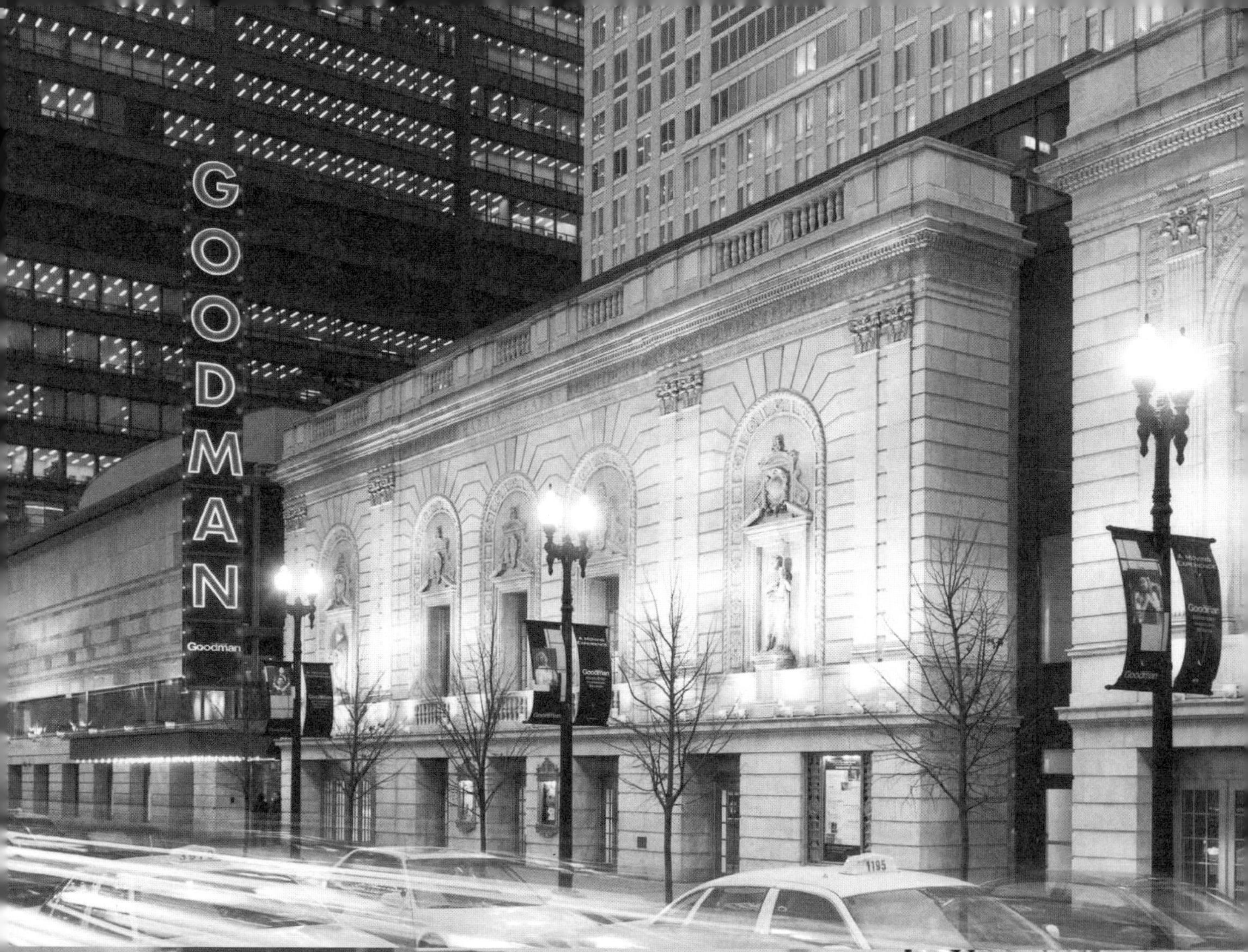
GOODMAN
Goodman

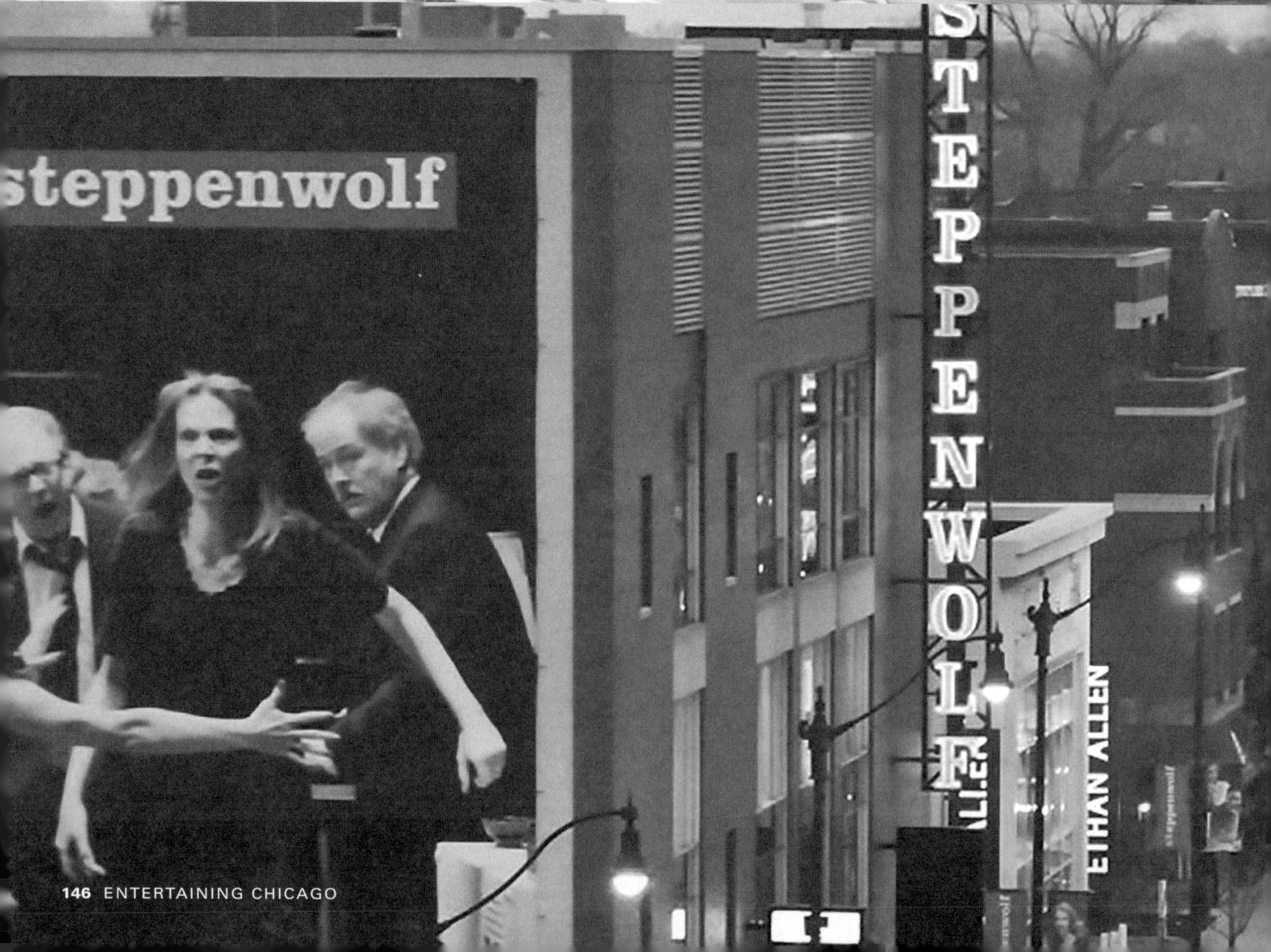
steppenwolf
STEPPENWOLF
ETHAN ALLEN

Gary Sinise at Steppenwolf, (Courtesy of the *Chicago Sun-Times*, Inc.), photographer–Carmen Reporto, Copyright, 1960. reprinted with permission

Breakfast Special JUICE 2 EGGS Bacon or Ham Toast, Jelly, Coffee $1.65

young people, many of whom had been students at Illinois State University.

The Body Politic, started by the Reverend Jim Shifflet at 2257 N. Lincoln Avenue, was truly a product of the youth movement of the late '60s and early '70s. When Jim opened that, he opened a theater as well as other branches of the visual and performing arts. One of his first residents in the Body Politic was Paul Sills' Story Theater, another groundbreaking theater. When Paul moved out, Stuart Gordon moved in with his Organic Theater, which had come to Chicago about a year or so earlier.

Victory Gardens was in operation in 1974, and Billy Peterson got active as an actor in the '70s. He was a student of Dennis Zochek at Victory Gardens on Clark Street. He starred in a play called *Dillinger* there, and then, Billy and a group of other actors formed Remains Theater in the late '70s. Again, it was a group of incredibly talented people including Billy, Amy Morton, Gary Cole, and Donnie Moffett, and they had a real ensemble heat among them. They were up in a little pie-shaped space on north Clark Street and did amazing work there.

By the mid to late-'70s, the foundation of Chicago theater was established. This included "poor" theaters, not in terms of quality but in terms of financial strength, such as the storefront and second floor theaters, which included Victory Gardens, Body Politic, and Wisdom Bridge. Later on, the Evanston Theater Company was formed, and that evolved into the Northlight Theater Company.

STEPPENWOLF THEATRE COMPANY

In 1974, Terry Kinney, Jeff Perry, and Gary Sinise founded the Steppenwolf Theatre Company at the Unitarian Church on Half Day Road in the northern suburb of Deerfield. The Company is now located at 1650 N. Halsted Street on Chicago's North Side in a new facility that offers a season of multiple plays each year. In 1982, the Sam Shepard play *True West* was offered, starring Sinise and Steppenwolf Theatre Company ensemble member and movie star John Malkovich. The famous ensemble includes such well-known names as Laurie Metcalf, Joan Allen, Amy Morton, William Petersen, Martha Plimpton, Tracy Letts, and Austin Pendleton. The Theatre Company has won many awards, including the Tony Award for Regional Theatre Excellence in 1985 and the National Medal for Arts in 1998.

GARY SINISE | ACTOR

I was born in 1955 and lived in Harvey until I was nine years old when we moved to Highland Park. In mid-seventh grade, my family moved again, this time to Chicago's western suburb of Glen Ellyn. We lived there through 7th and 8th grades and my freshman year at Glenbard West High School before moving once again, back north again to Highwood, the suburb just north of Highland Park along the lake.

I was playing guitar more, and I really began getting active with my music when I joined a band while we lived in Glen Ellyn. The move to Glen Ellyn was tough for me because I didn't know anybody in that suburb, and it's always hard when a young kid is new to a neighborhood. Luckily, I met somebody who also played guitar. He asked me to join their band, and we began playing at parties and doing various events. When I moved back to Highwood, I stayed in touch with the guys in Glen Ellyn and kept playing with the band. We even named the band after a street in Highwood, Half Day Road. My musical influences in the late '60s were Jimmy Hendrix, The Who, and Led Zeppelin, and, a little bit later, the Allman Brothers and Grand Funk. In fact, Gary Sinise and the Lieutenant Dan Band that I have today play an eclectic mix of genres: country, blues, pop, rock, and classics by these same artists who influenced me early on.

My acting career began with a minor role in a play at Glenbard West during my freshman year. I think it was an original play that a student wrote called *Who Says There's a War On?* I really got involved in acting at Highland Park High School, as a sophomore when I was in the musical *West Side Story* in the early '70s. I was standing in the school hallway one day with members of my rock band and we looked pretty scruffy. The drama teacher was walking down the hall, and when she passed us she turned around, walked back and said, "I'm doing *West Side Story* and you guys would be great gang members for the play. So, come to the audition." We kind of laughed, but a few of us went and auditioned and two of us were cast. That was when I really started doing theater, and, after that, I just wanted to be selected for every play they were producing at the high school.

I graduated from Highland Park High School in 1974, but didn't go to college, and, instead, started Steppenwolf Theater. We began doing plays at a Unitarian church on Half Day Road in Deerfield near I-294. It was a beautiful building, and my parents knew the architect. I asked them if they thought the church would let us do a play there, and the church agreed to it. They gave us a key so we could go in there after school and rehearse our plays. That was when and where Steppenwolf was born which I started with my friends Terry Kinney, Jeff Perry, and some others from Highland Park High School who were involved in those early days. We only did a few plays because Jeff and Terry were in college at that time. So, the three of us made a bond to get together when they completed college, start a theater company, and make a serious attempt to make it successful. We were watching Pacino, DeNiro, Brando, Robert Duvall, Gene Hackman, Dustin Hoffman, and guys like that in the early '70s. We were heavily influenced by them as well as Elia Kazan and John Cassavettes.

So, in 1976, Terry, Jeff, and I got together with John Malkovich, Laurie Metcalf, Moira Harris, who would be my future wife, and other actors and began working out of the basement of a catholic school on Deerfield Road in Highland Park where we had built an 88-seat theater. It was a talented group, and we remained in the basement until 1979 when we moved to the North Side of Chicago into the Jane Addams Center at Belmont and Broadway. We opened there in March of 1980 and were there for a couple of years until 1982. Then, we moved the

company to 2851 N. Halsted into a building that was a former milk company garage. The St. Nicholas Theater with David Mamet and William H. Macy had been started there in the early to mid 70's, but they went bankrupt about six years later, and the building sat empty. We were looking for a new space, so we took over that building in 1982 and were there until 1991 when we opened our new building at 1650 N. Halsted. I am still actively involved at Steppenwolf at the executive level and I raise money for the company. No matter what I do or where I go, Chicago will always be in my blood. I am always proud to say that I am from Chicago. My kind of town.

WILLIAM "BILL" PETERSEN | ACTOR

The first acting I did in Chicago was at the Jewish Community Center in Skokie. I read that they were having open auditions for a play called *Darkness At Noon* based on a book dealing with Russians captured by Germans in World War II and written in the 1950s by Arthur Koestler. The director wanted me to play the German prosecutor since there were all Jews there and I looked Aryan. It was a big thing even though it was only two weekends of performances.

I started the Remains Theater Company in 1979 and acted at Remains Theater, Victory Gardens, and Steppenwolf Theater during those years.

JOE MANTEGNA | ACTOR

I was born in 1947 and grew up on the West Side, first on Polk Street, across from the old Sears, Roebuck on Homan and Arthington. My mother worked at that Sears, and we lived in an apartment nearby. We moved west, but before going to Morton East High School in Cicero, I had no more desire to be an actor than the "man in the moon." However, it was the play and film, *West Side Story*, which had a huge impact on my acting career that developed in high school. When the movie came out, they had auditions for the play that fall when I was a junior in high school. I didn't know it was a play, and, at that point, I had only seen two plays in my life because my family did not go to the theater. The high school drama teacher wanted to cast as many kids as possible because the teacher needed all these guys to play the gang members. They were making a concerted effort to recruit kids from the school who normally wouldn't try out for plays.

There I was on the stage with the footlights in my eyes, and it was magical for me, like being in a fantasy world. I sang the song, *Maria*, heard applause in front of footlights, and, I swear at that instant I knew I wanted to become an actor. When I walked off the stage, I felt like I was floating, and I heard people saying "Thank you, thank you very much, that was wonderful!" I went home that night, and all I could think about was that audition and how badly I wanted to be in the play. It was so strange for me because 24 hours earlier I didn't even know about the play. The next morning, I got to school early because I wanted to see if my name was on the cast list. I looked at the list, and I was devastated to find that I hadn't been selected for the cast.

At that moment, I became aware that my interest in the theater was real. In fact, I decided to talk to the head of the drama department because I heard that one of the kids in the show had been injured during rehearsals. I thought that I could get into the play that way. I talked to the teacher who was directing the play and who was the head of the department. He said, "No, the kid just sprained his ankle and he'll be fine. But, I remember you from the audition, and I really like your enthusiasm. Why don't you come into my advanced drama class?" I was amazed by his offer since I had never taken a drama class in my life. I said, "Okay." So, I juggled my schedule, and the next thing I know I was taking drama during my junior year at Morton East High School.

I graduated from Morton East and then went to Morton Junior College for two years, which was on the same campus. It worked out well for me because it was the same drama department for the high school and the college, and they combined students from the junior college and the high school for a lot of the productions, as well as students from Morton West High School in Berwyn. One of my friends, who was a year ahead of me at the junior college, had enrolled in the Goodman School of Drama in the Art Institute, and he suggested that it was a cool place to go.

Again, I had no money and my parents had no money, so I couldn't go away to college. I applied for a government loan and used that money for the tuition, which was around $800. Although auditions were not required to be admitted to Goodman, you did need letters of recommendation, and I had such letters from Morton Junior College. I was admitted to Goodman, lived off the student loan, and went there for two years from 1967 to 1969. In my second year, I received a scholarship that paid for some of the costs. But, I still needed another government loan to have money to live on because, by that time, I had moved out of my parents' house and was living with friends in an apartment in Old Town.

In the summer of 1969, they had tryouts for the play *Hair*. It was a summer-long process, but ultimately, I was cast in the play about a couple of weeks before school would have started. I had to make the decision whether to join the cast of *Hair* or go back to school for my third, and final year at the Goodman. I met with the dean, and he said, "Look, you've been here two years. You go to the school in order to become a professional actor. So, since somebody offered you a job, go do it." Thus, in the fall of 1969, in Chicago, I began my professional acting career.

MIKE NUSSBAUM | ACTOR

I got into drama when I was in high school, and I was doing school plays, including *Romeo and Juliet*. I also used to do some kind of stand-up impressions of famous actors of the time. I was probably about 9 or 10 years old when I got my first interest in acting, and I started at Camp Ojibwa in Eagle River, Wisconsin, and it was one of the more important events of my life being able to go to that camp. I had rheumatic fever as a young boy, and I was unable to engage in a lot of activity. When I was cured of it, my parents sent me to camp and I suddenly discovered that I had athletic ability and that I also had the ability to act on stage. It was a seminal event when I went to Camp Ojibwa and it changed my entire life. The clean, cold air of northern Wisconsin was good for me as well as the fact that it was highly competitive and I found that I thrived under competition. One would have thought that was a bad thing, but, for me, it was good. When I came back to Chicago, and during high school, I got involved in drama classes and acting at Von Steuben. In 1941, I graduated and, first, I went to the University of Wisconsin for a year and a half and then I went into the war in March 1943.

During the '50s, I wasn't in any big plays, and I didn't get into acting professionally until the beginning of 1960 when I did a show with the Second City Repertory Company. This was an offshoot that had been started by Bernie Sahlins and Paul Sills and Sheldon Patinkin. We took over a theater called the Harper Theater in Hyde Park, but it failed. I was in the original company of the Body Politik that Paul Sills started, but when they moved the repertory company to LaSalle Street, I dropped out because it required more time than I was able to give to it.

In the early '60s, that was the beginning of Hull House, and in 1961 or 1962, Bob Sickinger came to Chicago. He had operated a theater in Philadelphia, and he somehow hooked up with Hull House run by Paul Jans, and created a little theater near Broadway and Belmont. That was the beginning of the Chicago theater renaissance and all of the 200 or so theaters that Chicago has today can trace their lineage back to Bob Sickinger and that theater at Hull House. Richard Christiansen would come to review the plays, and it was the first time that non-professional theater got reviews. The audiences represented the kind of intellectual seekers who had not, in the past, gone to that kind of theater. It was just a remarkable upsurge. David Mamet worked backstage as a 14-year-old kid while I was doing a play there, and I met him. That was the beginning of the theater program, and St. Nicholas, the Organic Theater, and Steppenwolf grew out of that environment. Subsequently, David Mamet and I did a play together that was written by Dick Cusack. It was a terrible play. One night, he gave me a copy of a play of his called *The Duck Variations* and

I realized that David didn't have to act because he was a brilliant playwright. I also got some small parts in movies that were being shot in Chicago, and, then, after a while, I went out to Los Angeles to look for work and it worked out nicely.

In 1970, I went into acting on a full-time basis. Until then, for about 10 years, I was doing a lot of commercials and theater, and whatever income came in from the commercials, I would put into the business as a subsidiary income. It made me feel that I could devote my time to acting. Eventually, I realized that it was unfair to my partner and to me to do acting on a part-time basis. Over the years, I have worked at almost every theater in Chicago.

COMEDY CLUBS

ZANIES COMEDY CLUB

Zanies was founded in November 1978 by Rick Uchwat. The club, which has other locations in Chicago, Nashville, Tennessee, St. Charles, Illinois and Rosemont, Illinois is considered by many to be the perfect comedy club and, for many, it became the king of Chicago's comedy clubs. Among the numerous big-name comedians who have performed there were Jerry Seinfeld, Kathy Griffin, Lewis Black, Richard Lewis, Jay Leno, Chris Rock, Tim Allen, Jimmy Fallon, Gilbert Gottfried, and Roseanne Barr.

MARC DAVIS | AUTHOR AND FREELANCE WRITER | CHICAGO, IL

I remember the great comedians performing in Chicago. For example, I saw Richard Lewis perform at Zanies in Vernon Hills. Lewis in a black suit, black shirt, matching dark circles under his eyes, raved and ranted relentlessly, for more than an hour without seeming to take a breath. His act consisted in large part of hilarious neurotic kvetching. If you didn't know he was a comedian, you'd think he was unloading on his long-suffering shrink.

ALL JOKES ASIDE

It was a popular, 275-seat comedy club located in the city's South Loop that catered primarily to African Americans. It was co-owned by Raymond Lambert, and during the 1990s it was considered by many to be one of the most influential comedy venues in the country. The club opened in 1992 and lasted for a decade, offering such well-known comedians as Cedric the Entertainer, Steve Harvey, Jamie Foxx, D.L. Hughley, Martin Lawrence, Bernie Mac, Chris Rock, and Donald Glover.

SECOND CITY

The premier improvisational comedy club in America, it also had programs operating at one time in Toronto and Los Angeles. Second City also produced television programs in both Canada and the United States including SCTV and *Saturday Night Live*. It grew from the Compass Players that operated in the Hyde Park neighborhood on the city's South Side. Its first show premiered in 1959 at 1842 North Wells Street in Old Town and then moved to 1616 North Wells where it is today. It was founded by Bernie Sahlins and Paul Sills and among its many notable alumnus have been Bill Murray, John Candy, Dan Aykroyd, Tina Fey, Steve Carell, Stephen Colbert, Harold Ramis, Martin Short, and such original members as Shelley Berman who began at Compass Players.

SHELDON PATINKIN | ACTOR | EDUCATOR

In high school, at U-High, I was in plays. Then, I became part of University Theater at the University of Chicago when I was 16 years old. I wanted to become an actor until I started working backstage at University Theater and discovered I liked that a lot better. In 1953, during the end of my second year in college, we opened Playwrights Theater Club and that ran for two years. Next, Compass Players opened in July 1956, then Second City in 1958. I wasn't part of Compass, and I was getting my MA and PhD in English Literature at that point. I didn't start at Second City until close to a year after it opened, and I just couldn't take graduate school anymore. Bernie Sahlins called me and asked me if I was going to be an English teacher for the rest of my life, and that was when things really changed and I started at Second City.

Playwrights Theater happened after we broke away from University Theater in 1953 and we opened our own space at North and LaSalle Streets on the city's North Side. Up until Playwrights Theater, except for an occasional itinerant group that would book a space and do a play, the only local theater was school, community, church/synagogue theater, and the Goodman Theater was a "school theater." In fact, until then, visiting a theater meant going downtown to the plays that had been sent from New York City, and there about eight or 10 legitimate theaters in those years, and a lot more than that in Chicago during the 1920s and 1930s.

Playwrights opened June 23, 1953 at 1516 N. LaSalle, above of a drugstore in a converted Chinese restaurant. The initial group included Paul Sills, David Shepherd, and Eugene Troobnik who were the original founders, and Bernie Sahlins replaced Troobnik after a few months. Actors included Ed Asner, Barbara Harris, Bern and Joyce Piven, Joyce Hiller, Mike Nichols, and Elaine May. Many of them came out of the University of Chicago. It was an odd time because there were no theater classes or department at the University of Chicago, so it was all extracurricular. We existed for almost two years during which time we did close to 30 plays. I was the box office manager, the production manager, the lighting designer, the costume designer (once), and the musical director and pianist, as well as assistant director, and an actor only when there were more roles than we had people to fill them. It was quite an exciting time.

The plays were very successful, even though we only seated 100-125 at a performance, but we were really very good. But, by that point, the desire was much stronger to do the improvised thing which is what had originally been the intention, but we weren't ready for that yet. Compass Players was the next logical step, and Compass was totally improvisational. It started with a somewhat different form from Second City, but it ended with exactly the Second City form. We did a living newspaper based on that day's newspaper, and then a seven-scene scenario which had been written by a member of the company and then improvised out. Then, they took suggestions and came back and improvised. After about a year, scenarios got harder and harder to agree on, and, more and more of the improvisational sets turned out to be repeatable. In the early years, Compass Players was located in Hyde Park near the University of Chicago. Actually, David Shepherd, who was producer, wanted to open it in Gary, Indiana, but he was talked out of that. He wanted to be where the people were. So, we opened it on 55th Street at the back room of Jimmy's Tavern and then at the Dock in Lake Park. Eventually, it moved to the North Side, and that's when Shelly Berman joined it.

The Compass Players started in Chicago and then moved to St. Louis because business didn't really work that well on the North Side at Devon, just south of Broadway. David Shepherd had an offer to bring the Compass to the new Gaslight Square in St. Louis, so he moved it there. He was producer of Playwrights and of Compass. Those who moved to St. Louis included Elaine May and Mike Nichols, and they were joined there by Alan Arkin, Jerry Stiller, Anne Meara, and Del Close. Barbara Harris didn't go to St. Louis. Then, in 1958, Bernie Sahlins opened the Studebaker for a year to do repertory, but that didn't work out too well either so Bernie and Paul decided to open Second City. It was really the Compass, but David wouldn't give them the name, although he gave them a lot of help. So, they named it after a series of articles in the New Yorker, by A. J. Liebling that was a really snotty investigation of Chicago, the second city.

The early days of Second City were very exciting. We had a built-in audience because everyone knew it was the Compass again, and, by that point, Old Town was exploding. We originally opened at the other end of Old Town at 1842 N. Wells that was then the last block of Wells, but it is now where Hemingway House is located. Within months of opening, *Time* Magazine had reviewed us and called us a "temple of satire." We were selling out two shows a night and three on Saturday. We called it the Club in those days. And, then, a year and a half later we built next door to us and half of what was our beer garden, at 1846 N. Wells and called it Playwrights at Second City. We opened with a first revue by Jules Pfeiffer, based on his comic strips. And, then we did an improvised jazz Chicago set, a variation on *Three Penny Opera* with Alan Arkin as McKie. Business wasn't really all that great at Playwrights at Second City, so we moved it next door to the old Second City, which was smaller. And we moved Second City to the bigger space at 1846 N. Wells. We continued with the revues at Second City and we did the first Chicago production at Playwrights at Second City of *The Caretaker, The Death of Bessie Smith, Krabbs Last Tape,* and *The Maze.* By that

point, we were selling out, and it became clear that we couldn't afford to continue an equity theater in a 125-seat house and make a profit. So, we closed it. Then, eventually we moved Second City to where we are now: 1616 N. Wells at Pipers Alley.

JOYCE SLOANE | CO-FOUNDER | SECOND CITY

I grew up in Chicago and got married in the '50s. After a trip to the West Coast we returned to Chicago, I decided to get a divorce. But I needed to find a job because my daughter had been born. I had a "Dutch uncle" named Hal Zeiger, and he produced a show called *The Borscht Capades* with Mickey Katz and Joel Grey. My cousin, Jack Hilliard, who was a singer in the show, told Hal about my job search, and Zeiger said to me, "As long as you're staying home to raise your daughter, why don't you sell theater parties?" I didn't even know what that entailed, but I soon discovered that I could get an organization to sponsor a performance. Hal also got me connected with the Erlanger Theater, and I sold theater parties for their show "*Once Upon A Mattress*" which became a big hit.

After that, I received a call from Al Weisman of Foote, Cone and Belding to work for a show called *Mr. and Mrs.* with Marilyn Maxwell and Jackie Coogan. It was sponsored and produced by Johnson Wax, and Al wanted me to sell theater parties for his company. Although I still had a baby at home, I needed the income and accepted the opportunity. I went to see Al, and he suggested that I should also contact Irving Seidner who was opening a little club on Wells Street. Irv sent me over to meet Bernie Sahlins, the founder of Playwrights at Second City, and during our meeting in early 1960, Bernie and I crawled through the theater that they were just building. We looked over the place and discussed the development of a strategy for making the place into a success.

The first show at Playwrights was going to be a production of Jules Pfeiffer's *The Explainers*. Bernie asked me to sell out the first week, but I didn't know that no theater opens with the entire first week sold out. I was so young that I did what I was asked to do, but I had a problem because there were two groups that wanted to buy out the opening night: the University of Chicago Cancer Research Foundation and the Travelers Aid Society Junior Board. I called Sheldon Patinkin, who partnered with Bernie, and he said, "It's not a problem. We'll make one of the shows a preview." We opened soon after, and that was the beginning of the original Second City which was located at 1846 N. Wells Street, north of the current location. After that, Bernie never thought that there was anything too difficult for me to accomplish.

In the mid to late '60s, Second City was doing fine in Chicago, even though we weren't selling out every night. Business wasn't as big as it is now, and, in 1967, we decided to move to our current location in Piper's Alley. Although we were doing okay, we had some lean times, and it was hard keeping track of our operations in Chicago and Toronto. Things were good on both fronts and we had a great cast in Toronto that included Dan Aykroyd, and his partner, Valerie Bromfield, one the funniest people I had ever known. Gilda came to see us when we were playing the Second City touring company in Ann Arbor, told us she wanted to join our company, so, of course, we hired her. It was a wonderful company that also included Eugene Levy and Jane Eastwood. *Second City Television* (SCTV) is what made Toronto a hit, and it became like a cult show. The great John Candy worked in Chicago before he worked in Toronto, and when he came here, supposedly for a week or so, he had about 12 bags of luggage when I picked him up at the airport. By the mid-to late-'60s, you literally couldn't drive down Wells Street when Old Town became so popular, the traffic was bumper-to-bumper, and Second City was so successful.

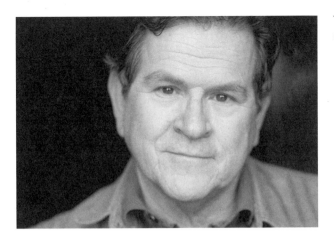

Tim Kazurinsky,
(Courtesy of Tim Kazurinsky).

TIM KAZURINSKY | PROFESSIONAL ACTOR AND FEATURED PERFORMER AT SECOND CITY AND A MEMBER OF THE *SATURDAY NIGHT LIVE* CAST

In 1976 I was working as a copywriter at the Leo Burnett Ad Agency and as a favor to one of the art directors, I agreed to help promote a play his friend had written that was being mounted at the Playwright's Center in Chicago. It was a wildly funny absurdist show called *The Mystical Body of the Meat Grinder*. I offered to do some PR work for them. When I met with them, I found out that there was a budget of $400. That was not the budget for promotion. That was the budget for the entire production—the set and everything. I thought, "Well, there's not much that can be done with the $30 they had left." So I came up with an idea for a funny flyer that the actors could hand out at L-stops near their homes during rush hour. (Believe it or not, this actually worked and we ended up with pretty good audiences at the production.)

When one of the actors had to drop out of the show, I was asked to take his place. It was a small role. Though I had never been in a show…I said I would do it. A few days later, the show's director came to rehearsal naked and freaked everybody out. After that, nobody would work with him. So the playwright, William Lederer, had to fire him. Then he asked me to finish directing the show. While I thought this was totally crazy, I agreed to do it. Then things went from crazy to insane. Right before opening night, the lead actor got very ill—and had to be hospitalized. Who the hell was Lederer going to get to do that role on such short notice? Why…me, of course. So now this ad man from Leo Burnett, who four weeks prior had volunteered to do some PR work for this production, was now the director and male lead in this show!

The show had a limited run of a few weeks. But here's the point: Immediately after doing this show, I flew to California to shoot a commercial for Oldsmobile that had a budget of $100,000. In 1976, that was a lot of money for a TV spot. Yet in the process of shooting the spot, I realized that I'd had a hell of a lot more fun and got a whole lot more satisfaction doing the absurdist play with a budget of $400… than I had doing that big budget TV commercial.

Now, continuing my job as an adman at Leo Burnett, I realized that I needed to strengthen my skills when presenting my storyboards to the creative review board at the agency. It was a three-man group that sat at the end of long table, and they would pass judgment on the copywriter's efforts. I was always nervous and not very good at presenting. These guys, most of who lived in Lake Forest or Glencoe, sat there in their expensive suits, chain-smoking whatever cigarettes the agency was in business with. They really intimidated me. As a result of the Playwright's Center experience, I decided to look into taking an improv acting course at Second City to help me get over my fear of presenting. It was great fun and I ended up joining a new improv group called *The Survivors*. There were six of us and after months of working for free, we landed our first paying job. It was to be part of what was called the Lincoln Avenue Poor Arts Festival. I think this was around 1977. Our director was a great guy named Dan. On the day we performed, Lincoln Avenue was closed off and it was the hottest day of the year. When we finished performing, all hot and sweaty, someone sent us to a place to cool off. It was the Body Politic Theater, which was under extensive renovation at the time. We went in, and it was very dark and I could barely see. We were steered to a stairway leading up to the second floor. I was the first one to enter the dark stairway. I remember there were lots of people laughing and in the dark, these cackling thespians picked me up and carried me up the stairs. While doing this, they began removing my clothes. When I was finally delivered upstairs, naked, wondering what the hell was going on, I was plunged into a bathtub that had been filled with cocktail-sized ice cubes—over which peppermint schnapps had been poured. It remains one of the most bizarre, aromatic, refreshing experiences of my life. Surrounded by a sea of merry pranksters laughing faces, I came to the epiphany that this was an infinitely more interesting way of life than the advertising business. And these loons were the people I wanted to be around for the rest of my life. These were theater people. And I wanted to try to become one of them.

FOOTNOTE: Dan, our director, took the $200 we made on that gig and bought himself a plane ticket to New York—where he went on to become a successful actor. None of us were upset about that. We actually thought it was hilarious. In fact, over the next few years, we would see his face in TV commercials and we were proud to have contributed $25 each to help jump-start his career.

One time on main stage at Second City, I was doing an intro for a spooky scene and I was trying to do an impersonation of Rod Serling. My lines went something like this: "Time. Space. Double-Time. Double-Space. You are now entering another dimension. A dimension known as…The Twilight Zone." As I delivered these lines, I exited the stage towards the left wing. But like an idiot, I wasn't looking where I was going and I walked straight INTO the stage left wing. Which was a solid, unforgiving wall. I smacked into it face-first. I literally knocked myself out. A few seconds later, I woke up sprawled on the stage and discovered the audience was laughing hysterically. My nose wasn't broken—but it was bleeding. The audience thought I was doing a "bit." I was dazed and confused and couldn't figure out why 350 people were laughing at my misfortune. Then I clawed my way off stage, slapped some ice on my face, and the show went on. As it always does.

In 1978, Second City was located above a restaurant and deli. And there was also some construction going on next door. One night, during intermission, a rat decided to make its entrance on the stage. We heard the audience gasp. We ran to the wings and saw the rat. It was taking its merry old time, casually wandering about the stage. The audience was horrified. And we were horrified we might lose our audience. So George Wendt and I quickly grabbed a couple of army helmets and prop wooden rifles. Then we crept out onto the stage, stalking the wily beast. As the rat made its way off the other side of the stage, George started singing, "Kill da wabbit…

Kill da wabbit." Instead of leaving in disgust, the audience started laughing—and stuck around for the second act. There's no business like show business, folks.

After I left the ad business, I was hired by Second City to do a show they had booked at the Chateau Louise resort out in Dundee (the hotel-restaurant-theater complex opened in 1961 and grew into 17 hotel rooms and became a 22-acre resort hotel complex with four restaurants, a dinner theater, and banquet hall, but closed in 1984). Not much of a resort, it resembled a collision of tractor-trailers. But it was a paying gig and for the better part of a year, I rode out there with George Wendt (who went on to play Norm Peterson on *Cheers*) and his soon-to-be wife, Bernadette Birkett. We would all pile into George's VW Bug—onto the front of which his father had attached a fake Rolls Royce grille—and we'd drive 40 miles out to Dundee to do eight shows a week. The resort had a large 500-seat theater there and one Wednesday matinee, we realized there were only two people in the audience. So the cast took up a collection and tried to bribe them so we wouldn't have to do a show. We offered them $50 and free tickets for the evening performance. But the couple told us it was their 20th wedding anniversary. They'd had hired a babysitter, driven down from Wisconsin, and had to be back home that evening. So of course we did a performance for them. And it turned out to be great fun. When any of the actors weren't in a scene, we'd run out and sit next to our "audience." We heckled and made catcalls to the other actors on stage. I remember yelling, "Where's the little guy? I really miss the little guy!" It became a memorable performance not only for our two-person audience—but for us as well.

SHELLEY BERMAN | COMEDIAN | ACTOR
I grew up on Chicago's West Side. After high school and serving in the military during WWII, I didn't know what to do with my life in the mid-1940s, so I decided that maybe I should find an easy college to attend, and that turned out to be the Goodman Theater, located just east of the Art Institute of Chicago.

But I had to talk my parents into letting me go. The GI Bill of Rights had just taken effect, but my father didn't want me to be an actor and my mother thought that I was wrong to pick that career. They knew that I was funny at parties, but I had no intention of being a comedian. None. I was funny in the Navy, but it never dawned on me that I could do this professionally. I thought that maybe I could become an actor.

At Goodman, I had a nice girlfriend by the name of Geraldine Page, and a good buddy just a half-year behind me who was Harvey Korman. After a while I met Sarah Herman and soon we decided to get married in April 1947. But, at that time I didn't know what to do with myself in terms of a career. I had heard about this stock company that had been formed in Woodstock, Illinois called the Woodstock Players, so I joined the company. Sarah came out with me and we lived in Woodstock, all of us living on one floor of a rented house. There were people from Goodman in the company, including Lois Nettleton, who would do very well in our industry, a fellow by the name of Tom Bosley—and Geraldine Page. We were a non-equity group and we did a play a week. We would open on a Thursday, close on Sunday night, and strike the set. The new set would be up by Monday morning and nobody ever had a day off. We were subsidized by the town of Woodstock, and were all making about $30 a week. We struggled with each other, and we played all the classics, including Shakespeare, Shaw, and Ibsen. If we needed a wardrobe or a girl needed a special gown, all of a sudden a window would be missing its drape. When the show was over, we would hang it back on the window. We learned to do our own props, our own lighting, our own box office—we all did duties. You were a star one week and a flunky the next. The Woodstock Players were very successful, and the year I left the company a guy by the name of Paul Newman, who didn't have much of a career in acting, started at the Woodstock Opera House.

When our run at Woodstock ended in the late 1940s, Sarah and I sought to make our fortune. I tried to be a social director at a hotel in Florida, but I was terrible at it. They fired me, and Sarah and I hitchhiked across the country to California where I finally wound up as an Arthur Murray dance instructor for a while as well as taking odd jobs and acting whenever I could. Then, Geri Page came out to do a movie called *Hondo* with John Wayne. She said to me, "What are you doing just sitting around?" She made me go to New York, a place that I hadn't been to. So, I tried my route in and out of live theater, including Goodyear Playhouse, Philco Playhouse, and other television shows like them. While I was there I met a guy in the Stanley Wolf Players who did some summer stock in the Catskills. But that was the closest I ever got to the Catskills.

I'll tell you how I got started in acting, and it certainly wasn't in the Catskills. I got a job with a group of performers as an actor, and we were touring with Stalag 17. One of the guys in the cast was another star-to-be, Martin Landau, who was part of that group. After the play closed, we were looking for work and Marty was accepted by Actors Studio in New York, which was thrilling for him—I was jealous because I had tried it and blew it. A Chicago group called up Landau because they needed somebody to fill a spot vacated by one of the players and Marty said to them, "I have a job, but there's another fellow I work with and maybe you can use him." So, they brought me in to be a part of the Compass Players.

When I got there a lot of these kids were younger than me, and it bothered me that I was still struggling with my career. I thought that here they were actually doing things while I was wondering if I was ever going to get started in life because I hadn't made it yet. I met Barbara Harris there, and I also met another girl who was marvelous—Elaine May—and a skinny, pale kid named Mike Nichols. I also met Paul Sills, who loved to intellectualize things into oblivion and he and Mike Nichols would go round and round. But I learned what that was: it was not just oblivion—it was creativity.

In those days, I thought that you went on stage just to be funny. So, I tried that a couple of times, to everyone's dismay, including my own. No, that wasn't the purpose. You got out there and you

Second City, 1965 (Courtesy of Second City)

improvised. And when you improvised you were not just trying to "out funny" everybody out there, or get all the laughs. You were out there to communicate with each other and make it all happen together.

The Compass Players were located on the South Side of Chicago at a place called The Dock, which was just a little bar. These people were fabulous, and we did things together that I never dreamed I could do. I found myself capable of improvising and playing something quite seriously and getting laughter as a result. The technique was quite extraordinary, but it was exactly what Uta Hagen had been teaching me for the longest time which was don't go out there just to act, go out there for a reason. Well, in a month or two, I had it. Still I was driven because I was a little older than they were by about five years, and I was getting scared that I hadn't made a career for myself—and I was coming up on 30 years old. I was scared to death,' but I knew that I had the talent and the will. So, I began to get along and work with these marvelous people. I never stopped admiring them—never. Working with them was such a pleasure and such a gift given to me.

I was with Compass Players almost three years until they left Chicago and moved to St. Louis in 1957. I decided to stay in Chicago although I didn't know what I was going to do for my career. But I knew that I had to do something. Around that time, I had developed an act doing some phone calls where I could play the thing by myself, but in reality the other "person" was supposedly on the other end of the line. That was the technique— I would sit down and make a phone call, and I would swear that the other person was talking to me. It wasn't a gimmick— it never occurred to me. However, it started me as a monologist, although I didn't realize that was happening. Now, as far as I was concerned these were marvelous phone calls, but what the hell was I going to do with them? I couldn't imagine doing this in a nightclub with people smoking and drinking!

You've got to have these big, strong powerful jokes—that's the way the comedians who I had seen worked in those places.

I watched Second City change over the years, and it used to be that the actors put scenes together and did dramatic scenes onstage and improvise those wonderful dramatic things, sometimes funny and sometimes serious. I saw Second City gradually metamorphose into the emphasis on games shared with the audience. What was happening there was that somebody would start talking about a topic, and the next guy would tell the big joke. He would get all the attention for telling the joke, but the thing had started to build so this guy could tell the big joke.

BEN HOLLIS | BROADCASTING LEGEND HOST OF EMMY AWARD WINNING SHOW, *WILD CHICAGO*

Not Late Night With Ben Hollis— The Talk Show That's Not On TV

I want to talk about a place that could be described as a kind of underdog Chicago venue. In fact, it's so obscure, that when I do an Internet search, I can't find it. It was called the Chicago Comedy Showcase, and I was playing guitar and singing funny songs—a kind of musical standup act, you might say. I grew up wanting to be like Johnny Carson. In fact, I wanted to be Johnny Carson—sit in that chair and act cool. Joke around with whoever could be my version of Ed McMahon. I liked what looked like to me, the reduced pressure of sitting behind a desk and being funny, versus the pressure of doing stand-up. Now, I knew there was no school to attend to learn how to be a talk-show host, so I thought I'd just invent one myself and we'll put it into a comedy club and go from there. So, I bought a desk and a couch and planned to talk to local luminaries. We didn't need any cameras, but it gave birth to a show called *Not Late Night With Ben Hollis*. Chicago Comedy Showcase was actually located in a functioning church. I don't recall the denomination, it was on Diversey just west of Sheffield, and they were open to the idea. We did shows on Thursday, Friday, and Saturday nights with the proviso that we had to clear the pews of empty beer bottles and remnants of other trash so that they'd be ready to conduct services on Sunday morning. It was a BYOB kind of place. There were other acts that performed there—singers, stand-up comedians, and the like. There were some that went on to a little bit bigger things, but nothing huge. I remember one comic, Mark Nutter, who had a group called Friends of the Zoo. They achieved some notoriety as they were featured on the front page of the *Chicago Tribune* Entertainment section and they were being heralded as being right up there with Second City. A guy named Jim Shea ran the club and when I started appearing there, I asked about the pay. Of course, he could never tell me because it would be based upon how much came in at the door. But the first time I appeared there, at the end of the night, he handed me a hundred bucks! I was delighted. I thought this was very cool and I then knew that if I did two shows of a night, it was possible to walk out with a hundred and $150 or more. Of course, it was intoxicating to play there, in such a relaxed atmosphere and do my 20-minute set and receive standing ovations. How cool was that? The idea for the talk show came later.

The Chicago Comedy Showcase then moved to another location, near DePaul University. For the move, we actually took the old church pews. Then, I told Jim Shea that I wanted to introduce *Not Late Night With Ben Hollis*—The Talk Show That's Not On TV and he agreed that we could do it on Thursday nights. So, I found a desk in an alley and someone gave us a vinyl couch—it was white and gave the guests on the show a place to sit. There was a piano in the place, so we got it tuned and we had a pianist, Tim Hillman, sit in on the show and we were off and running. We had some "regulars" one the show—they were ringers, kind of like Steve Allen had on his show that played different characters. People like Tom Poston and Louie Nye and Don Knotts. One of them was Nora Dunn, who went on to *Saturday Night Live* for several seasons. She talked with me about developing characters to play on the show. She did one, Babbette, an international sex kitten. She did another where she was a 7-year old little girl. Of course, one that was developed for *Saturday Night Live* was Pat Stevens. I'm not sure

what she was, but the character was this very uptight, carefully put together businessperson or business coach and it was greatly received. That was a big boost to the show because everybody loved her. My buddy at improv class, where I got my training—it was called Players Workshop of the Second City—was Christine Zander. We improv-ed together and she came on, created a bunch of characters and then she went on to New York to join Nora at *Saturday Night Live*. While she did a handful of appearances, she was really a writer and she did that for SNL and I believe she's still doing it to this day—after 35 years!

While at *Saturday Night Live*, Christine Zander, Nora Dunn, and Jan Hooks developed The Sweeney Sisters—a party singing act that was a major hit on the show. Back to *Not Late Night*, I attempted to bring on local celebrities to appear on the show. A great big help to me when I launched the show was a local PR person by the name of Cheryl Lewin, who volunteered to some promotion work—gratis! Al Lerner, of Channel 5–WMAQ, came with a camera crew to do a little feature for the 10 O'clock News, but the one that really gave us a big push was Ron Grossman, who did a big feature in the *Chicago Tribune* and that really got our name out there. I discovered then and there that I was much funnier sitting down than doing stand-up. The show did well. People were coming to see it, not that they were beating the doors down, but it did pretty good. At that point, Charna Halpern from I.O. got in touch with me and said that she wanted to bring the show over to Cross Currents. This venue was well above the Chicago Comedy Showcase. They had the budgets to promote and advertise. They were regularly in *The Reader*. They were anchored by a show called Council Wars that started up right after Harold Washington became mayor of Chicago. Charna said she thought it would be great for us to do our show on Saturday nights, right after Council Wars. Essentially, that meant doing a midnight show, but I didn't see any problem in doing that, particularly in a place that already had an audience. After all, this was a big upward leap for my show. She went on to say that she could get me great guests. She said she could get me Kup (columnist Irv Kupcinet) and to me, that was a great coup. And she got him. Not only did she get him, but also he was the guest on our opening night! At one point in the interview, I took an elongated pause and he said, "C'mon, Ben. Let's keep it moving!" Obviously, this wasn't broadcast, but it was the equivalent of dead air and he was used to being the interviewer. For a moment, it kind of ticked me off, because I'd listened to some of his things on the air and he was kind of a bumbler. But then I realized he was being very generous with his time in agreeing to do the show. I'm sure it was probably past his bedtime.

TOM "BONES" MALONE | PROFESSIONAL MUSICIAN AND ORIGINAL *BLUES BROTHERS* BAND MEMBER

When we were filming the *Blues Brothers* movie in Chicago, it became apparent that we couldn't just go anywhere and hang out. So John Belushi knew of a small, private bar that was available to rent. It was down at the end of a little dead end street, right across from Second City. John's friend, Steve Bashakis, was the manager of the place. So, John made arrangements to rent it and now, we could hang out anytime we wanted and not be bothered.

One of John's bodyguards, Bill "Superfoot" Wallace, was guarding the door one night. Bill was a World Karate Association Middleweight champion of nine years. He was about 5'11" and 165 pounds. On this night, six members of The Charlie Daniels Band came to the door. Bill said, "Where do you think you are going?" They were all 6'6" and 250 pounds. One of them said, "We're going inside." So, Bill said, "I don't think so." He then started breathing deeply, took his stand and was ready to move into action. The six guys took off—abruptly.

HAROLD RAMIS | ACTOR DIRECTOR | COMEDIAN

In the early '60s, I became interested in playing a musical instrument and began going to the Old Town School of Folk Music for music lessons. My friends played guitar, I played the five-string banjo, and we used to perform for whoever would listen. In 1960, I was attending Senn High School, singing in the high school chorus, performing in an all-city chorus at the Chicago Symphony Orchestra, and serving as an extra at the Lyric Opera. I was in a lot of skits and shows at Senn, as well as being a member of the school theater group. Our little band was playing in coffee houses by the time I was 16 years old, and although I wasn't doing formal improvisation yet, we were making stuff up just like the improvisational skits I would do later at Second City.

When I was growing up, the big deal was to take the "L" downtown, meet under the clock at Marshall Field's, and go to a movie at the Chicago Theater, State-Lake, Roosevelt, Oriental, or Michael Todd Theaters and then, maybe walk over to the Art Institute. But, by the time I came back to Chicago in 1962 from attending Washington University in St. Louis, the action had shifted to Old Town, The Mother Blues club, Earl of Old Town, and Second City as the Near North began to develop into the center for entertainment for my generation. I became more interested in show business around 1966 and took 12 workshops in 1967 and 1968 at Second City with Josephine Forsberg. There was an opening in the touring company, but when she didn't select me, I stopped going to the workshops. I actually started teaching a workshop at the Old Town Players, which was at a church in Old Town. That was fun and, while I was still teaching, in 1967, I began freelancing for the *Chicago Daily News* working for Richard Christiansen. I was writing entertainment features, and he assigned me to cover movies on various locations. Christiansen also allowed me to review major rock and roll concerts like The Cream and The Doors and Jefferson Airplane, as well as the Joffrey Ballet, and Dick continued to print all my pieces in the newspaper. When I finished a second semester of teaching in 1968, I took my published stories to *Playboy* and got hired in the summer of 1968 as party joke editor at the magazine. After about two months, they moved me up to assistant editor and then, in a few more months, I became associate editor and stayed with *Playboy* for 18 months before leaving in 1970.

In 1968, Dick Christiansen called and said that a friend of his, Michael Miller, had become the new director of Second City. Dick asked if I would be interested in auditioning for Miller. So, I called Michael and he told me to come in on a Saturday night. To my surprise, my audition involved going onstage in front of a full house in an improv set. I was told to just go up there and see what I could do. I think that I did well because when Michael formed a new touring company, he included me in it. The stage was ours on Monday nights at Second City, and we actually did very little touring. At that time, Bernie Sahlins and Joyce Sloane were around, but Sheldon Patinkin had already left. My company included Brian Murray, Joe Flaherty, David Blum, Jim Fisher, Roberta McGuire, and Judy Morgan. Then, in 1969, Bernie moved the entire Second City cast out and sent them to New York and made the touring company the main stage group.

BILL ZWECKER | TELEVISION PERSONALITY AND ENTERTAINMENT REVIEWER

In the 1970s, I went to Second City a lot. One thing that comes to mind that I will never forget was when I was having dinner with Tina Fey and others. It is sort of funny when you realize what happened with their careers and how they took off. The one thing that really stands out was related to Chris Farley. I happened to be having dinner at the next table from him and his parents at That Steak Joynt. It was the night that he found out that he was going on *Saturday Night Live* and he was so excited that he bought drinks for everybody in the restaurant.

I remember watching Chris perform at Second City as well as seeing Steve Carrell and a bunch of other people from that era who were so talented and went on to great fame. It was such a unique kind of a comedy format in those days. Then, there was the time Tom Dreesen introduced me to Frank Sinatra when both were in town to perform. I had gone to see them perform when Tom said to me that I should come over to the Ambassador East and the Pump Room. Tom escorted me over to Frank and introduced me to the "Chairman of the Board" and was very exciting to meet Frank Sinatra. I remember seeing the great Judy Roberts when she was playing at the Hotel Intercontinental at the piano bar there for years.

The thing that I think back on is that were such a range of things to see and do in Chicago. For example, the Lyric Opera has grown to a world class quality over these many decades and I knew Ardis Kranick very well and went to a lot of operas during her heyday.

When I was a kid, I remember my parents talking about places like Mister Kelly's but I never had the chance to go there. I did go to the Earl of Old Town back in the late '60s and early '70s as well as Steppenwolf when Gary Sinise and Terry Kinney started out in the early days. Of course, the old Goodman Theater was a place that we used to go to a lot, and I would see Ramsey Lewis at Ravinia. It was a place I went to a lot over the years starting when I was a little kid. The first thing I remember about going there in the early '50s was sitting on the benches and, one time, seeing *Peter and the Wolf* narrated by Peter Ustinov.

As for jazz music, I went to the Jazz Showcase and the Green Mill, a place I loved to hear jazz, but when we traveled to Uptown, the neighborhood was already changing.

CLASSICAL AND OPERA MUSIC

CHICAGO SYMPHONY ORCHESTRA AND ORCHESTRA HALL

Originally known as the Chicago Orchestra when it was founded in 1891 by Theodore Thomas, it later was called the Chicago Symphony Orchestra. It first performed at the Inter-State Industrial Exposition Building on Michigan Avenue which would later become the site of the Art Institute of Chicago.
In 1904, the Symphony Center was built at 220 S. Michigan Avenue and Orchestra Hall would be able to seat more than 2,500 music patrons. The Hall was designed by famous architect Daniel Burnham, and Thomas became the first conductor the world renowned orchestra. The Hall had major renovations in the 1960s and was transformed again in the late 1990s. The Chicago Symphony Orchestra also began to perform in a series of free concerts each summer at a site east of Michigan Avenue at the Petrillo Bandshell in Grant Park, further south of downtown beginning in 1935. A new and modernized bandshell was opened in 1978 in Grant Park near Monroe Street, and, in 2004, the Jay Pritzker Pavilion was opened in the new Millennium Park and became the summer home of the Chicago Symphony Orchestra. The Orchestra also performs each summer at the Ravinia Festival in the city's northern suburb of Highland Park.

RAVINIA FESTIVAL

The Ravinia Festival, located in Highland Park, Illinois, along Sheridan Road and just east of the Chicago & Northwestern Railroad, is the oldest outdoor music festival in the United States, and offers a series of concerts and performances each summer on its 36 acre property. First opened in 1905, it has been the summer home of the Chicago Symphony Orchestra since 1936, and its Pavillion provides a 3,400-seat venue while the grounds accommodates thousands more guests to the various concerts. Artists who have performed at Ravinia over the years have included such popular stars as Tony Bennett, Peter, Paul and Mary, Aretha Franklin, Diana Ross, Lady Gaga, Dolly Parton, Josh Groban, Patti LaBelle, Santana, Gladys Knight, Ramsey Lewis, and John Mellencamp.

EDWARD KENNEDY ELLINGTON II (DUKE ELLINGTON'S GRANDSON) MANASQUAN, NEW JERSEY

When you're traveling in a band and you're doing a lot of one-nighters, you tend to look for beauty because generally, all you're seeing is airports and hotels and the bus. Face it... they're not the most aesthetically pleasing. When we got to Ravinia and we got out of the bus, there were all of these lush lawns and magnificent trees and it kind of made you homesick—but your home doesn't look that good. It's located on the North Shore of Lake Michigan and you kind of stood there and thought, "God, I can't get back on the bus." You know, being on the road the way we were was difficult. It hurts people because it's such a grind. I toured with Mercer and the band for five years, but we had musicians who would sign on and then quit after a while because they just couldn't take the stress of constantly being on the road. We had a magnificent pianist, the now late, Mulgrew Miller, who joined the band coming out of college and he stayed with us for about a year. One day, he just kind of wandered off and said, "I can't do this anymore. I'm out of here." This is not a criticism. It's just the way things were and he was right to do so for his own sanity. There were times when we'd go to Europe and we'd play seven nights a week—all one nighters, for weeks on end, so Ravinia looked like paradise.

MILLENNIUM PARK

Constructed on the site of the original Grant Park, the 24-1/2 acre Millennium Park first opened in 2004. As part of the new Park, the Jay Pritzker Pavillion was designed with the Grant Park Orchestra and Chorus under the direction of Carlos Kalmar in mind by world-renowned architect Frank Gehry. The concert area has 4,000 fixed seats and space on the park lawn for another 7,000 people.

Civic Opera Building
Lyric Opera Building (Opera House)

CIVIC OPERA BUILDING

The Civic Opera Building is a 45-story structure located at 20 North Wacker Drive along the south branch of the Chicago River. It opened on November 4, 1929 and contains a 3,503-seat opera house, the Civic Opera House, which is the second largest opera auditoriums in North America, and is the permanent home of the Lyric Opera of Chicago. The structure was envisioned by businessman Samuel Insull who directed the construction of the building which was designed by architects Graham, Anderson, Probst & White.

LYRIC OPERA OF CHICAGO

Opera was first presented in Chicago in 1850, and the city's first opera house opened in 1865 but was destroyed in the Great Chicago Fire in 1871. The second venue for opera opened in 1889. The current opera house opened in 1929, although resident opera companies began in the city in 1910 with the Chicago Grand Opera Company. The Lyric Opera was formed in 1954 by Carol Fox who brought Maria Callas to perform. Among the great opera artists to perform in Chicago over the years were Rudolph Nureyev, Maria Tallchief, Birgit Nilsson, Renata Tebaldi, Placido Domingo, Jose Carreras, and Anna Moffo.

PHIL PASCHKE | LEWISVILLE, TX

The Opera House in Chicago played a big part in my life. My parents were involved in a big benefit show for the Polish Jewish refugees and other displaced persons who had fled Poland because of Hitler. My parents were members of the chorus that was performing an opera called Halka. The performance took place at the Civic Opera House around 1940 after Hitler had invaded Poland. A humorous footnote (pun intended) was my mom getting ready to perform a dance number and she kicked off her shoe and it hit my father square in the eye. That's how they met.

My mother and father were members of a performing ensemble called the Polonaires. It was founded by William Wolski and Lydia Pucinski, the mother of Congressman Roman Pucinski. The Polonaires performed classic operas in Polish— Carmen, Faust, The Merry Widow, The Bartered Bride and so forth. Personally, I was involved in show business the first 33 years of my life and my first stage performance was in the opera, Carmen. I was in the children's chorus and I sang the opera in Polish. The core of the Lyric Opera company was made up of members from The Polonaires—about 20 of them. An interesting side note about the Polonaires is that Carol Lawrence, who went on to star in the original Broadway production of West Side Story, was a ballerina in the group. To this day, that group of singers from The Polonaires is recognized as the foundation of the Lyric Opera company.

The Civic Opera House is where my parents would take me to their rehearsals. I could just roam around the theater. I would go to the Civic Theater and I would watch the performances and telecasts of Kukla, Fran and Ollie. They broadcasted from that theater on WMAQ-TV. I would also sneak in and watch the telecasting of Super Circus, which Claude Kirchner and Mary Hartline. Mary Hartline—how shall I put it …was probably every young boy's first fantasy. Another show that originated from the Civic was the Tom Duggan Show. He was one of the first controversial talk show hosts, but he wasn't mean like some of today's personalities.

In the 60s, I was the assistant technical director for the Civic Opera House. We did live productions for opera, stage plays, and Broadway musicals. From my office backstage, I handled all sorts of functions, including crew payroll, scenery inventory—all the things that audiences never even think about. A funny story—this took place during a production of La Boheme. I took my cues from the stage manager, and it was right at the beginning of the Second Act at the Cafe Momus. I thought the stage manager had given me the cue to get the curtain open. So, I signaled to a stage hand to pull the cord that opened this massive stage curtain. Only problem was . . . that he hadn't. So the curtain opened and there were all of the stage hands running around, putting scenery and props in place, much to the amusement of the audience! Needless to say, all hell broke loose, but the crew kept me from getting murdered by the head of production.

Another interesting event that occurred took place during the Cuban Missile Crisis in 1962. I had taken a "smoke break" outside of the theater. I was standing on the corner of Wacker Drive and Washington Boulevard and a limousine pulled up at the corner. I was able to look inside the limo and inside were Mayor Daley and President John F. Kennedy. This particular night was one where the president and the mayor were to have an extended meeting, but Kennedy had gotten called to come back to Washington, immediately. It was at the time of the Cuban Missile Crisis.

I have a follow-up to the story about JFK and the Cuban Missile Crisis. On November 22, 1963, I was walking up the backstage stairs and encountered Alfredo Kraus who was performing in *The Barber of Seville*. He had tears in his eyes and pointed his hand as if he were holding a gun and said in a French accent, "Boom, boom—President Kennedy killed." That's how I found out about the assassination. Of course, the show for that night was canceled. The next night, November 23, as I was standing in the backstage wings, I witnessed Danny Newman as he walked to the front of the curtain before the opening of Don Pasquale and offered Lyric's condolences on President Kennedy's death followed by the entire audience standing and singing *The Star Spangled Banner* conducted by Oskar Danon. It was performed before every performance until the burial of President Kennedy. My mother, Helen, was the union rep of the American Guild of Musical Artists (AGMA) and she sent a condolence telegram to Jackie Kennedy on behalf of Lyric Opera's Chorus and Ballet. She received a thank-you note from Jackie Kennedy, which I still have in my possession.

In 1969, I was hired to be the controller for Lyric Opera. The musicians' union had gone on strike and shut Lyric down for an entire season. They were hurting. My first negotiating session I did with the

union was with their head guy—Dan Garamoni. I really had no idea who he was and I kind of came down hard on him, only to receive a friendly elbow in the ribs from my people and to be told to "cool it." But, in the end, I was able to get the Lyric Opera back in the black before too long. Also, we received some significant grants along the way. We were the first opera company to receive grants from the National Endowment for the Arts and also a grant from the Ford Foundation. Danny Newman was the head of marketing and promotion, and he and I worked on developing the grant and we got it. Danny became known as The Godfather of Subscriptions Series. That was his invention. So, any time you see subscription series for the Performing Arts, that was Danny's idea and Lyric Opera was the first performing arts group to offer such a premium. His wife, Dina Halpern, was also a famous Polish-born actress of the Yiddish theater. In total, I produced 33 productions for the Lyric Opera between 1969 and 1972, when I left the opera company. So, I had a history with the Lyric stretching from the time I was a little kid, along with my grandparents and parents. We were kind of like a Polish von Trapp family at the Lyric.

Another interesting story concerning Lyric is about their musical and artistic director of more than 20 years—Maestro Pino Donati. He was an Italian Jew and when Mussolini came into power, they were rounding up Italian Jews and sending them to concentration camps. Donati was among those destined for the camps. Mussolini was also a big fan of the opera and Donati's wife, Maria Coniglia, was a celebrated dramatic soprano. Mussolini made a deal with Donati's wife—that if she would do a private performance for him, he would release Donati and spare him from the camps. And, that's what happened. She did the performance and Mussolini kept his word. Donati went on to become one of the main consultants for Lyric. He helped select the operas, the singers like Tito Gobbi and stage directors like Franco Zeffirelli. He was the man when it came to the productions for Lyric in terms of artistic and musical direction.

CHICAGO SPORTS

Throughout the 20th century, sports teams and sporting events provided Chicagoans with a wide variety of popular entertainment. Chicago had many teams that celebrated sports championships, beginning with the Cubs who would appear in 10 World Series, including one in 1945; the White Sox who were the American League champions in 1919 but were given the name Black Sox for allegedly throwing the World Series but who were in the Series against the Dodgers in 1959; the Bears who won several NFL world championships including 1963; and the Super Bowl in 1985; the Cardinals who won the NFL title in 1947; the Bulls who would win six NBA titles in the 1990s; the Blackhawks who won the Stanley Cup in the 1930s and again in 1961; the Loyola Ramblers who won the NCAA title in 1963; the Chicago Sting soccer team that won the North American Soccer League Championship in 1984; the University of Chicago Maroons with championship football teams in the early part of the 20th century, and Northwestern University that won the Rose Bowl in 1949.

In addition, Chicago sports enthusiasts were able to witness and participate in a broad array of athletic events that ranged from bowling, basketball, tennis, and 16" softball to boxing, wrestling, and midget car racing. As television gained in popularity beginning in the late '40s and early '50s, many of Chicagoans' favorite sports were broadcast on television on a regular basis, including Friday night boxing and wrestling and professional bowling.

Professional football was a major part of Chicago's sports tradition, especially during the years when there were two professional teams in the city: the Bears who played their games at Wrigley Field, and the Cardinals at Comiskey Park. The Chicago Cardinals won their only NFL Championship in 1947 when they beat the Philadelphia Eagles, and, in 1948, they had a chance to make it two in a row, only to lose the championship to the Eagles, 7-0. The Chicago Cardinals would never win the title again, and, in 1959, the team was moved to St. Louis, thus ending an era when there were two NFL teams in Chicago. The Chicago Bears won several NFL championships during the 1940s (1940, when they beat the Washington Redskins 73-0; 1943, when they once again defeated the Redskins by a score of 41-21; and, in 1946, in a 24-14 victory over the New York Giants). The Bears would play in another championship game in 1956, but this time they lost to the Giants by a score of 47-7. The situation was reversed on December 29, 1963 when the Bears won the NFL Championship by defeating the New York Giants in frozen Wrigley Field, 14-10, and in 1985 the team won its only Super Bowl by defeating the New England Patriots.

Chicago baseball fans have been able to enjoy a century-old rivalry between its two major league baseball teams, the Cubs and the White Sox. Although the Cubs had been involved in 10 World Series since 1906, the last one being in 1945, it was the White Sox that were the dominant Chicago baseball team of the 1950s with such stars as Billy Pierce, Nelson Fox, and Luis Aparicio. Meanwhile, the Cubs continued to struggle from 1945, when they lost the World Series to the Detroit Tigers, through the '50s and into the early '60s. Many Cub players came and went at Wrigley Field, including Andy Pafko and Hank Sauer, but one Cub, who came to be known as "Mr. Cub" proved to be the bright light on the North Side: Ernie Banks. Banks came up to the major leagues in September 1953 and would star with the team until the early '70s. He won National League MVP honors in 1958 and 1959, but his team was never in the pennant races until the late 1960s. He would end up with 512 career home runs and membership in baseball's Hall of Fame. By the early '60s, some future Cub star players reached the team, including Baseball Hall of Famers Billy Williams, Ron Santo, and Ferguson Jenkins, but their glory years didn't happen until the end of the decade, including 1969 and into the 1970s and when the Cubs finally won the National League title again in 1984, led by Hall of Famer Ryne Sandberg, before losing to the San Diego Padres in the playoffs, and being in the playoffs several times in the 1980s and 1990s.

Professional hockey was also an important part of the sports scene in Chicago from the late '40s through the early '60s. The Chicago Blackhawks, who played their games at Chicago Stadium, struggled in the '40s and '50s, and in a 13-season span, from 1946–47 through 1957–58, the Hawks made the NHL playoffs only one time, and for 15 years, from '46–'47 through '59–'60, they had losing regular-season records. However, things began to change for the team when they acquired goalie Glenn Hall during the 1957–58 season. They also added several star players from their junior teams and minor leagues: Bobby Hull, Stan Mikita and Pierre Pilote. In 1960–61, they Hawks finally went over the .500 mark during the regular season, beat the Montreal Canadiens in the semifinals, and surprised the Detroit Red Wings to win the Stanley Cup in six games. The next year, Bobby Hull broke hockey's 50-goal barrier for the first time, the Chicago Stadium began an era of 14 years of consecutive sellouts, and Stan Mikita joined Hull as one of the Hawks' all-time greats during those years.

Chicago was a focal point for professional boxing from the late '40s through the 1950s, and several championship fights were held at Chicago Stadium, Soldier Field, and Comiskey Park. On July 16, 1947, Rocky Graziano knocked out Tony Zale in the sixth round. Two years later, on June 22, 1949, Ezzard Charles defeated Jersey Joe Wolcott in 15 rounds. On February 14, 1951, Sugar Ray Robinson knocked out Jake LaMotta in the tenth round, and, two years later, on May 15, 1953, the great heavyweight, Rocky Marciano knocked out Jersey Joe Wolcott in the first round to win that fight. The Chicago Stadium was the location for the heavyweight championship fight on November 30, 1956 when Floyd Patterson knocked out Archie Moore in the fifth round to win the title. The next year, there were two major championship fights in Chicago: Ezzard Charles won a unanimous decision against Joey Maxim at Chicago Stadium on May 30; and, on July 16, Rocky Graziano defeated Tony Zale in the 6th round. Finally, on May 25, 1958, Sugar Ray Robinson defeated Carmen Basilio in a 15 round decision.

Bowling was a very popular pastime in the Chicago area during the '50s and '60s, and local professional bowlers like Carmen Salvino who went on to become a member of the bowling Hall of Fame. The sport was so popular that parents and children could be found at bowling alleys throughout the week, often as members of teams in leagues. The sport was also televised, and many fondly remember "Whispering" Joe Wilson who announced the sport on local television, as well as Chris Schenkel who was on ABC-TV.

Basketball at the high school, college, and professional level was also very popular throughout the years.

BASEBALL
CHICAGO WHITE SOX

BILL GLEASON | SPORTS JOURNALIST

A significant thing about the 1950s was that the White Sox took over as the city's baseball team. For ten out of eleven years, the White Sox outdrew the Cubs, and the Cubs only averaged about 600,000 in attendance. There was tremendous excitement on the South Side because there had been such a long, long wait for White Sox fans. The Cubs had been in the World Series in 1945, while the Sox hadn't been in one since 1919. We had Jimmy Dykes as a manager and the players that the Comiskeys bought when Grace Comiskey got a loan from the First National Bank. The great years for the Sox really began in 1950-51 with the beginning of the "Go-Go" Sox and with Paul Richards as the manager. Richards knew how to get a team ready in spring training, and that way they would build a lead early in the season and sell tickets early because people became so excited about the team. And, they were exciting teams with so many heroes.

They had somebody on that team for everybody, and I said that they even had a guy for the men who came out of Stateville Prison...Jim Rivera, who had been in Leavenworth. Then, they had Jim Landis, Minnie Minoso, Nelson Fox, Chico Carrasquel, Luis Aparicio, Sherman Lollar, and that wonderful pitching.

Bill Veeck used to say that the great pitchers don't draw at home because people can see them pitch 20 times a year. But, Billy Pierce had such a hold on the fans that they wanted to see him pitch. And, part of it was so "South Side," because usually he would pitch brilliantly and lose to Whitey Ford by the score of 2-1. Every year there was hope, and Richards made headlines by things he did, like taking Pierce out of the game and moving him to first base because a big right-handed hitter was coming up, and then make the switch again and bring Pierce back to pitch. Paul Richards was so far ahead of the game, and had such a tremendous baseball mind.

The team was so exciting. Every batter who came to bat excited you, and they would do impossible things like sweeping the New York Yankees in four straight. And, there was the time when Tommy Byrne, the relief pitcher, hit a grand slam home run. The thing that I loved about Paul Richards, and guys don't think about it today, he was working with 10 pitchers, not with 11 or 12. He would take a guy out in the first inning, and that was so wildly entertaining. Then, when Veeck came, the team won the pennant in 1959. He brought so much excitement to the city, and he made a few deals and got Ted Klusewski from the Cincinnati Reds to play first base, and Early Wynn from the Indians. Klusewski was the only power hitter in my memory to be an "arms" hitter, it was all with his arms and he overpowered the ball.

BILLY PIERCE | ALL-STAR PITCHER, CHICAGO WHITE SOX

I came to Chicago for the 1949 season. I had recalled being here with the Detroit Tigers in 1948, and what I remembered, mainly, was that during the night games the aroma from the Stockyards was brutal. I figured that this was one place I would never like to come. But, it turns out that the aroma left, the wind blew it away, the Stockyards were leaving, and Comiskey Park became a beautiful place to play. The fans were always fantastic in Chicago even though the team didn't have a winning year for quite a while. As it turned out, we brought some excitement back to the city and the White Sox fans

because we had players like Nellie Fox, Luis Aparicio, Chico Carrasquel, Minnie Minoso, and Jimmy Rivera running the bases. It made for exciting ball games and we acquired a lot of good players.

In 1949, the team ended up in fifth place, but that was an improvement from eighth place the previous year. The New York Yankee ballclub was the top team coming into town for most of the '40s and the '50s. They had a great ball club, and the Cleveland Indians were coming up at that time. Cleveland always had good pitching, and then they had Larry Doby, Al Rosen, Luke Easter, and Jim Hegan, but New York had everything: good pitching, hitting, and very great fundamentals. In the good years for the White Sox, it was us, the Yankees, and the Indians fighting it out for the pennant. Everyone remembers the Friday night Yankee games and the four-game weekend series that included Friday night, Saturday, and the Sunday double headers. We did that two or three times during the year and that probably accounted a third of our total annual attendance. Since there was no television coverage of the games, the only way to see it was to have tickets to the games.

Salaries were a joke in those early years, in comparison with today. In 1945, the minimum salary was $600 a month for five and a half months, so maybe it was $3,600 a year. But, by 1949, the minimum salary was about $6,000 or $7,000 up to about $20,000. We only traveled by train in those days, and we only went to the East Coast but no further west than St. Louis since there were only eight teams each in the American and National Leagues, and we would only would play 154 games a year in those days.

When I first started with the White Sox, Whitey Ford wasn't up yet with the Yankees. It was Raaschi, Reynolds, and Lopat, and they had a good pitching staff and a good team. Joe DiMaggio was still playing for them, Yogi was with them at the time. Yankee Stadium to me was the big thrill, and going into that ballpark after being a kid who listened to games in the World Series on radio with Mel Allen, the New York Yankees, and Yankee Stadium, that was a big thing. So, the first time I went in there and seeing that big façade out there in right field and left field and the monuments in center field, that was baseball. It was just baseball, the top echelon of baseball. It seemed that the World Series were always in New York.

In Fenway Park, I pitched a little differently because when I would throw the ball I would use my right hand and try to push the left field wall back. You tried to pitch away from hitters, mostly in Fenway Park, and into left handed hitters. The left hand hitters could hit that wall. I remember two things about Boston: the fence and a man named Ted Williams. I never forgot him. According to the records, I did fairly well against Williams, but to me he was always the best.

When I first started out, I had two pitches: a fastball and a curve ball. And, then, in '53, I came up with a slider. Paul Richards tried to get me to work on one and to hold it one way. I finally got the grip for the pitch. A slider, in those days, was a hard, small breaking ball and you could have very good control of it. I could hang the curve ball you could hang it and it covered more area, but the slider was a hard throwing ball that maybe moved six or eight inches, and it wasn't a strikeout pitch. But, it worked well in going along with a fastball and a curveball. I also threw some slow curves, but I didn't have a change-up. Before they had the Cy Young award in both leagues, in '56 and '57, I was the pitcher of the American League. I won 20 games both of those years. By '53 and '54, our shortstop Chico Carrasquel was traded and Luis Aparicio came up, and he moved up into the number one hitting spot, with Nellie Fox hitting second. It was a great 1-2 punch. Luis would get on base a lot, and Nellie could bunt or hit him over, he could do anything with the bat. That was a big thing having that 1-2 punch. And, then Minnie Minoso, who came to White Sox in '51, he batted third in the lineup. We never had a really strong 4-5 in our lineup. Some teams do that win pennants like the Yankees and Mantle and Maris. Sherman Lollar was our catcher, but he didn't knock in 100 runs each year. We didn't have the home run power in the 4-5 slots. Third base was a changing position for us, as first base was during those years. We had Eddie

Robinson toward the end of his career. Moose Skowron didn't come to the Sox until the '60s. Also, Minnie wasn't there in '59 when we won the American League pennant since he had been traded to Cleveland.

We had Jim Landis as our great centerfielder. So the outfield was Al Smith in left field, Landis in center, and Jim Rivera in right field. Three good defensive outfielders and very fast runners, and we needed them to catch our mistakes. Our pitching staff in the mid-'50s included Joe Dobson, Jack Harshman, and Virgil Trucks, but the great Early Wynn didn't come to the White Sox until 1957. As for managers, we started with Jack Onslow in '49, and when he left, Marty Marion took over, and then Paul Richards. He was the best teaching manager, and between him and Doc Kramer, they made Nellie Fox into a ballplayer. They changed his bat, they worked with him on double plays, they taught him how to bunt…I mean they did a lot of things with Nellie and it worked out wonderfully. He had a regular thin-handled bat and they got him into a bottle-bat. They worked on bunting by the hour, and he got to be the best left-handed bunter, without a doubt, in the league, while Phil Rizzuto of the Yankees was the best right-handed bunter. Nellie was MVP in 1959 when we won the pennant. So, we had a good ball team with Aparicio, Fox, and Minoso. We were the "go-go" Sox who would win ball games with a single, stolen base, sacrifice and fly ball.

I had my almost perfect game in 1958 when Ed Fitzgerald, a catcher for the Washington Senators, got the only hit and there went the perfect game, but I was happy to win the ballgame, 1-0, and I think that as years go by I would love to have the pitch back again and try something else since I couldn't do any worse. I had four one-hitters in my career, but never in the ninth inning with the first hit. I had one against New York, one against St. Louis, and two against Washington.

In 1959, the only changes in players that affected our team during the pennant year was the acquisition of Ted Kluszewski in the middle of the year from Cincinnati. Ted didn't hit that many home runs, but he hit lots of singles that knocked in some key runs for us. Bob Shaw came out of the blue as a rookie and pitched very, very well for us, Dick Donovan pitched well, and Early Wynn had the best year he had had over a period of years. Nellie Fox had a fantastic year, and between Nellie and Luis, they were on base all the time. The records show that we won so many one-run ballgames that year. Of course, they had me warming up in Cleveland for the clinching game because Tito Francona, the left-handed hitter, was the next batter after Vic Power. But the ground ball came to Luis Aparicio, and he stepped on second and it was all over and the White Sox had won the pennant in September 1959. We didn't know much about the sirens that were set off in Chicago that night. When we came in to Chicago it was about one or two o'clock in the morning, and there was a big crowd at Midway Airport waiting to greet us. I remember that when we got off, Earl Torgeson and I got a cab and we were going down Garfield Boulevard and there were flares out on the lawn and people were sitting on their steps. They were just sitting out there because they were excited that the White Sox had won the pennant.

The World Series of 1959 started out fantastic. Kluszewski hit a couple of home runs, and we were winning 11-0. Until the second game, Sherm Lollar got thrown out at home plate. Until that play it looked like we were going to walk away with the Series against the Los Angeles Dodgers. You have to be a little lucky in this game. But, the White Sox lost the Series in six games. I can't say much about that series because I didn't pitch much. I relieved for three innings in Los Angeles. Once we got into L.A., they didn't like left-handers to pitch too much because of the short fence in the old Coliseum. But, of course, I pitched three innings out there and nobody hit the fence. They had 92,000 people at each game for three days in a row, the biggest crowd that has ever seen a ballgame. There were two games in Chicago and then three games in L.A., and then the final two games in Chicago. It was an exciting time, and during the World Series there was bunting all around the stadium like an All-Star game. To me that was baseball at its best.

MARY FRANCES VEECK | WIFE OF BILL VEECK | OWNER OF CHICAGO WHITE SOX

In 1959, Bill bought the White Sox from Grace Comiskey. When we were in Chicago, famous newsman Edward R. Murrow came to our apartment in Hyde Park before we had anything unpacked and did his *Person To Person* show on CBS-TV. We lived in the Shoreland Hotel, and one of the key things was that almost all of the White Sox ballplayers lived at the Del Prado Hotel on the South Side. I think that was one of the differences that built team morale instead of now when most players live wherever they feel like it and they go out to the suburbs and they don't live together. But, Bill always maintained that when the teams rode the trains they were together over a longer period of time and that fostered camaraderie and a closer situation, and it wasn't the same after the teams started flying everywhere.

The deal for Bill to buy the White Sox was finished at the end of 1958. I remember that we arrived in Chicago on the first day of spring in 1959 and it was quite wonderful. Bill did the same thing in Chicago that he did in Cleveland. Some people didn't really know what he was doing but he would always say that there was no way that we could win the pennant with this team because you can't win with just a hit batsman, a fly ball, a walk and a sacrifice bunt. He kept saying that, and, as I understand it, he followed the same *modus operandi* in Cleveland with Boudreau as his player-manager. This was Bill using his old psychology, and we really believed that we had a chance with the White Sox. He had enormous respect for Al Lopez, the manager of the White Sox, and Bill brought in a couple of other players. But the team was basically, pretty well set.

His contribution, the one thing that Bill could always bring to a baseball club, was the excitement. He loved baseball and, owning a team, he thought it was wonderful. He thought the idea that he could make a living in this business that he really did love, and his love for the game were the special things that he brought to baseball. Every once in a while, people wondered out loud what Bill really did, but I didn't get upset at that because I knew what he had accomplished.

I do remember the day in September 1959 when the team clinched the pennant against Cleveland. Bill called me and he said, "Dizzy Trout will pick you up and drive you out to the airport, and I will meet you out there." It was so exciting, and when we got to the tarmac, Mayor Daley was there with Mrs. Daley, and, all of a sudden I realized that I had lost my shoe. So, I was kind of limping and Mrs. Daley inquired as to the problem. I said, "I lost my shoe, I guess that I must have stepped out of it." So, she tells the mayor and he turned to somebody and said, "Find her shoe!" So, someone finally found it and held it up as if it were on a silver tray. Of course, it was just an incredibly wonderful, wonderful time. Finally, everybody went to their own homes and Bill and Hank Greenberg and I stayed up all night, went to a couple of places, and sat and talked and talked. We were so happy, and, then, finally we went to bed. Then, the phone calls started, so, finally, I decided to just take a long walk along the lake. It was just an incredibly wonderful time. At that time, you couldn't buy whole blocks of tickets for the series, and you could only get a certain number of seats. Bill felt that anybody who had been a White Sox fan for years and supported them should have the opportunity to buy a ticket, if humanly possible.

As for the air raid sirens that night that were set off in celebration of the victory, we heard them but we didn't know it was going to happen. It was something that I think was done by Fire Commissioner Quinn, himself, and I am not certain that Mayor Daley knew it was going to happen. I thought that when the sirens went off it was just celebratory, and it seemed wonderful, so I wasn't panicked at all. After all, it was just a magical night and I thought that the whole heavens had opened up, and Hank and Bill and I had our share of champagne that night in celebration of the victory. We just wanted to remember the excitement of the moment.

Then, we traveled out to California for the World Series and Bill gave the box that the owners had to the Comiskeys and Bill and I sat up in the stands and had a great time. He felt very strongly that the Comiskey family should have the box after all those

years of owning the White Sox. Everything just blended together and while I don't remember much about the series, it was very "heady" when we won the first game. However, it was a big letdown when we lost the series to the Dodgers.

BILL JAUSS | SPORTS JOURNALIST

I remember Nellie Fox and Luis Aparicio and Minnie Minoso because they were the cornerstones of those White Sox teams. They had become the "Go Go" Sox and were managed in those years by Paul Richards and they played with defense, speed, verve and daring. Jimmy Landis was their centerfielder and there was no one better than Landis, while Aparicio and Fox were "magicians" around shortstop and second base. During the '50s they had good pitching that included Early Wynn, Billy Pierce, and Bob Shaw. The White Sox had a tremendous increase in attendance as the team began to win and the "Go Go" Sox concept took effect. The fans became very excited with the team, as well as their great defense. Paul Richards used the players that Frank Lane had brought to Chicago, and they had speed, and excitement. Another factor in the White Sox's success was their persistence because they had to plug away for the whole decade of the '50s until they won the pennant in 1959. I also remember the Yankee-White Sox games during the '50s. When I came back to Chicago in my early days of journalism, I wasn't covering baseball and I was still going to the games as a fan. When they were playing the Yankees, it seemed like it was always a weekend series and there would be one game where Billy Pierce would be pitching against Whitey Ford and Pierce would be magnificent and get beat 2-1. Inevitably, the White Sox would take leads into the seventh inning.

In 1959, when the White Sox clinched the pennant in Cleveland, the game was televised back to Chicago. We had started the celebration, the Sox had won, and then the air raid sirens went off.

As for the Cubs in the '50s, there was one star in any one year, either Hank Sauer in the early '50s or Ernie Banks from 1954 to the end of the decade. At the start of the '50s, the Cubs had a centerfielder named Frankie Baumholtz. Baumholtz had been a professional basketball player who played in the NBA, and he was very fleet of foot. He had to be because he had Hank Sauer playing in left field and Ralph Kiner in right field. So Frankie had to play all of three outfield positions. During the decade, Wrigley Field had sparse attendance and only twice did the Cubs break a million in attendance. But, the upside of that situation was you were able to get there at game time and pick a good seat anywhere in the park.

By the early '60s, things started to turn upward for Chicago sports. Dick Butkus enrolled at the University of Illinois and he ended in Illinois winning the Big Ten and going to the Rose Bowl in 1963. Then, George Ireland expanded outside of the Chicago recruiting market, got Jerry Harkness and Ron Miller from New York, Les Hunter and Vic Rouse from Nashville, and they became the basis of the team that won the NCAA Basketball Championship in 1963. And, the Bears finally came out of a decade of lethargy and put together the components of the NFL Championship team in 1963. The Blackhawks won the Stanley Cup in 1961 with exciting stars that featured Bobby Hull, Stan Mikita and Glenn Hall.

CHICAGO CUBS

ANDY PAFKO | OUTFIELDER
CHICAGO CUBS

I first came to Chicago at the tail end of the season of 1943. I played at the Pacific Coast League, in Triple A, and when our season was over there, the Cubs had about 13 games left to play, so they brought four of us up from the Triple A club, and I was one of them. Of course, I had never been to Chicago before and I never saw Wrigley Field until I played there. That was quite a thrill for me and I'll never forget my first time at bat. I think that I had an extra base hit and drove in a couple of runs, and then I got another hit and drove in a couple of more runs. I broke in kind of good, and it was a good feeling. I will never forget the feeling of walking into Wrigley Field in Chicago the first time. I had never been to Chicago before, and the four of us took a cab to Wrigley Field.

I'll never forget walking into the clubhouse, and I opened the door and the first guy I ran into was Stan Hack, Cub third baseman, and I recognized him. I'll never forget what he said, "Andy Pafko, welcome to the big leagues, welcome to Chicago!" That was the greatest moment of my life, I mean, just getting into a big league clubhouse and then playing in Chicago as long as I did. The Cubs radio announcer, Bert Wilson, used to call me "the kid from Boyceville."

I played outfield, and primarily I was a center-fielder, but I played right and left field, and eventually I even played third base for the Cubs, when Stan Hack retired. They had no third baseman so I filled in and I had a good year and I made the All-Star team as a third baseman. To me, it was just a thrill to be in the Big Leagues. I think that the Cub fans are the best fans in the country.

The year the Cubs were in the World Series in 1945 was a great year. We were battling the Cardinals for the championship, and I drove in the winning run to clinch it for the Cubs that year. I hit a fly ball to right field and that put us into the World Series and, of course, playing in the World Series was a tremendous, tremendous feeling. There is nothing like it, and, ultimately, when you get to the Big Leagues, your number one thing is to someday get into the World Series. I was very fortunate in my career because I played on three different clubs and they all went to the World Series. I'll never forget the first one in 1945, though, that was thrilling.

Wrigley Field was a beautiful place to play baseball. A lot of people complained that the wind blows in, and of course, it does blow in. But, I think that it was a fair ballpark. They said that it was a pitcher's park, but they didn't like to pitch when the wind was blowing out. But, it's a fair park and the distances are fair for the pitcher and hitter. If you hit a home run you deserve it at Wrigley Field. It was not like a lot of other ballparks where I played like the old Polo Grounds. You could drop kick the ball over the left field fence, it was so close, about 280' down the line. So, Wrigley Field was a fair park for both pitchers and hitters. I hit 36 home runs one year and only struck out 30 times, and I think that is a record for a home run hitter. I am kind of proud of that fact. I had good seasons with the Cubs, and I appreciated that the fans of Chicago were loyal to me, but of course, I always gave it 100%.

JIM BROSNAN | PITCHER
CHICAGO CUBS

In 1956, I went to spring training and made the team—and I met Mr. Wrigley. He would go to one game in spring training and one game during the regular season—that was it. Then, when I went Wrigley Field for the first time it was amazing—that walk up to the field from behind home plate is like no other! In one of my few starts that year I beat the Giants by a score of 7-0 and struck out Willie Mays three times. About 10 years later, Jerome Holtzman wrote a story about that game because he thought it was one of the biggest achievements of my career. My record that year was 5-9, and every once in a while they would pick me to start a game, but in those years we had Bob Rush, Paul Minner, Moe Drabowsky, and Dick Drott. Minner helped me a lot, Howard Pollett taught me how to throw a slider, and Max Lanier helped me with my breaking ball.

In 1957, Bob Rush, the ace of the Cubs' staff, had pneumonia, Drabowsky and Drott were doing their military service for six months, and I was the number one pitcher on the team during spring training. We opened the season in St. Louis against the Cardinals and I beat them. I struck out Stan Musial twice on 3-2 curve balls in that game, which he didn't expect, because nobody had ever seen me throw a curve ball before in the Major Leagues. A week later, we were up in Chicago at Wrigley Field against the Cardinals. I was the starting pitcher and Musial was hitting fourth. I went to a count of 2-2 against him, and he looks at a pitch that he could have hit and which I thought was a strike. The umpire called it a ball, and now we are at a 3-2 count. Then, Stan had this smile on his face. I figured he damn well knew that I was going to try and get him out with the same pitch. So, I figure, no, he will be looking for something else—anything but that curve ball. So, I threw him another 3-2 curve ball—

a good one—and Musial hit it about half way up into the right center field bleachers. He was laughing to himself as he rounded the bases, and when he crossed home plate he tipped his hat to me—there you go rookie! I was traded to the Cardinals in 1958, and the tenth word out of his mouth was, "Do you remember the curve ball on that 3-2 pitch?" And, he had kind of a giggle that went on and on.

KENNY HOLTZMAN | PITCHER
CHICAGO CUBS

By 1967, most of the younger Cub players had at least a year of experience, and we started to play quite well. Amazingly, although I was absent at times for National Guard duty, I wound up pitching in 12 games and finished the season 9-0. That year, Ferguson Jenkins, Bill Hands, Rich Nye, and Joe Niekro started to mature and, combined with the performances of our three great players—Ernie Banks, Billy Williams, and Ron Santo—the club started to be competitive. That year, we challenged the Cardinals for the lead in the National League well into the season although they went on to win the World Series. Other teams in our league began to take us seriously, and when the season ended, we had an 87-74 record, which meant that we were over .500 for the first time in many years.

I threw my first no-hitter on August 19, 1969 which we won 3-0 against the Atlanta Braves. That year became the culmination of the previous three years. All the players who had been brought up and traded for, young players who were the nucleus of the team, were with the Cubs by then and we felt that we had a legitimate chance to win the pennant. It was the first year of the divisional races, and there were six teams in each of the east and west divisions of the American and National Leagues. We were in the same division with the Cardinals, Mets, Expos, Phillies, and Pirates, and, in April 1969, we started the season like a "house on fire." Right away, we had an amazing won-loss record in the first month and we shot into first place. Little by little, over the first three or four months of the season, support grew in Chicago so that it seemed like there were

Chicago Cubs, 1952 (Courtesy of Walter Jacobson)

40,000 people at Wrigley Field each game. In addition, there were crowds of fans before and after the games to get players' autographs. It was just very, very exciting, but, unfortunately it didn't turn out the way we wanted.

The Mets were similar to us in many ways. They had invested in a lot of time and money in the development of their young players in the mid-1960s, including Nolan Ryan, Tom Seaver, Jerry Koosman, Tug McGraw, Tommie Agee, Cleon Jones, and Rusty Staub. They did what we did by bringing to the majors a bunch of young players, who also matured, and by 1969, they had two or three years of experience. By late August, they had passed us in the standings and won the pennant going away. Everybody said that the Cubs folded at the end of the season, but I don't agree. I would argue that the Mets were quite probably a deeper 25-man team and, over the course of the full six-month season, outlasted us.

US DISTRICT COURT JUDGE MARVIN ASPEN

I remember going to Wrigley Field. I think that I first had a sense of awareness of baseball in 1944, and I think that both St. Louis teams were in the World Series that year: the old St. Louis Browns and the St. Louis Cardinals. Burt Wilson was the Cub announcer on radio and there was no television. He'd begin each game, no matter what the weather was, by announcing, "It's a beautiful day in Wrigley Field." We got hooked on baseball by listening to Burt Wilson on the radio. In those days, when the Cubs played away, he didn't go with the team because it would have been too expensive, but he would get the report from the wire services on the ticker tape and he would make things up. For example, the ticker tape would say that the batter had flied out to left field on a 2-2 count. Wilson would create the situation and have him fly out to right field. So, we listened to baseball and we got hooked on it. I think that I first went to a baseball game with my father in 1945 when the Cubs won the pennant and lost to the Detroit Tigers in the World

Series. The bleachers were there by then and they were a fun place to sit. I think that a ticket cost $.25 and it was $.10 for a hot dog and $.05 for a Coke. But, we started going to baseball then.

U.S. CONGRESSMAN DAN ROSTENKOWSKI

As for baseball, the Cub games used to start at 3 p.m. each day in the '30s and '40s. If you had a ticket from the day before, the nuns would let you get out at 2:30 p.m. from school. If you went there after 3 p.m., and you got to the stadium, they would give you a little ticket. The next day, you would go in there and wipe the seats off at Wrigley Field, and you could watch the ballgame for nothing. Wrigley started Ladies Day, and Pat Flanagan was the radio announcer, and Pat Piper was the field announcer. In those days, Stan Hack was at third base, Billy Jurges was at short stop, Billy Herman was at second base, Rip Collins was at first base, Frank Demaree was in right field, Hank Lieber was in center field, Augie Galan was in left field, and Gabby Hartnett was the catcher. As for the pitchers, they included Big Bill Lee, Claude Passeau, and then they traded for Dizzy Dean from St. Louis. The Yankees came to town and won the World Series in four straight, and that was in 1938. I was on Clark and Addison with my dad the day that the Cubs played the Pittsburgh Pirates and Gabby Hartnett hit the "homer in the gloaming." They were going to call the game because it was dark and foggy that day. I was 10 years old and my dad put me on his shoulders, turned me around and said, "Danny, look at all these people. You'll never see happier people in your life."

HONORABLE IAN LEVIN | U.S. FEDERAL MAGISTRATE

I went to see the Cubs and Detroit's Hank Greenberg when I was six years old. My first clear memory of the Cubs was in 1946 when I became a lifelong Cub fan. My dad took us to Wrigley Field , and it was very nice on his part since he was a Sox fan from his years of growing up on the South Side. In 1947, Dad took me out of school, which he rarely did, to go see Jackie Robinson when he first came to the major leagues with the Brooklyn Dodgers. They were playing at Wrigley Field, and he was the first black player in the majors. It was very exciting and although I had heard all about Robinson I was only vaguely aware that something important was happening, although I didn't understand the total ramifications. I don't remember any fans around us taunting him, and I don't think that there was a lot of tension because he was playing. I then started to go to the games with my friends because we lived two blocks from the "L" stop at Lunt and Morse in Rogers Park, and you could take the "L" to the Addison Street stop and be at Wrigley Field. And, I used to sneak into the Bears games in those years, because they had turnstiles in those days that if the guy turned his head you could race past him and get in free into the stadium. Or if you worked the turnstiles at Wrigley Field for the ticket taker, then they would let you into the games.

JACK ROSENBERG | WRITER | PRODUCER | WGN-TV, CHICAGO

I came to Chicago in 1954 to work for WGN-TV. It was Ernie Banks' first full season in the major leagues with the Cubs as well as the beginning of the major league career for Walter Alston with the Dodgers who went on to manage them and lead them to several championships. So, the three of us came together and that put me in pretty good company. Occasionally, we would get together before a game and I would kiddingly point out to them that I had done pretty well, but I hadn't heard much about those two guys. They used to laugh at that. To this day, Walter Alston was one of my all-time favorite managers, along with Al Lopez of the White Sox.

I remember Al and Walter as being two of the greatest gentlemen I ever met. Al was a great manager who knew the game inside out and had been a tremendous catcher with the Cleveland Indians. He was part of one of the greatest baseball seasons any of us have ever seen in Chicago in 1959 when the White Sox won the pennant and played the Dodgers in the World Series. Jack Brickhouse of WGN-TV was picked by NBC-TV to telecast the series,

and I got the opportunity to work with him. It was a great series even though the White Sox lost. I remember 1959 because each Sox game was usually won by scratching and clawing for runs. They were basically a defensive team with great pitching. Winning a pennant in Chicago was something that we thought we would never see. There we were on the brink of it in 1959, and the excitement was unparalleled and the Sox had to go to Cleveland for what they hoped would be the pennant clincher. A double play ended the game, and the team came back to Chicago amid all the great excitement, and Mayor Daley and Fire Commissioner Quinn decided to turn on the air raid alarms as part of the celebration. That was talked about for many, many years after as to whether that was the right thing to do because a lot of people who may not have been baseball fans wondered if the city was facing some catastrophe. Fortunately, it was a celebration and something that I think we will always remember.

Billy Pierce of the White Sox was one of the greatest left-handers ever. I recall that in April of '59 our daughter Beth was born. I went from Presbyterian-St. Luke's Hospital directly to Comiskey Park for the baseball opener. What was ironic was that Jack Brickhouse had one daughter, Jeannie, who was born on opening day of a Cub season in 1949. Beth was born in April 1959, and I went directly to the clubhouse and Billy was getting ready to pitch the season opener. I said, "Billy, I've never done this with any athlete in all the years I've been in sports, but, we just had our first daughter to go with David, our son, and if you win this game today against Kansas City, as Beth grows up I will make sure that you will always have a warm place in her heart." Billy said, "Jack, I'm going to win this game for Beth." He did, and he shut out Kansas City on four hits, 2-0, and as the years went by he and I would occasionally and this incident would invariably come up. One day, after Harry Caray had succeeded Jack in the announcing booth, it was time for another opener at Wrigley Field. I told him the story about Beth and Billy Pierce, and he had me go on during a nationally-televised game and tell the whole story. Just about everybody knows about Beth.

Ernie Banks was very quiet when he came up to the Cubs in 1953. He was very nice, and he got by with the least amount of conversation that he could do. All he really wanted to do was to get out to his shortstop position and play, and get in the batter's box and hit the baseball. He turned out to be an incredible part of Chicago sports lore as we know it because he, like so many of the '69 Cubs, gave of themselves to the community. They gave it back and they were not just out there playing baseball. You would always see them standing by the brick wall at Wrigley Field signing autographs, and when they went out to the parking lot after the games they would always acknowledge the fans. That is why, all these years later, the '69 Cubs are remembered with such warmth and adulation. I don't think that there is any substitute for what they did, and Ernie was the "ring leader." The fact that he was "Mr. Cub," he really enjoyed being called that. He was great, and, even while playing on lackluster teams in the late '50s, he was selected as MVP twice in the National League in 1958 and 1959. I thought that Ernie was a great human being, and he was just a joy to be around.

I produced the telecasts of the Cubs and the Sox on television, and the Bears on WGN radio. We did the Bears games for 24 years, and Irv Kupcinet and Jack were the announcers. As for the 1963 Bears, I remember that year well. One of the big games that season was against the Detroit Lions, and it turned out to be one of Jack Brickhouse's greatest calls. In fact, it is still replayed today whenever his name comes up. It was the call when Davey Whitsell intercepted a pass, turned the tide in the game, and the Bears won it. I remember when the Bears played the New York Giants for the title that year on December 29, 1963 at Wrigley Field, and how cold it was that day with the wind blowing off Lake Michigan to make it feel like it was -50 degrees. Jack was tapped to do the television announcing and Jack Quinlan was picked to do the radio coverage. The Bears won the game 14-10 although it was in doubt until the end. But quarterback Billy Wade scored both touchdowns, and Larry Morris had a key interception.

MILO HAMILTON | BASEBALL HALL OF FAME TELEVISION BROADCASTER

I was with the Cubs doing the radio broadcasts in the 1950s on WIND, beginning in 1955 through 1957, and then, with the White Sox in the '60s. Covering the Cubs back in 1955, calling them "lean years" is probably being generous. The Cubs had Monte Irvin, Frankie Baumholtz, Hank Sauer, and Ralph Kiner as the team's outfielders, and then along came Gene Baker and Ernie Banks, as well as Dee Fondy and Handsome Ransom Jackson as the infielders, and Harry Chiti as the team's main catcher. Stan Hack was the manager in those years. Bob Rush was probably the best pitcher, as well as the youngsters including Moe Drabowsky and Dick Drott. They looked like they were going to be the saviors of the franchise, but never blossomed. Later, there was Walt "Moose" Moryn, who made the great catch to save the no-hitter for Don Cardwell on June 16, 1960. It was Cardwell's first start after being traded to the Cubs from St. Louis.

The White Sox was the best baseball team in town in the 1950s because they had Al Lopez as a manager, and they had a great group of players including Nellie Fox and Luis Aparicio along with Billy Pierce. I later worked with Bob Elson in the 1960s doing radio broadcasts.

Ernie Banks would have told you that I was the first guy who interviewed him when he got to Chicago. All pre-game shows now are taped, but then it was live right by the screen in Wrigley Field next to where Pat Piper was the public address announcer and presented the lineups to the fans. The engineer up in the booth pointed at you to go, and that was how you got your cue. So, I was doing the show when Banks came to the Cubs. Of course, not only was he a great ballplayer but we learned from the start that he had a dynamic personality. He was always a guy who remembered you.

CHICAGO BLACKHAWKS

HARVEY WITTENBERG | PUBLIC ADDRESS ANNOUNCER | CHICAGO STADIUM

In the early 1950s the Blackhawks were the cellar dwellers of the six-team National Hockey League, and they didn't make the playoffs too often. A major change came when Arthur Wirtz and James D. Norris purchased the Blackhawks in 1954. When Wirtz and Norris took over, they started to rebuild the team. They hired Tommy Ivan as general manager, who was the coach of the Detroit Red Wings, and had led Detroit to four first-place finishes and two Stanley Cups. The team struggled, and there was a series of coaches that Ivan hired and fired because the team was just doing terribly. The Chicago Stadium was pretty empty.

Then, in the late '50s, Tommy Ivan made a trade with the Detroit Red Wings to get Glenn Hall as goalie, and that was when the Blackhawk franchise started turning around. When Glenn Hall played for the Hawks he never wore a mask, and he never came to training camp because he played every game during the 60-game season—he just didn't want to go through all the rigors of playing in exhibition games. Next, Bobby Hull and Stan Mikita came up from the juniors, as well as Pierre Pilote, who had toiled in the minors in Buffalo. Pilote was a very popular player, and he was clearly ahead of his time as an offensive-minded defensive player. Pilote was the first defenseman, outside of Doug Harvey, who moved up on the play. As a fan, I had a clear sense in 1957 that the team was turning around—they had made it back to the playoffs.

In the 1960-61 season, the Blackhawks won the Stanley Cup. The Hawks finished in third place in the season standings, so they were matched against the first place team, the Montreal Canadiens—and beat them. The Hawks then faced Detroit and beat them four games to two—and won the Stanley Cup. It was a great series, and the Hawks should have won at least three or four Stanley Cups in the '60s. They had some great talent in those years—Bobby Hull and Stan Mikita were the greatest one-two punch in the league. Pound for pound, Stan Mikita was the best player, while Bobby Hull was the most exciting player. Today, Mikita, Hull, Pilote, and Hall are all in the Hockey Hall of Fame.

BILL "RED" HAY | PAST PRESIDENT NHL HALL OF FAME, AND CENTER CHICAGO BLACKHAWKS

My rookie year with the Blackhawks was in the 1958-59 season. We had some good young players who had come up through the Montreal chain, including Ab McDonald and Murray Balfour. The stars of our team, at that time, were Stan Mikita, Bobby Hull, and, of course, Glenn Hall. The team also included Dollard St. Laurent, Tex Evans, Al Arbor, and Moose Vasko. We melded together, learned how to win, and became an exciting team.

My initial impression of the Chicago Stadium was that it was so much bigger and more crowded than anyplace we had played in Canada. I remember one time when Rudy Pilous, the Blackhawks coach, was talking about how much faster the Zamboni machine was going than most of his skaters between the second and third periods. I leaned over to Bobby Hull and said, "What number is this Zamboni guy wearing? He sounds like he's having a pretty good game!" It was a big building, but it didn't take long to get used to it because we got to know people who ran the building.

The Stadium actually shook when we came up the stairs to the hockey rink. Of course, the person who contributed to atmosphere there was the famous organist, Al Melgard. The thing that was so nice about it was that, as we began winning, the place really filled up and once it was full, it was noisy. NHL teams didn't like coming into the Chicago Stadium because it wasn't a new building, it wasn't like their buildings, and that gave us a "leg up." In fact, the Stadium rink was a little smaller in size, and that helped us against certain teams. The slap shot was just coming into its own, so the shooting power was gaining momentum and Stan and Bobby were curving their sticks. Bobby could shoot a puck from his own goal line and break the glass at the other

Chicago Blackhawks Stanley Cup Team, 1961
(Courtesy of Glenn Hall)

end, and that got to be dangerous. We won close games because Glenn Hall was by far the best goal tender in the NHL and kept us in games. When we won the Stanley Cup in 1961, it was the special teams that really out performed the other teams when we beat Montreal, and then beat Detroit for the Cup.

In the '60s, Jim Norris and Arthur Wirtz were the owners of the Blackhawks and knew how to run an organization and manage it. They hired Tommy Ivan, and Tommy hired Rudy Pilous and they were allowed to operate the team without the interference that you see today. We developed into a pretty good team, and there was nothing finer and nothing more exciting than the '61 team that won the Stanley Cup. The 1961 team was exciting because we were young, we were together, and could have a lot of fun on a six-pack. Nobody had agents. We grew up together, and we lived together. The wives got along very well together, as did the players. Eddie Litzenberger was our captain, and he was a strong leader. We worked very, very hard, and, of course, Bobby was coming into his own and was playing with Murray Balfour and me on the "Million Dollar Line." Bobby learned how to score goals by being in the right spot. Of course, Stan Mikita, Ab McDonald, and Kenny Wharram played on another great line.

What I remember about the '60-'61 season was seeing Bobby Hull getting 51 goals, and that was the first time that had ever been done in the history of the NHL. And, our entire team developed into an offensive powerhouse while still being able to play solid defense, especially since the goal tenders on the other strong teams were so good. With the curved sticks and the way our guys started to shoot, we were able to score from out around the blue-line, and sometimes even further. So, the Blackhawks opened up the game and made it great for the fans. It was a new mentality of the Hawks. There were a lot of young guys coming in, and we didn't know how they had played before and how they lived.

We beat Montreal first in six games. We didn't let them score on the power play, and Glenn really played well. We took away their power play, and that

was the strength of all those Montreal winning teams. They had won the Cup five years in a row, but in the 1960-1961 season, we developed momentum and won the Stanley Cup. I remember that during the final series in Detroit, we had a little tussle with them in the third game at home, and that got us back the momentum. And, then, we knew that we could beat them. It was very close, and once we got by Montreal, we knew that we weren't going to lose it because the year before we had come close. For several years after, we came close and should have won, but we couldn't keep the team effort together as well as it should be.

GLENN HALL | NHL HALL OF FAME GOALIE | CHICAGO BLACKHAWKS

I came to the Blackhawks in 1957 and thought it was great to be in Chicago and play in the Chicago Stadium. At that time, it wasn't a very good team and they weren't drawing many fans. I was just there to play hockey and was happy to go to a team that wanted me. But, after I came to Chicago, we really began to improve because the Blackhawks had a strong farm team (junior team), and they brought Bobby Hull up from the minors that year. We realized from the start that he was going to be a great, great hockey player, and, then, a few years later, they brought up Stan Mikita.

During our Stanley Cup year of 1960-61, I remember how good it was to win the Cup. We had a good team, although I think we had better teams in later years. We weren't as successful after 1961, and it was obvious that the opposition had better teams too. I think that with the addition of such players as Bill "Red" Hay, Stan Mikita, Reggie Fleming, and Murray Balfour, we had a lot of guys who had come in and played very well that year. I think that, if anything, the team that gets along together does well. During that season, we were a team that worked well together and was closer than at any other time, and when one of us went one direction, we all went in the same direction.

In 1960-61, the Blackhawks finished the season in third place, and at that time, in the playoffs, the first-place team played the third-place team, and the second-place team played the fourth-place team. It never made much sense to me since you would have thought that the first place team would have played the fourth place team. In the first round, we defeated the Montreal Canadiens, and then we played the Detroit Red Wings for the Stanley Cup. Montreal had been the dominant team all those years, yet we always believed we could beat them. If you don't believe that you can defeat the opposition, don't get dressed. We knew that they were tough, had played against them 14 times in the regular season, and I'm sure that we were able to beat them some of the time. So, if you can beat them some of the time, you can beat them all of the time if you put your mind to it, things break the right way for you, and you play to the best of your ability. I remember playing very well against Montreal, and I always liked the challenge of playing against good teams. You got more satisfaction in beating a good team than beating a team that you should beat. So, there was a lot of satisfaction in defeating the Canadiens. As it turned out, that was the only Stanley Cup team I was on during my career, although I was the backup goalie to Terry Sawchuck when the Detroit Red Wings won the Cup in the '50s, and my name was on the Cup as the goal keeper coach in Calgary in 1989.

After we beat Montreal, we had to face Detroit in the finals of the Stanley Cup. I can remember the last game of the series, and I believe that the Blackhawks were down 1-0 in the game when Reggie Fleming got a short-handed goal and Kenny Wharram got a couple goals, including the fifth goal late in the third period that clinched the victory and the Cup. It was a very special feeling to win the Stanley Cup. The Blackhawks had good teams throughout the 1960s even though we didn't win another Stanley Cup. We were better offensively than we were defensively. If you take a look at Montreal, they were the dominant team because they were so good offensively and defensively, while the Toronto Maple Leafs were the best defensive team and we were close to Montreal as an offensive team. I have always had a special feeling about my opportunity to play in the National Hockey League with the quality of players who were in the NHL.

Throughout my years in Chicago, I never wore a face mask, although I wore one during my last two-plus years when I played for the St. Louis Blues. It was quite scary to play without a face mask, so I played the game a little bit differently. You held your hand up, you made sure that you saw the puck, and you encouraged your defensemen not to deflect the puck at you and to let you see the puck. As long as you saw the puck, you were generally in a position to kick it out of the way. I was more concerned about getting out of the way than getting in the way while stopping the puck because I wanted to stay alive and avoid major facial injuries, which were the major puck-related injuries for goalkeepers at that time. I think that I got hurt bad three times, with two of them deflections and the other one a shot that came through a screen. I was with the Blackhawks until 1967 when there was expansion of the NHL.

In terms of my well known dislike of coming to training camp each year, there were a number of reasons. First, in those days, training camp was a focus on conditioning where you were expected to get in shape. I always felt that I kept myself in pretty good shape and I didn't need training camp. Second, there was the issue of Bobby Hull and Stan Mikita shooting the puck at four million miles an hour. That didn't make it a fun situation, and the two-a-day practices and putting on that cold, wet, sweaty equipment was not a lot of fun. I think that the biggest issue was that I didn't think I needed the training camp, and I felt that it hurt me. In fact, even today, I think that the practices hurt a lot of the players. If the team wanted me to play well, I always needed a day off.

Years later, the Blackhawks moved from the Chicago Stadium to the new United Center. My friend said to me, "Remember telling Nancy, my wife, about the noise in the Chicago Stadium?" I said, "You know what, I do remember." The story was that his wife asked me, "How do you handle the noise in the Chicago Stadium?" I said, "You simply blank it out."

Glenn Hall in Nets
(Courtesy of Glenn Hall)

I think that the noise in the Stadium was absolutely great, and I think that when they moved to the United Center, they did a reasonably good job, but the acoustics were perfect for the Chicago Stadium and it was great to play under those conditions. I was received quite well when I played goalie for the Blackhawks, as all of us were. A lot of the fans were loyal fans and had been there when the team wasn't doing very well. When the Blackhawks started playing well, they had something to compare it to, and it was a nice situation. Chicago was a great city, the fans were so supportive, and I really appreciated the opportunity to play with the Blackhawks.

CHICAGO BEARS

GALE SAYERS | NFL HALL OF FAME RUNNING BACK | CHICAGO BEARS

My first reaction to playing in Wrigley Field was quite simple: it didn't matter to me where I played, including the field or the fans since every football field is 50 yards wide and 100 yards long. I wasn't distracted by the fans yelling and screaming since I was just out there trying to do my job, make the team, and win ballgames for the Bears. I had no concept about how old Wrigley Field was or that we were playing football on a baseball field. It was a nice field, and the fans were close to us and we had home field advantage. But, things like that didn't enter my mind and I didn't play any differently there. When we defeated the Rams in Chicago by a score of 31-6, I scored a touchdown, and even though we had lost our first three games, the Bears ended up with a winning season record of 9-5. We lost our last game of the season, 24-17, to the Minnesota Vikings, and came in second to the Packers who won the division title with a 10-4 record.

It was a great rookie year for me. In the 49er game, I set an NFL record by scoring six touchdowns, and, then, in our first game against the Vikings, I scored four touchdowns in Minnesota. My teammates really supported me, and they knew that all they had to do was make a block for me and I could break into the open. It was a good

season, and I was selected Rookie of the Year. My teammate, Dick Butkus, was second in the voting. I also went to the Pro Bowl, but Vince Lombardi, the Pro Bowl coach that year, decided not to play me too much. We wanted to win every game we played, and although the Packers beat us in the first game, when they came to Wrigley Field in late October, we "killed" our main division rivals by a score of 31-10. It seemed that during my football career, the Packers would always beat us in Green Bay while we would beat them in Chicago.

I had caught the other teams by surprise in my first year, but I wasn't sure it would happen in my second year. However, I did improve, led the league in rushing in 1966, went to the Pro Bowl, and was selected as Most Valuable Player in the Pro Bowl. In 1966, our record was 5-7-2, losing both games played with the Packers, even though we thought we had a very good team. Many of my teammates were in their 30s and might have been past their prime and thinking about retiring. However, we did have some very good young players, including Mike Ditka, Dick Butkus, Dick Gordon, Jimmy Jones, Ronnie Bull, and Ralph Kurek. But, we didn't have too many choices in the annual NFL draft, and I think that was why we didn't do well for the next several years. It was too bad since we had some players who would eventually go into the NFL Hall of Fame.

In 1967, we were 7-6-1 and I ran for 880 yards. Then, in 1968, we had a chance to be in contention before I badly injured my knee against the 49ers in the ninth game of the season. Green Bay beat us late in the year by one point, 28-27 and knocked us out of the playoffs. My backups at running back were Ronnie Bull, Brian Piccolo, and Ralph Kurek. Our quarterbacks were Virgil Carter and Jack Concannon, but it seemed like we were changing quarterbacks every two games. Successful teams have consistency at quarterback, but the Bears didn't have it then. When I played, our focus was running and defense, and when I came back from my knee injury in 1969, we picked up Bobby Douglas out of Kansas, a left-handed quarterback who could throw the ball through the wall. That year, the Bears were 1-13 under Jim Dooley after Halas had retired, and I was the only person in the NFL to gain 1,000 yards for the season. I made All-Pro and was selected as the MVP again of the Pro Bowl.

In 1970, we were 8-8 under Abe Gibron, who had been selected as the head coach. Abe was head coach for a couple of years, and I decided to retire after the 1971 season. Although my first knee injury was very bad, when I came back in 1969, the injury never bothered me and I didn't even wear a brace. Then, in 1970, I was returning a kick-off and I got hit and I stretched a ligament. They operated on it and tightened the ligament back up. I was out for that season and came back to play in 1971. But, it never felt good again, and with the introduction of Astroturf, it was tougher when you fell on it. So, after the 1971 exhibition season, I decided to retire.

I was very surprised to make the NFL Hall of Fame since I had only played in 68 games over 4 1/2 years in my career in the NFL, and most people who are in the Hall of Fame had careers that lasted 10 to 12 years. I had no idea that I would be considered for the Hall of Fame or be in it. But, in 1977, I got the call and they said that I would be inducted. I believe what got me in the Hall of Fame was being the first NFL running back to return kick-offs and punts, run from the line of scrimmage, and catch passes.

MIKE PYLE | STAR DEFENSIVE LINEMAN, CHICAGO BEARS

I graduated from Yale in 1961, but I hadn't thought about playing professional football, although I was curious whether I might be drafted by the NFL. But, when I got drafted by the Chicago Bears, I was able to make a quick decision. The players who were drafted in 1961 included Mike Ditka from Pittsburgh, Bill Brown from the University of Illinois, and Roosevelt Taylor. Ditka was Rookie of the Year in 1961, and, then, in 1962, Ronnie Bull was Rookie of the Year, and in 1963, we won the NFL Championship.

As for the championship year of 1963, that was one of my better years. During my first two years with the Bears, the co-captains were Bill George and Stan Jones. In the fall of 1963, George Halas came up to Mike Ditka and me, and asked us if we would be the co-captains of the offensive team, and Joe Fortunato and Larry Morris, the two great outside linebackers to be the defensive captains.

We beat Green Bay twice that year, and that year the Bears played the Packers in the first game of the regular season. Our feeling was that if we could beat the Packers, we had a chance to win the conference, and we did play teams from the other western division. It was a 14-game season, so after we won the conference we played the New York Giants for NFL Championship. In 1963, we were able to beat the Packers in the first game. Then, Halas said to us, "Okay guys, we've got to do it this year." But, we didn't know how good we were. Then, we won one or two more games, and then we went to the West Coast to play the Rams and the 49ers. We lost to the 49ers, and that was the only game we lost that year. But, we were building a confidence level that we could win it all, and it was just a wonderful feeling as it grew and grew.

Then, in the third week of November, President Kennedy was assassinated on Friday, November 22. I think of the assassination more in a personal vein than in terms of the impact on football and the Bears. There was a tremendous feeling of shock for everybody as individuals that this kind of thing could happen. I remember that Friday afternoon when I heard about it because they told us the news at the end of practice. As it turned out, Pete Rozelle and the NFL decided to play the scheduled games that weekend, although other sports cancelled their schedules. But, the NFL also decided to not have radio or television coverage of the games. We went to Pittsburgh to play the Steelers and almost got beat. We tied the game and Ditka made the greatest run I have ever seen on a football field as he avoided one tackler after another, although he never did get into the end zone.

After the tie game, which was our second tie of the season, we really were focused on the rest of the year. Our final record was 11-1-2, the tie games didn't count as losses, and we beat Green Bay

Chicago Bears 1963 Title Game, (Courtesy of the *Chicago Sun-Times*, Inc.), photographer—John Arabinko, Copyright, 1963, reprinted with permission.

twice that season. The last game of the season was against Detroit at Wrigley Field when Davey Whitsell intercepted the pass and ran in for the touchdown.

The championship game in which we beat the Giants was the most amazing time I ever had in Chicago. Everybody was a part of the buildup for that game, because the last football championship game that was played in Chicago went back to the 1940s. I remember Halas getting very excited about us winning the game, and there were 13 days in December that year where the temperature was below zero. We couldn't wear gloves, not even in practice, and we would practice at the harbor at Montrose and the lake because they wouldn't take the cover off the turf at Wrigley Field. And, throughout my career, whenever the ground was too wet because of the rain, we would practice in the Chicago Armory on Chicago Avenue where they also played polo, which meant dirt and horse manure. It was very cold on the day of the championship game, and by the fourth quarter it was -15 degrees. But, everybody in Chicago wanted to help us win the game, and people had to go all over to watch the game because television had blacked out coverage in the city. So, it was just the greatest build-up I had ever been in.

The final score was 14-10, and Richie Pettibone made the final interception in the end zone to ice the victory for the Bears.

JOHNNY MORRIS | STAR RECEIVER CHICAGO BEARS | AND TELEVISION BROADCASTER

When I got to the Bears in 1958, we were 8-4 my first year, and second to the Baltimore Colts during my first couple of years. Remember, the Bears had gone to the NFL Championship in 1956 and lost to the New York Giants. Then, we were hanging around 8-4, but we started getting better in 1961 and 1962, and we had a good defense. Of course, in 1963 we won the NFL Championship. I set the reception record with 97 catches in 1964.

It was a great feeling to be on the championship team in 1963. Just like everything else, we felt that we were the best. In any profession, if you feel

that you are the best, it can't get any better than that. It was a great feeling to rise to the top of your profession, and we had a really good team with a great defense and a good offense. While our offense wasn't explosive, we were able to control the ball and help the defense by keeping the other team off the field. We didn't score a lot of points, but the backbone of our team was the defense.

I have memories about three particular games that highlighted the 1963 season. We beat the Green Bay Packers twice that year, and we only won the division by a half game over Green Bay. That game when J.C. Caroline made the tackle on that kick-off in Wrigley Field against the Packers. That hit raised the intensity of the crowd and got us excited, and I think that we beat the Packers by the score of 24-7. It was the key point of the season and really led to the victory against Green Bay. The second thing that I remember was when we had to play the game in Pittsburgh only two days after President Kennedy was assassinated on November 22. Most of us didn't want to play, but NFL Commissioner Rozelle decided to play on that Sunday. There weren't that many people at the game against the Steelers, and we ended up getting a tie out of it on a pass and catch by Ditka. That, too, got us into the championship game, but nobody wanted to play that game, and I'm sure that it was also the same for the other team. We just didn't have our hearts in it. The fact that we were able to escape from that game with a tie, that became the second "key" of the season.

The last thing was a game in Wrigley Field in December against the Detroit Lions in the last game of the regular season. We had to beat them in order to get in the championship game because the Packers had already won out on the West Coast on a Saturday. We were down 10-0 at the half, and George Allen was our defensive coach, and I remember him coming to me and saying, "Can you get us a couple of touchdowns? Then we can pull this out." So, I just said, "I'll get you a touchdown." I'll never forget it because, a few minutes later, I heard him tell the defense, "Johnny said he's going to get us a couple of touchdowns." Anyway, I did get one touchdown and got us back in the game, and then Ditka got us another one and we ended upwinning the game. Then, Davey Whitsell made an interception at the end of the game that wrapped up the victory. It was pretty close after Ditka's touchdown put us ahead 14-7. Detroit was driving down the field to tie us or beat us, and Whitsell got an interception and that wrapped it up. Billy Wade was the quarterback on our team, and he was a good, steady quarterback.

When we played in the championship game against the Giants on Sunday, December 29, 1963, it was very cold and uncomfortable playing at Wrigley Field. The field was like a rock, but it was great to win the game and the defense really controlled it. I didn't do much in that game after Erich Barnes of the Giants hit me on the sidelines after I caught a pass and I was out for about a quarter. I did get back in the game, but I didn't do much. But, I'll tell you, our defense did and our offense with Ditka and Wade did just enough, and we won the game and we were the champs. The feeling is kind of hard to explain except the fact that when you want to be the best in your profession, and I was only 27 or 28 and we had won the world championship. It was the pinnacle of my career and that was a great feeling. After I was done with football, my challenge was to do well in television. A lot of other guys who retired after that had their own challenges, but I'll bet you that was the peak of their lives.

JIM MCMAHON | STAR QUARTERBACK CHICAGO BEARS

When I first got to Chicago, the team wasn't very good. The first year I came to the Bears, 1982, was a strike year, and we only played nine games. I didn't play right away, and I didn't start until the third game of the year. We were 3-6 that year and we struggled.

In 1983, the Bears were 8-8. We won five of our last six games and showed that we were getting better. We had a big draft that year that included Willie Gault, Jimbo Covert, and

Richard Dent. Walter Payton had been with the Bears since 1975, so by 1984 we sensed we had a chance to win the NFL title. We were 6-3 that year when I blew my kidney out against the Los Angeles Raiders. We finished with a 10-6 record and won the division. Steve Fuller led us to victory in the first round of the playoffs, but we lost the NFC Championship game that year to the San Francisco 49ers and we felt that we should have won the title.

Coming into training camp in 1985, I knew that we had a really good football team because we had picked up Wilber Marshall in 1984 and Mark Bortz and Otis Wilson were already with the Bears, so the majority of our defense was in place for the '85 season. We won the opener, but surprisingly we didn't play well defensively in the early part of the season. The key game for us was Week 3, in Minnesota. Mike Ditka said that I wasn't going to play because I had missed practice for three days, so, there I was watching the game, and we were getting beaten. I finally bugged Ditka enough to get him to put me in the game, and we won.

After Minnesota, we got on a roll, winning nine in a row until Miami beat us for our only loss of the season. I don't think that we should have lost that game. I had missed two days of practice because of a sprained ankle so Mike said Steve Fuller would be the quarterback. Miami had the worst rush defense in the league, so Walter should have had 300 yards that night. But, Miami scored quickly and Coach Ditka decided to start throwing the ball. I didn't get in that game until there were six minutes to go. The loss didn't bother Ditka because we were already in the playoffs and had already won the division with a month to play.

After Miami, we swept through the rest of the season, including Super Bowl XX against New England. For the next five years we had the best players and best team in the NFL but we just never brought it home again.

Gale Sayers and Chicago Bears (As published in the *Chicago Daily News*), photographer—Gary Settle, Copyright, 1972 by the *Chicago Sun-Times*, reprinted with permission.

CHICAGO CARDINALS

DON STONESIFER | ALL-AMERICAN RECEIVER | NORTHWESTERN UNIVERSITY AND STAR RECEIVER | CHICAGO CARDINALS

After graduating from Schurz High School in 1945, I went into the Army for a year and was sent to Germany, where I was also able to play some football. Soon after I returned from military service, I enrolled at Northwestern University and went there from 1947 to 1950. I was selected as an All-American football player as an offensive end. I held all the Big Ten records for receptions, and I went to the Rose Bowl in 1949 when we beat the University of California by the score of 12-7.

When I was a senior, it was time for the NFL draft and my father had been a Chicago Bears fan for 40 or more years. We had gone to the Bears games since I was 12 years old. When I graduated from Northwestern, George Halas, the owner and coach of the Bears, told me that he was going to draft me for the team. However, I was drafted third in 1951 by the Chicago Cardinals because they were higher in the draft. Since my father was a lifelong Bears fan, he was quite disappointed but he ended up coming to the Cardinal games for the next six years. But while he fully supported me, he would say, "I hope that you have a good game, except against the Bears."

I got to the Cardinals in the summer of 1951 as a rookie. In those days, training camp began in August and then we would have four or five exhibition games. We spent about three weeks in Lake Forest, with twice-a-day practices in the heat. So, if you weren't in shape, you would tighten and lose your coordination, and nothing has changed. You might not be the biggest or fastest player, but if you came to camp in shape it worked in your favor. That was my theory about being prepared to play football with the Cardinals. When my first season began, I was a starter for some of the games as offensive end and I played both ends, but mainly right end. I played with the Cardinals from 1951 through 1956 and was the all-time receiver for the Chicago Cardinals.

In my fourth year, I broke all the records for the team for number of passes caught and yardage.

COLLEGE BASKETBALL

RAY MEYER | COACH | DEPAUL UNIVERSITY

I came to coach at DePaul in 1942 after two years at Notre Dame. Then the big thing happened. I had about 24 players and the Selective Service draft came along and all of them were called except George Mikan, who was too tall, and Dick Tripto, who was 4-F. They were going to cancel the schedule, so I called Bill Shea, who I played basketball with and who was coaching at St. Phillips High School. Bill said that he had a lot of 4-F's over there, so we got about four of them and played the schedule. We had about eight players, and when we practiced, the team manager and I played so that we would have 10 players. We were successful because we had Mikan. George was about 6' 9." The following year we lost Tripto to graduation, so we took some more young kids who were coming along. Actually, it was really tough to deal with the situation at that particular time. Travel was rough because we had to take the train all night to get to New York to play games and we couldn't afford individual compartments on the train. So the players sat up all night or slept in their seats. It was very difficult at that time to even get a schedule of games, especially with Mikan, because the schools didn't want to lose to us. When I first started, we played some of the Big Ten schools and played our home games at Chicago Stadium because all we had was something that we called "The Barn" that only seated about 2,000 people. So, you couldn't play the big teams there, but you could play the Division II or III teams, and maybe a few lesser teams. We played 15-16 games at Chicago Stadium, and we always played doubleheaders with Northwestern and Loyola and drew very well at the Stadium. But overall, it was a struggle for us.

PROFESSIONAL BASKETBALL CHICAGO BULLS

JOHNNY "RED" KERR | COACH | CHICAGO BULLS

I graduated from the University of Illinois in 1954 and was drafted by the Syracuse Nationals. At that time, there were eight teams in the NBA, with the four teams in the East being New York, Boston, Philadelphia, and Syracuse. I stayed with Syracuse for nine years until they moved to Philadelphia. The Warriors moved to the West Coast and became Golden State, and we moved to Philadelphia. Wilt Chamberlain was with the Philadelphia Warriors when they moved out, but, a year later, they traded him and he became a member of the 76ers. I played against Wilt for seven or eight years and then played with him for about a year. When Wilt came to the team, I knew that I wasn't going to be playing much, even though I had worked for the owner of the team, Irv Kozloff, in his paper business. I said to him, "You know, Koz, this isn't going to go work out since Wilt is used to playing an entire game, and I would like to play." I had played in a continuous streak of 844 games. "I'd like to play one more year. Why don't you see if you can do something to trade me to another NBA team?" It wasn't a demand, but I wanted to play. I was traded to Baltimore for Wally Jones, a guard, and I finished my career at Baltimore after one more year. I was going to play maybe one additional year, but the expansion job of head coach opened in Chicago.

The Chicago Bulls were initially owned by Dick Klein, and he hired me in 1966. Chicago had several professional basketball teams before the Bulls, including the Gears, the Stags, the Zephyrs, and the Packers. Then, the Bulls came in, and we were playing at the Amphitheater before moving our games to the Chicago Stadium. The Amphitheater was just about the right size stadium for a team that was trying to make it back in Chicago. Then, in 1967, there was a fire at McCormick Place, and Mayor Richard J. Daley wanted everyone out of the Amphitheater because the city needed the facility for

trade shows. So, we moved to the Chicago Stadium, which was just a high-rent arena for us compared to the Amphitheater. At the Stadium, we didn't draw too many fans and there was almost no media coverage of the team. In fact, after the games, I would walk around with about $5 in change in my pockets so that I could call the media and tell them about the results of the games. I would call a newspaper and say, "This is Johnny Kerr, coach of the Bulls, and I'm just calling give you the score of the game." They would say, "What happened? Who was the leading scorer?" And, I would usually say, "That was Bob Boozer." They would often say, "How do you spell that?" Then I would call the other papers, radio, and television stations.

It was great to be with this new team, and, at that time, Jerry Colangelo worked in the Bulls' front office. The players on the team during the first year included: Guy Rodgers, a flashy guard from Villanova who had played with Wilt on the Warriors and set a record that first year for us with 21 assists in a game; Bob Boozer, who was from Kansas, the captain of our team, and one of the top scorers; and, Jerry Sloan, whom I wanted the Bulls to draft. Although I wasn't a player/coach with the Bulls, I had to be in the expansion pool. It was great going from a player to a coach because I missed the camaraderie and everything else. And, I could still do all the things I still liked to do in basketball. I was selected as Coach of the Year in our first year, and the team won 33 games as an expansion team. No other expansion team has ever come close to that victory total. We also made the playoffs, which no other first-year team has done. In fact, when they asked Richie Guerin of the St. Louis Hawks, "How do you think the Bulls will do?" He responded, "They'll be lucky if they win 12 games." But, we went out and won 33 games, and I ended up coaching the Bulls for two years. In our second year, we won 29 games and one game in the playoffs.

After I was a coach, I left Chicago and went to Phoenix where Jerry Colangelo was the new general manager of the team. I was head coach there for two years. In fact, I think that I am the only expansion coach that ever won his first two games with two different expansion teams. My roommate for many years at Syracuse was Al Bianchi, and we were always very close friends. When I came to Chicago, I chose Al as my assistant coach with the Bulls. He left, got the job in Seattle, and coached there for a couple of years before he went to the Virginia Squires in the ABA (American Basketball Association). He called me when he got to Virginia and he said, "Johnny, I need a guy who can come out here and help me run the front office of the franchise." As a matter of fact, one of my claims to fame was that I signed Julius Irving and George Gervin to contracts in the ABA.

NORM VAN LIER | BASKETBALL PLAYER, CHICAGO BULLS | TELEVISION BROADCASTER

When I came back to Chicago in 1971, I was excited that we started drawing bigger crowds and people loved the Bulls. My teams included Bob Love and Chet Walker at forwards, Tom Boerwinkle and Cliff Ray at center, and me, Jerry Sloan, and Bobby Weiss as the backcourt players. Jerry and I played around seven years together as the guards. We were set and we started winning and we were in the Western Conference in those days that included the Los Angeles Lakers, Milwaukee Bucks, Detroit Pistons, and the Golden State Warriors, and all of those teams were tough. Then, in the not too distant future, the Eastern Conference began to include tough teams. I was still with the Bulls when Artis Gilmore came here from the ABA, and many of my former teammates had retired. I was a very young guy on the Bulls in the '70s.

I retired in 1979 and after I was gone, Jerry Sloan became head coach of the Bulls. I left Chicago for eight years and I was not in broadcasting here but worked for ESPN on the West Coast. I came back to Chicago just one year before the Bulls won their first championship in 1991, and I started broadcasting. By 1990 I knew that there was something special about the Bulls. They were always putting on their "war clothes" and going to battle with the Detroit Pistons. No other team seemed to bother them

at that time. In my opinion, what turned everything around for their championship team to go forward was Horace Grant. To me, he changed the whole outlook of the Bulls, because he was ready to fight. I'll never forget him wearing those goggles, and he was just ready to "go to war" and it seemed like he took the team on his back in a different direction as far as their attitude about being physical, and from that point it was "history."

In my opinion, he was the workhorse. As for Phil Jackson, he was a good coach who had learned from Red Holtzman of the Knicks how to be a great coach. At the same time, he was Michael Jordan's coach. When Michael left in 1993, there was an 18-month gap but during those championship years, he was great and you can't argue with winning those championships. And, in my opinion, it could have lasted even longer.

My best memory about those six championships is just how they played together and the defense that they really applied. To watch that team grow and do what they did and to maintain the drive and the will that Michael Jordan had with that team was amazing to me. The main guy was Michael, and deservedly so, but it was a team with a lot of heroes that allowed them to win so many championships. Phil Jackson was good at keeping everybody together to play and win the game.

Of the six championship teams, I thought that the best one was in 1992. Maybe not the best record, but the most versatile team, the most physical team.

BOWLING

CARMEN SALVINO | HALL OF FAME PROFESSIONAL BOWLER

It all began in 1945 when, at the age of 12, I went to work setting pins in a local bowling center (there were no automatic pinsetters then) to help my family and that started my career in bowling. By the age of 17, I had become an accomplished bowler and was the youngest bowler to ever compete in the then famous "Chicago Classic League" and was tagged with the nickname "Chicago's Boy Wonder."

Bowling started to become very popular, and it was an era of famous bowling teams in cities like Chicago, Detroit, St. Louis, and Minneapolis. The competition between these teams was fierce.

In 1954, Matt Niesen, a Chicago bowling proprietor, put together a bowling show for a local television station and called it "Championship Bowling." The format was two bowlers who would bowl each other for three games, and the winner of the match would come back the following week. I was 19 then, stayed on the show for eight consecutive weeks, and it helped me to become better known. The show helped put bowling in Chicago on the map, and new bowling centers were popping up everywhere. Bowling was a sport where everyone could participate, young children and adults alike. At that time we had 100 million people throughout the world bowling.

During the '60s, the sport of bowling was very popular and I continued to bowl in the classic league until the Professional Bowlers Association was formed in 1958 by its founder, Eddie Elias, a lawyer from Akron, Ohio. I was one of the seven original chartered members. Our PBA tour consisted of 35 tournaments, the show was televised on ABC every Saturday afternoon, and bowling became even more popular.

SOCCER
CHICAGO STING

LEE STERN | OWNER | CHICAGO STING, PART OWNER, CHICAGO WHITE SOX | AND BROKER | CHICAGO BOARD OF TRADE

As a pure soccer player, Arno Steffenhagen was recognized as probably one of the four or five best players ever to play in the North American Soccer League, and even Clive Toye, coach of the Chicago Sting, would tell you that. We had a very colorful team, including Karl-Heinz Granitza, Steffenhagen with his big moustache, Davie Huson, blowing kisses to the fans, and Pato Margetic, with his long hair. And, nobody was more colorful than our coach Willy Roy. Today, my guess is that if you think about

baseball and hockey players, over 50% of them are not American born and come from many different nationalities. Then there are the soccer-style kickers in professional football who were all foreign based, and there are many foreign born players in professional basketball. So, now, nobody pays attention to the issue, but, in those days, it was a big negative for soccer, although we had the best bunch of American players in the NASL. That was due to Willy Roy because he played them when he was my head coach. You had to play a certain number of them: three or four at all times. But, he would bring in somebody as a substitute. Willy is one of my favorite "love-hate" guys because we had what might be described as a love-hate relationship...but not really.

One important thing I will say about sports, and the Sting, goes back to the parade that we had down LaSalle Street in 1981 after winning the NASL Championship. I was asked what I thought about that event, and my answer was, "Anybody who ever thought they would lead a parade down LaSalle Street was either nuts, had an ego surpassing anybody in the world, or should be in an insane asylum somewhere. Why would anybody think that they would ever lead a parade down LaSalle Street?" I think that if our coach Willy Roy had another year of experience we would have probably won the Championship in 1980 as well as 1981. But, by the time we won it again in 1984, the League was reduced to nine teams.

Chicago Sting 1981 North American Soccer League
Championship Parade, (Courtesy of Lee Stern)

INTERVIEWEE INDEX

SUBJECT INDEX